# Android Application Testing Guide

Build intensively tested and bug free Android applications

Diego Torres Milano

[PACKT] PUBLISHING

BIRMINGHAM - MUMBAI

# Android Application Testing Guide

Copyright © 2011 Packt Publishing

All rights reserved. No part of this book may be reproduced, stored in a retrieval system, or transmitted in any form or by any means, without the prior written permission of the publisher, except in the case of brief quotations embedded in critical articles or reviews.

Every effort has been made in the preparation of this book to ensure the accuracy of the information presented. However, the information contained in this book is sold without warranty, either express or implied. Neither the author, nor Packt Publishing, and its dealers and distributors will be held liable for any damages caused or alleged to be caused directly or indirectly by this book.

Packt Publishing has endeavored to provide trademark information about all of the companies and products mentioned in this book by the appropriate use of capitals. However, Packt Publishing cannot guarantee the accuracy of this information.

First published: June 2011

Production Reference: 1170611

Published by Packt Publishing Ltd.
32 Lincoln Road
Olton
Birmingham, B27 6PA, UK.

ISBN 978-1-849513-50-0

www.packtpub.com

Cover Image by Asher Wishkerman (a.wishkerman@mpic.de)

# Credits

**Author**
Diego Torres Milano

**Reviewers**
Paul Bourdeaux
Noah Eltzroth
Tomas Malmsten
Gabor Paller
Abhinav Tyagi

**Acquisition Editor**
Tarun Singh

**Development Editor**
Chris Rodrigues

**Technical Editor**
Conrad Sardinha

**Project Coordinator**
Joel Goveya

**Proofreaders**
Aaron Nash
Stephen Silk

**Indexer**
Hemangini Bari

**Graphics**
Nilesh Mohite

**Production Coordinator**
Kruthika Bangera

**Cover Work**
Kruthika Bangera

# About the Author

**Diego Torres Milano** has been involved with the Android platform since its inception, at the end of 2007, when he started exploring and researching the platform possibilities, mainly in the areas of User Interfaces, Unit and Acceptance Tests, and Test Driven Development.

This is reflected by a number of articles mainly published in his personal blog (http://dtmilano.blogspot.com) and his participation as a lecturer in some conferences and courses like Mobile Dev Camp 2008 in Amsterdam (Netherlands) and Japan Linux Symposium 2009 (Tokyo), Droidcon London 2009, Skillsmatter 2009 (London, UK), and he has also authored Android training courses delivered to various companies in Europe.

Previously, he was the founder and developer of several Open Source projects, mainly CULT Universal Linux Thin Project (cult-thinclient.sf.net) and the very successful PXES Universal Linux Thin Client project (that was later acquired by 2X Software, www.2x.com). PXES is a Linux-based Operating System specialized for thin clients used by hundreds of thousands of thin clients all over the world. This project has a popularity peak of 35M hits and 400K downloads from SourceForge in 2005. This project had a dual impact: big companies in Europe decided to use it because of improved security and efficiency; organizations, institutions, and schools in some developing countries in South America, Africa, and Asia decided to use it because of the minimal hardware requirements to have a huge social impact providing computers, sometimes recycled ones, to everyone.

Among the other Open Source projects that he has founded we can mention Autoglade, Gnome-tla, JGlade, and he has been contributing to various Linux distributions such as RedHat, Fedora, and Ubuntu.

He also has been giving presentations in Linux World, LinuxTag, GUADEC ES, University of Buenos Aires, and so on.

He has been developing software, participating in Open Source projects, and advising companies worldwide for more than 15 years.

He can be contacted at dtmilano@gmail.com.

Firstly, I would like to thank my family: Laura, Augusto and Octavio for their patience and consideration. The time I borrowed to achieve this goal was mostly theirs.

Secondly I would like to thank my personal friend and IN3 Integracion Informatica co-founder, Caludio Palonsky, with whom we started this amazing adventure more than 15 years ago when we pioneered the provision of Linux services and support to enterprises in South America. He certainly taught me to be a bit more consultant and a bit less hacker (but I'm a very bad student :-)). And special thanks to Ricston's Peter Delia with whom we started providing Android training services throughout Europe as early as mid 2008 when Android was just a beautiful dream of having a mainstream Open Source operating system in the mobile arena. This is now a reality dictated by the market.

And lastly I would like to thank all the reviewers and the Packt Publishing team who gave me their opinion, suggestions, and corrections on early manuscripts; without them the book would never have had the quality it endowed.

# About the Reviewers

**Paul Bourdeaux** is the Senior Software Engineer and Application Development Team Lead at Sundog, a marketing and technology company based in the Midwest. He has a strong background in traditional software engineering, has authored several white papers relating to mobile marketing and software engineering, and has presented at both national and regional software engineering conferences. Paul is the mobile marketing expert at Sundog, and his passion lies in mobile and cloud based software engineering.

**Noah Eltzroth** teaches dynamic web development at the Sullivan College of Technology and Design in Louisville, Kentucky. He enjoys working on a variety of different software projects including business-oriented portals, data processing, and Android applications. In his free time, Noah enjoys programming in both Java and PHP.

**Tomas Malmsten** has been working with software development for over a decade. During this time he has had the opportunity to work with a vast variety of technologies in various different business settings. His main focus has been the Java ecosystem where he has worked with everything from large enterprise systems to Android application development.

Tomas is a passionate software craftsman who strives for excellence in all aspects of programming. From customer service and interaction to well crafted maintainable programs.

You can get in touch with Tomas through any of the following means:

- Blog: http://www.tomasmalmsten.com
- Twitter: http://twitter.com/tomasmalmsten
- E-mail: public@tomasmalmsten.com
- LinkedIn: http://se.linkedin.com/in/tomasmalmsten

**Gábor Paller** received his MSc. and PhD. degrees from the Technical University of Budapest in 1992 and 1996, respectively. Dr. Paller joined Nokia in 1998 and held positions in Nokia R&D and Nokia Research Center. His interests included wireless protocol development, mobile device management, mobile Java and middleware. He was also involved in standardization and joint research program activities. After having left Nokia, he worked at OnRelay Ltd. on fixed-mobile convergence technologies, and then in 2010 he joined Ericsson where he works on IMS. Gabor Paller runs the popular My Life with Android blog and reviewed a number of Android books.

**Abhinav Tyagi** is a Computer Science graduate from Pune. He also holds a post graduate diploma in Advanced Computing from CDAC, Pune. He developed several Android applications while working as a Software Engineer at Antarix Networks, Mumbai.

He is currently working on telecom protocols as a Research & Development Engineer at Nokia Siemens Networks.

> I would like to thank Joel Goveya and Tarun Singh for giving me this wonderful opportunity.

# www.PacktPub.com

## Support files, eBooks, discount offers and more

You might want to visit www.PacktPub.com for support files and downloads related to your book.

Did you know that Packt offers eBook versions of every book published, with PDF and ePub files available? You can upgrade to the eBook version at www.PacktPub.com and as a print book customer, you are entitled to a discount on the eBook copy. Get in touch with us at service@packtpub.com for more details.

At www.PacktPub.com, you can also read a collection of free technical articles, sign up for a range of free newsletters and receive exclusive discounts and offers on Packt books and eBooks.

**PACKTLIB®**

http://PacktLib.PacktPub.com

Do you need instant solutions to your IT questions? PacktLib is Packt's online digital book library. Here, you can access, read and search across Packt's entire library of books.

## Why Subscribe?

- Fully searchable across every book published by Packt
- Copy and paste, print and bookmark content
- On demand and accessible via web browser

## Free Access for Packt account holders

If you have an account with Packt at www.PacktPub.com, you can use this to access PacktLib today and view nine entirely free books. Simply use your login credentials for immediate access.

# Table of Contents

| | |
|---|---|
| **Preface** | **1** |
| **Chapter 1: Getting Started with Testing** | **7** |
|   **Brief history** | **7** |
|   **Software bugs** | **8** |
|     How bugs severely affect your projects | 9 |
|   **Why, what, how, and when to test** | **9** |
|     What to test | 11 |
|       Activity lifecycle events | 12 |
|       Database and filesystem operations | 12 |
|       Physical characteristics of the device | 12 |
|   **Types of tests** | **13** |
|     Unit tests | 13 |
|       The test fixture | 15 |
|       The setUp() method | 15 |
|       The tearDown() method | 15 |
|       Test preconditions | 16 |
|       The actual tests | 16 |
|     Integration tests | 20 |
|     Functional or acceptance tests | 20 |
|       Test case scenario | 22 |
|     Performance tests | 22 |
|     System tests | 23 |
|   **Android testing framework** | **23** |
|     Instrumentation | 23 |
|     Test targets | 25 |
|   **Summary** | **26** |
| **Chapter 2: Testing on Android** | **27** |
|   **JUnit** | **28** |
|   **Creating the Android main project** | **28** |
|   **Creating the Android test project** | **29** |

| | |
|---|---|
| **Package explorer** | **31** |
| **Creating a test case** | **32** |
| Special methods | 36 |
| Test annotations | 36 |
| **Running the tests** | **37** |
| Running all tests from Eclipse | 37 |
| Running a single test case from Eclipse | 38 |
| Running from the emulator | 39 |
| Running tests from the command line | 41 |
|     Running all tests | 42 |
|     Running tests from a specific test case | 42 |
|     Running a specific test by name | 42 |
|     Running specific tests by category | 43 |
|     Running performance tests | 44 |
|     Dry run | 44 |
| **Debugging tests** | **45** |
| **Other command-line options** | **47** |
| **Summary** | **47** |
| **Chapter 3: Building Blocks on the Android SDK** | **49** |
| **The demonstration application** | **50** |
| **Assertions in depth** | **50** |
| Custom messages | 52 |
| Static imports | 52 |
| **View assertions** | **53** |
| **Even more assertions** | **55** |
| **The TouchUtils class** | **57** |
| **Mock Objects** | **58** |
| MockContext overview | 59 |
| The IsolatedContext class | 59 |
| Alternate route to file and database operations | 60 |
| The MockContentResolver class | 60 |
| **The TestCase base class** | **61** |
| The no-argument constructor | 61 |
| The given name constructor | 62 |
| The setName() method | 62 |
| **The AndroidTestCase base class** | **62** |
| The assertActivityRequiresPermission() method | 63 |
|     Description | 64 |
|     Example | 64 |
| The assertReadingContentUriRequiresPermission method | 64 |
|     Description | 64 |
|     Example | 65 |

|  |  |
|---|---|
| The assertWritingContentUriRequiresPermission() method | 65 |
| Description | 65 |
| Example | 66 |
| **Instrumentation** | **66** |
| The ActivityMonitor inner class | 66 |
| Example | 67 |
| **The InstrumentationTestCase class** | **68** |
| The launchActivity and launchActivityWithIntent method | 69 |
| The sendKeys and sendRepeatedKeys methods | 69 |
| The runTestOnUiThread helper method | 71 |
| **The ActivityTestCase class** | **72** |
| The scrubClass method | 73 |
| **The ActivityInstrumentationTestCase2 class** | **74** |
| The constructor | 75 |
| The setUp method | 75 |
| The tearDown method | 76 |
| The testPreconditions method | 76 |
| **The ProviderTestCase2<T> class** | **76** |
| The constructor | 77 |
| Example | 78 |
| **The ServiceTestCase<T>** | **78** |
| The constructor | 79 |
| **The TestSuiteBuilder.FailedToCreateTests class** | **80** |
| **Using external libraries in test projects** | **80** |
| **Summary** | **84** |
| **Chapter 4: Test Driven Development** | **85** |
| **Getting started with TDD** | **85** |
| Writing a test case | 86 |
| Running all tests | 87 |
| Refactoring the code | 87 |
| What is the advantage? | 88 |
| Understanding the requirements | 88 |
| **Creating a sample project—the Temperature Converter** | **88** |
| The list of requirements | 89 |
| User interface concept design | 89 |
| Creating the projects | 90 |
| **Creating the TemperatureConverterActivityTests project** | **92** |
| Creating the fixture | 96 |
| Test preconditions | 97 |
| Creating the user interface | 97 |
| Testing the existence of the user interface components | 98 |

| | |
|---|---|
| Getting the IDs defined | 98 |
| Translating requirements to tests | 99 |
|     Empty fields | 100 |
|     View properties | 100 |
| Screen layout | 104 |
| **Adding functionality** | **104** |
| Temperature conversion | 104 |
| The EditNumber class | 105 |
| TemperatureConverter unit tests | 110 |
| The EditNumber tests | 114 |
| The TemperatureChangeWatcher class | 119 |
| More TemperatureConverter tests | 123 |
| The InputFilter tests | 125 |
| **Viewing our final application** | **126** |
| **Summary** | **128** |
| **Chapter 5: Android Testing Environment** | **129** |
| **Creating Android Virtual Devices** | **129** |
| **Running AVDs from the command line** | **132** |
| Headless emulator | 133 |
| Disabling the keyguard | 134 |
| Cleaning up | 135 |
| Terminating the emulator | 136 |
| **Additional emulator configurations** | **136** |
| Simulating network conditions | 137 |
| Additional qemu options | 140 |
| **Running monkey** | **142** |
| Client-server monkey | 143 |
| **Test scripting with monkeyrunner** | **144** |
| Getting test screenshots | 145 |
| Record and playback | 147 |
| **Summary** | **148** |
| **Chapter 6: Behavior Driven Development** | **149** |
| **Brief history** | **149** |
| **Given, when, then** | **150** |
| **FitNesse** | **151** |
| Running FitNesse from the command line | 151 |
| Creating a TemperatureConverterTests subwiki | 152 |
|     Adding child pages to the subwiki | 153 |
|     Adding the acceptance test fixture | 155 |
|     Adding the supporting test classes | 156 |

| | |
|---|---|
| **GivWenZen** | **158** |
| Creating the test scenario | 159 |
| **Summary** | **165** |
| **Chapter 7: Testing Recipes** | **167** |
| **Android Unit tests** | **167** |
| **Testing activities and applications** | **170** |
| Applications and preferences | 170 |
| The RenamingMockContext class | 170 |
| The TemperatureConverterApplicationTests class | 171 |
| Testing activities | 175 |
| **Testing files, databases, and ContentProviders** | **181** |
| The BrowserProvider tests | 185 |
| **Testing exceptions** | **191** |
| **Testing local and remote services** | **192** |
| **Extensive use of mock objects** | **196** |
| Importing libraries | 198 |
| The testTextChanged test | 198 |
| Introducing Hamcrest | 202 |
| Hamcrest matchers | 203 |
| The hasToString matcher | 204 |
| **Testing Views in isolation** | **205** |
| **Testing parsers** | **209** |
| Android assets | 209 |
| The parser activity | 210 |
| The parser test | 211 |
| **Testing for memory leaks** | **212** |
| **Summary** | **215** |
| **Chapter 8: Continuous Integration** | **217** |
| **Building Android applications manually using Ant** | **218** |
| **Git—the fast version control system** | **224** |
| Creating a local git repository | 224 |
| **Continuous Integration with Hudson** | **225** |
| Installing and configuring Hudson | 226 |
| Creating the jobs | 227 |
| Obtaining Android test results | 231 |
| **Summary** | **240** |
| **Chapter 9: Performance Testing and Profiling** | **243** |
| **Ye Olde Logge method** | **244** |
| **Performance tests in Android SDK** | **246** |
| Launching the performance test | 246 |
| Creating the LaunchPerformanceBase instrumentation | 246 |

| | |
|---|---|
| Creating the TemperatureConverterActivityLaunchPerformance class | 248 |
| Running the tests | 249 |
| **Using the Traceview and dmtracedump platform tools** | **251** |
| **Microbenchmarks** | **255** |
| Caliper microbenchmarks | 256 |
| Creating the TemperatureConverterBenchmark project | 257 |
| Running caliper | 258 |
| **Summary** | **261** |
| **Chapter 10: Alternative Testing Tactics** | **263** |
| **Building Android from source** | **264** |
| Code coverage | 264 |
| EMMA features | 265 |
| System requirements | 266 |
| Downloading the Android source code | 266 |
| Installing repo | 267 |
| Creating the working copy | 267 |
| The Building Steps | 268 |
| **TemperatureConverter code coverage** | **270** |
| Generating code coverage analysis report | 274 |
| Covering the restoring the instance state | 279 |
| Covering the exceptions | 281 |
| Bypassing access restrictions | 282 |
| Covering the options menu | 283 |
| **The undocumented Ant coverage target** | **284** |
| **Introducing Robotium** | **285** |
| Downloading Robotium | 286 |
| Configuring the project | 286 |
| Creating the test cases | 286 |
| The testFahrenheitToCelsiusConversion() test | 286 |
| The testOnCreateOptionsMenu() revisited | 289 |
| **Testing on host's JVM** | **291** |
| Creating the TemperatureConverterJVMTest project | 291 |
| Comparing the performance gain | 296 |
| Adding Android to the picture | 297 |
| **Introducing Robolectric** | **299** |
| Installing Robolectric | 299 |
| Creating a new Java project | 299 |
| Writing some tests | 299 |
| **Summary** | **303** |
| **Index** | **305** |

# Preface

It doesn't matter how much time you invest in Android design, or even how careful you are when programming, mistakes are inevitable and bugs will appear. This book will help you minimize the impact of these errors in your Android project and increase your development productivity. It will show you the problems that are easily avoided, to help get you quickly to the testing stage.

*Android Application Testing Guide* is the first and only book providing a practical introduction to the most commonly-available techniques, frameworks, and tools to improve the development of your Android applications. Clear, step-by-step instructions show how to write tests for your applications and assure quality control using various methodologies.

The author's experience in applying application testing techniques to real-world projects enables him to share insights on creating professional Android applications.

The book starts by introducing Test Driven Development, which is an agile component of the software development process and a technique where you will tackle bugs early on. From the most basic unit tests applied to a sample project to more sophisticated performance tests, this book provides a detailed description of the most widely used techniques in the Android testing world in a recipe-based approach.

The author has extensive experience of working on various development projects throughout his professional career. All this research and knowledge has helped create a book that will serve as a useful resource to any developer navigating the world of Android testing.

## What this book covers

*Chapter 1, Getting Started with Testing* introduces the different types of testing and their applicability to software development projects in general and to Android in particular.

*Chapter 2*, *Testing on Android* covers testing on the Android platform, Unit testing and JUnit, creating an Android Test project, and running tests.

*Chapter 3*, *Building Blocks on the Android SDK* starts digging a bit deeper to recognize the building blocks available to create the tests. It covers Assertions, TouchUtils, intended to test User Interfaces, Mock objects, Instrumentation, and TestCase class hierarchies featuring UML diagrams.

*Chapter 4*, *Test Driven Development* introduces the Test Driven Development discipline. It starts with a general revision and later on moves to the concepts and techniques closely related to the Android platform. This is a code intensive chapter.

*Chapter 5*, *Android Testing Environment* provides different conditions to run the tests. It starts with the creation of the Android Virtual Devices (AVD) to provide different conditions and configurations for the application under test and runs the tests using the available options. Finally, it introduces monkey as a way to generate simulated events used for testing.

*Chapter 6*, *Behavior Driven Development* introduces Behavior Driven Development and some concepts such as like the use of a common vocabulary to express the tests and the inclusion of business participants in the software development project.

*Chapter 7*, *Testing Recipes* provides practical examples of different common situations you will encounter applying the disciplines and techniques described before. The examples are presented in a Cookbook style so you can adapt and use them for your projects. The recipes cover Android Unit tests, Activities, Applications, Databases and ContentProviders, Local and Remote Services, UIs, Exceptions, Parsers, and Memory leaks.

*Chapter 8*, *Continuous Integration* introduces this agile technique for software engineering that aims to improve the software quality and to reduce the time taken to integrate changes by continuously applying integration and testing frequently.

*Chapter 9*, *Performance Testing* introduces a series of concepts related to benchmarking and profiles from traditional logging statement methods to Creating Android performance tests and using profiling tools. This chapter also presents Caliper to create microbenchmarks.

*Chapter 10*, *Alternative Testing Tactics* covers building Android from source, code coverage using EMMA, Robotium, testing on hosts, and Robolectric.

# What you need for this book

First of all, you need practical Android development experience as we are not covering the basics. It is assumed that you already have some Android application or at least you are familiar with the topics described extensively in the Android Dev Guide (http://developer.android.com/guide/index.html). Also it is very helpful having followed some of the Sample Code projects (http://developer.android.com/resources/browser.html?tag=sample), probably starting with API Demos and then moving to other more involved topics. This way you will get the most of this book.

To be able to follow the examples in the different chapters you need a common set of software and tools installed and several other components that are described in every chapter in particular including their respective download locations.

All the examples are based on:

- Ubuntu 10.04.2 LTS (lucid) 64 bit, fully updated
- Java SE version "1.6.0_24" (build 1.6.0_24-b07)
- Android SDK tools, revision 11
- Android SDK Platform-tools, revision 4
- SDK Platform Android 2.3.1, API 9, revision 2
- Android Compatibility package, revision 2
- Eclipse IDE for Java Developers, Version: Helios Service Release 1 (3.6.1)
- Android Development Toolkit, Version: 10.0.1.v201103111512-110841
- Dalvik Debug Monitor Service, Version: 10.0.1.v201103111512-110841
- Apache Ant version 1.8.0 compiled on April 9 2010
- Git version 1.7.0.4
- Subversion version 1.6.6 (r40053) compiled Mar 23 2011, 13:08:34

The UML diagrams presented in the book were created using BOUML release 4.21.

Screenshots were taken and edited using Shutter 0.86.3.

Manuscripts were edited using OpenOffice.org 3.2.1.

# Who this book is for

If you are an Android developer looking to test your applications or optimize your application development process, then this book is for you. No previous experience in application testing is required.

# Conventions

In this book, you will find a number of styles of text that distinguish between different kinds of information. Here are some examples of these styles, and an explanation of their meaning.

Code words in text are shown as follows: "To invoke the `am` command we will be using the `adb shell` command".

A block of code is set as follows:

```
@VeryImportantTest
public void testOtherStuff() {
  fail("Not implemented yet");
}
```

When we wish to draw your attention to a particular part of a code block, the relevant lines or items are set in bold:

```
public class MyFirstProjectTests extends TestCase {
  public MyFirstProjectTests() {
    this("MyFirstProjectTests");
  }
}
```

Any command-line input is written as follows:

```
$ adb shell am instrument -w -e class com.example.aatg.myfirstproject.test.MyFirstProjectTests com.example.aatg.myfirstproject.test/android.test.InstrumentationTestRunner
```

Any command-line output is written as follows:

**08-10 00:26:11.820: ERROR/AndroidRuntime(510): FATAL EXCEPTION: main**

**08-10 00:26:11.820: ERROR/AndroidRuntime(510): java.lang.IllegalAccessError: Class ref in pre-verified class resolved to unexpected implementation**

**New terms** and **important words** are shown in bold. Words that you see on the screen, in menus or dialog boxes for example, appear in the text like this: "Select the test project and then **Run As | Run Configurations**".

> Warnings or important notes appear in a box like this.

> Tips and tricks appear like this.

## Reader feedback

Feedback from our readers is always welcome. Let us know what you think about this book—what you liked or may have disliked. Reader feedback is important for us to develop titles that you really get the most out of.

To send us general feedback, simply send an e-mail to `feedback@packtpub.com`, and mention the book title via the subject of your message.

If there is a book that you need and would like to see us publish, please send us a note in the **SUGGEST A TITLE** form on `www.packtpub.com` or e-mail `suggest@packtpub.com`.

If there is a topic that you have expertise in and you are interested in either writing or contributing to a book, see our author guide on `www.packtpub.com/authors`.

## Customer support

Now that you are the proud owner of a Packt book, we have a number of things to help you to get the most from your purchase.

### Downloading the example code

You can download the example code files for all Packt books you have purchased from your account at `http://www.PacktPub.com`. If you purchased this book elsewhere, you can visit `http://www.PacktPub.com/support` and register to have the files e-mailed directly to you.

## Errata

Although we have taken every care to ensure the accuracy of our content, mistakes do happen. If you find a mistake in one of our books—maybe a mistake in the text or the code—we would be grateful if you would report this to us. By doing so, you can save other readers from frustration and help us improve subsequent versions of this book. If you find any errata, please report them by visiting `http://www.packtpub.com/support`, selecting your book, clicking on the **errata submission form** link, and entering the details of your errata. Once your errata are verified, your submission will be accepted and the errata will be uploaded on our website, or added to any list of existing errata, under the Errata section of that title. Any existing errata can be viewed by selecting your title from `http://www.packtpub.com/support`.

## Piracy

Piracy of copyright material on the Internet is an ongoing problem across all media. At Packt, we take the protection of our copyright and licenses very seriously. If you come across any illegal copies of our works, in any form, on the Internet, please provide us with the location address or website name immediately so that we can pursue a remedy.

Please contact us at `copyright@packtpub.com` with a link to the suspected pirated material.

We appreciate your help in protecting our authors, and our ability to bring you valuable content.

## Questions

You can contact us at `questions@packtpub.com` if you are having a problem with any aspect of the book, and we will do our best to address it.

# 1
# Getting Started with Testing

This chapter introduces the different types of testing and their applicability to software development projects in general and to **Android** in particular.

We will avoid introductions to Android and the **Open Handset Alliance** (http://www.openhandsetalliance.com) as they are covered in many books already and I am inclined to believe that if you are reading a book covering this more advanced topic you will have started with Android development before.

However, we will be reviewing the main concepts behind testing and the techniques, frameworks, and tools available to deploy your testing strategy on Android.

## Brief history

Initially, when Android was introduced by the end of 2007, there was very little support for testing on the platform, and for some of us very accustomed to using testing as a component intimately coupled with the development process, it was time to start developing some frameworks and tools to permit this approach.

By that time Android had some rudimentary support for unit testing using JUnit (http://www.JUnit.org), but it was not fully supported and even less documented.

In the process of writing my own library and tools, I discovered Phil Smith's **Positron** (originally at http://code.google.com/p/android-positron and now renamed and moved to http://code.google.com/p/autoandroid), an Open Source library and a very suitable alternative to support testing on Android, so I decided to extend his excellent work and bring some new and missing pieces to the table.

Some aspects of test automation were not included and I started a complementary project to fill that gap, it was consequently named **Electron**. And although positron is the anti-particle of the electron, and they annihilate if they collide, take for granted that that was not the idea, but more the conservation of energy and the generation of some visible light and waves.

Later on, Electron entered the first **Android Development Challenge (ADC1)** in early 2008 and though it obtained a rather good score in some categories, frameworks had no place in that competition. Should you be interested in the origin of testing on Android, please find some articles and videos that were published in my personal blog (http://dtmilano.blogspot.com/search/label/electron).

By that time Unit Tests could be run on Eclipse. However, testing was not done on the real target but on a JVM on the local development computer.

Google also provided application instrumentation code through the `Instrumentation` class. When running an application with instrumentation turned on, this class is instantiated for you before any of the application code, allowing you to monitor all of the interaction the system has with the application. An Instrumentation implementation is described to the system through an `AndroidManifest.xml` file.

During those early stages in the Android development evolution, I started writing some articles in my blog filling the gaps on testing. This book is the evolution and completion of that work in an orderly and understandable manner to paradoxically let you be bitten by the Android testing bug.

# Software bugs

It doesn't matter how hard you try and how much time you invest in design and even how careful you are when programming, mistakes are inevitable and bugs will appear.

Bugs and software development are intimately related. However, the term **bugs** to describe flaws, mistakes, or errors has been used in hardware engineering many decades before even computers were invented. Notwithstanding the story about the term 'bug' coined by Mark II operators at Harvard University, Thomas Edison wrote this in 1878 in a letter to Puskás Tivadar showing the early adoption of the term:

> *"It has been just so in all of my inventions. The first step is an intuition, and comes with a burst, then difficulties arise – this thing gives out and [it is] then that 'Bugs' – as such little faults and difficulties are called – show themselves and months of intense watching, study and labor are requisite before commercial success or failure is certainly reached."*

## How bugs severely affect your projects

Bugs affect many aspects of your software development project and it is clearly understood that the sooner in the process you find and *squash* them, the better. It doesn't matter if you are developing a simple application to publish on the Android Market, re-branding the Android experience for an operator, or creating a customized version of Android for a device manufacturer, bugs will delay your shipment and will cost you money.

From all of the software development methodologies and techniques, **Test Driven Development**, an agile component of the software development process, is likely the one that forces you to face your bugs earlier in the development process and thus it is also likely that you will solve more problems up front.

Furthermore, the increase in productivity can be clearly appreciated in a project where a software development team uses this technique versus one that is, in the best of cases, writing tests at the end of the development cycle. If you have been involved in software development for the mobile industry, you will have reasons to believe that with all the rush this stage never occurs. It's funny because, usually, this rush is to solve problems that could have been avoided.

In a study conducted by the **National Institute of Standards and Technology** (USA) in 2002, it was reported that software bugs cost the economy $59.5 billion annually. More than a third of this cost could be avoided if better software testing was performed.

But please, don't misunderstand this message. There are no *silver bullets* in software development and what will lead you to an increase in productivity and manageability of your project is discipline in applying these methodologies and techniques to stay in control.

## Why, what, how, and when to test

You should understand that early bug detection saves a huge amount of project resources and reduces software maintenance costs. This is the best known reason to write software tests for your development project. Increased productivity will soon be evident.

Additionally, writing the tests will give you a deeper understanding of the requirements and the problem to be solved. You will not be able to write tests for a piece of software you don't understand.

# Getting Started with Testing

This is also the reason behind the approach of writing tests to clearly understand legacy or third party code and having the ability to confidently change or update it.

The more the code covered by your tests, the higher would be your expectations of discovering the hidden bugs.

If during this coverage analysis you find that some areas of your code are not exercised, additional tests should be added to cover this code as well.

This technique requires a special instrumented Android build to collect probe data and must be disabled for any release code because the impact on performance could severely affect application behavior.

To fill this gap, enter EMMA (`http://emma.sourceforge.net/`), an open-source toolkit for measuring and reporting Java code coverage, that can offline instrument classes for coverage. It supports various coverage types:

- class
- method
- line
- basic block

Coverage reports can also be obtained in different output formats. EMMA is supported to some degree by the Android framework and it is possible to build an EMMA instrumented version of Android.

We will be analyzing the use of EMMA on Android to guide us to full test coverage of our code in *Chapter 10, Alternative Testing Tactics*.

This screenshot shows how an EMMA code coverage report is displayed in the Eclipse editor, showing green lines where the code has been tested, provided the corresponding plugin is installed.

```
main.xml    TemperatureConverterActivityTests.java    TemperatureConverterUnitTests.java    TemperatureConverterActivity.java    TemperatureConverter.java
 6  /**
 7   * @author diego
 8   *
 9   */
10  public class TemperatureConverter {
11      public static final double ABSOLUTE_ZERO_C = -273.0d;
12      public static final double ABSOLUTE_ZERO_F = -459.4d;
13
14      private static final String ERROR_MESSAGE_BELOW_ZERO_FMT = "Invalid temperature: %.2f%c below absolute zero";
15
16      public static int celsiusToFahrenheit(int c) {
17          return (int)Math.round(celsiusToFahrenheit((double)c));
18      }
19
20      public static double celsiusToFahrenheit(double c) {
21          if (c < ABSOLUTE_ZERO_C) {
22              throw new RuntimeException(String.format(ERROR_MESSAGE_BELOW_ZERO_FMT, c, 'C'));
23          }
24          return (c * 1.8d + 32);
25      }
26
27      public static int fahrenheitToCelsius(int f) {
28          return (int)Math.round(fahrenheitToCelsius((double)f));
29      }
30
31      public  static double fahrenheitToCelsius(double f) {
32          if (f < ABSOLUTE_ZERO_F) {
33              throw new RuntimeException(String.format(ERROR_MESSAGE_BELOW_ZERO_FMT, f, 'F'));
34          }
35          return ((f - 32) / 1.8d);
36      }
```

Unfortunately, the plugin doesn't support Android tests yet, so right now you can only use it for your JUnit tests. An Android coverage analysis report is only available through HTML.

Tests should be automated, and you should run some or all of them every time you introduce a change or addition to your code, in order to ensure that all the previous conditions are still met and that the new code still satisfies the tests as expected.

This leads us to the introduction of **Continuous Integration**, which will be discussed in detail in *Chapter 8, Continuous Integration*. This relies on the automation of tests and building processes.

If you don't use automated testing, it is practically impossible to adopt Continuous Integration as part of the development process and it is very difficult to ensure that changes do not break existing code.

# What to test

Strictly speaking you should test every statement in your code but this also depends on different criteria and can be reduced to test the path of execution or just some methods. Usually there is no need to test something that can't be broken, for example it usually makes no sense to test getters and setters as you probably won't be testing the Java compiler on your own code and the compiler would have already performed its own tests.

## Activity lifecycle events

You should test that your activities handle lifecycle events correctly.

If your activity should save its state during `onPause()` or `onDestroy()` events and later restore it in `onCreate(Bundle savedInstanceState)`, you should be able to reproduce and test these conditions and verify that the state was correctly saved and restored.

Configuration-changed events should also be tested as some of these events cause the current Activity to be recreated, and you should test for correct handling of the event and that the newly created Activity preserves the previous state. Configuration changes are triggered even by rotation events, so you should test your application's ability to handle these situations.

## Database and filesystem operations

Database and filesystem operations should be tested to ensure that they are handled correctly. These operations should be tested in isolation at the lower system level, at a higher level through `ContentProviders`, and from the application itself.

To test these components in isolation, Android provides some mock objects in the `android.test.mock` package.

## Physical characteristics of the device

Well before delivering your application you should be sure that all of the different devices it can be run on are supported or at the least you should detect the situation and take appropriate measures.

Among other characteristics of the devices, you may find that you should test:

- Network capabilities
- Screen densities
- Screen resolutions
- Screen sizes
- Availability of sensors

- Keyboard and other input devices
- GPS
- External storage

In this respect Android Virtual Devices play an important role because it is practically impossible to have access to all possible devices with all of the possible combinations of features but you can configure AVD for almost every situation. However, as was mentioned before, save your final testing for actual devices where real users will run the application to understand its behavior.

# Types of tests

Testing can be implemented at any time in the development process, depending on the method employed. However, we will be promoting testing at an early stage of the development effort, even before the full set of requirements have been defined and the coding process has been started.

There are several types of test available depending on the object being tested. Regardless of its type, a test should verify a condition and return the result of this evaluation as a single Boolean value indicating success or failure.

## Unit tests

Unit tests are software tests written by programmers for programmers in a programming language and they should isolate the component under test and be able to test it in a repeatable way. That's why unit tests and mock objects are usually placed together. You use mock objects to isolate the unit from its dependencies, to monitor interactions, and also to be able to repeat the test any number of times. For example, if your test deletes some data from a database you probably don't want the data to be actually deleted and not found the next time the test is run.

JUnit is the de-facto standard for unit tests on Android. It's a simple open source framework for automating unit testing, originally written by Erich Gamma and Kent Beck.

Android (up to Android 2.3 Gingerbread) uses JUnit 3. This version doesn't use annotations and uses introspection to detect the tests.

A typical JUnit test would look something like this (the actual tests are highlighted):

```
/**
 * Android Application Testing Guide
 */
package com.example.aatg.test;
```

```java
import JUnit.framework.TestCase;
/**
 * @author diego
 */
public class MyUnitTests extends TestCase {
  private int mFixture;
/**
 * @param name test name
 */
  public MyUnitTests(String name) {
    super(name);
  }
/* (non-Javadoc)
 * @see JUnit.framework.TestCase#setUp()
 */
  protected void setUp() throws Exception {
    super.setUp();
    mFixture = 1234;
  }
/* (non-Javadoc)
 * @see JUnit.framework.TestCase#tearDown()
 */
  protected void tearDown() throws Exception {
    super.tearDown();
  }
/**
 * Preconditions
 */
  public void testPreconditions() {
  }
/**
 * Test method
 */
  public void testSomething() {
    fail("Not implemented yet");
  }
}
```

> **Downloading the example code**
>
> You can download the example code files for all Packt books you have purchased from your account at http://www.PacktPub.com. If you purchased this book elsewhere, you can visit http://www.PacktPub.com/support and register to have the files e-mailed directly to you.

The following sections explain in detail the components that build up our test case.

## The test fixture

A test fixture is the well known state defined as a baseline to run the tests and is shared by all the test cases, and thus plays a fundamental role in the design of the tests.

Generally it is implemented as a set of member variables and, following Android conventions, they will have names starting with `m`, for example `mActivity`. However, it can also contain external data, as specific entries in a database or files present in the filesystem.

## The setUp() method

This method is called to initialize the fixture.

Overriding it you have the opportunity to create objects and initialize fields that will be used by tests. It's worth noting that this setup occurs *before* every test.

## The tearDown() method

This method is called to finalize the fixture.

Overriding it you can release resources used by the initialization or tests. Again, this method is invoked *after* every test.

For example, you can release a database or a network connection here.

JUnit is designed in such a way that the entire tree of test instances is built in one pass, and then the tests are executed in a second pass. Therefore, the test runner holds strong references to all Test instances for the duration of the test execution. This means that for very large and very long test runs with many Test instances, none of the tests may be garbage collected until the end of the entire test run. This is particularly important in Android and when testing on limited devices as some tests may fail not because of an intrinsic problem but because of the amount of memory needed to run the application plus its tests exceeding the device limits.

Therefore, if you allocate external or limited resources in a test, such as `Services` or `ContentProviders`, you are responsible for freeing those resources. Explicitly setting an object to null in the `tearDown()` method, for example, allows it to be garbage collected before the end of the entire test run.

## Test preconditions

Usually there is no way to test for preconditions as the tests are discovered using introspection and their order could vary. So it's customary to create a `testPreconditions()` method to test for preconditions. Though there is no assurance that this test will be called in any specific order, it is good practice to keep this and the preconditions together for organizational purposes.

## The actual tests

All `public void` methods whose names start with `test` will be considered as a test. JUnit 3, as opposed to JUnit 4, doesn't use annotations to discover the tests but introspection to find their names. There are some annotations available on the Android test framework such as `@SmallTest`, `@MediumTest`, and `@LargeTest`, but they don't turn a simple method into a test. Instead they organize them in different categories. Ultimately you will have the ability to run tests for a single category using the test runner.

As a rule of thumb, name your tests in a descriptive way using nouns and the condition being tested.

For example: `testValues()`, `testConversionError()`, `testConversionToString()` are all valid test names.

Test for exceptions and wrong values instead of just testing for positive cases.

During the execution of the test some conditions, side effects, or method returns should be compared against the expectations. To ease these operations, JUnit provides a full set of `assert*` methods to compare the expected results from the test to the actual results after running with them throwing exceptions if conditions are not met. Then the test runner handles these exceptions and presents the results.

These methods, which are overloaded to support different arguments, include:

- `assertEquals()`
- `assertFalse()`
- `assertNotNull()`
- `assertNotSame()`
- `assertNull()`
- `assertSame()`
- `assertTrue()`
- `fail()`

In addition to these JUnit assert methods, Android extends Assert in two specialized classes providing additional tests:

- `MoreAsserts`
- `ViewAsserts`

## Mock objects

Mock objects are mimic objects used instead of calling the real domain objects to enable testing units in isolation.

Generally, this is done to ensure that correct methods are called but they can also be of help, as mentioned, to isolate your tests from the surrounding universe and enable you to run them independently and repeatably.

The Android testing framework supports several mock objects that you will find very useful when writing your tests but you will need to provide some dependencies to be able to compile the tests.

Several classes are provided by the Android testing framework in the `android.test.mock` package:

- `MockApplication`
- `MockContentProvider`
- `MockContentResolver`
- `MockContext`
- `MockCursor`
- `MockDialogInterface`
- `MockPackageManager`
- `MockResources`

Almost any component of the platform that could interact with your Activity can be created by instantiating one of these classes.

However, they are not real implementations but stubs where every method generates an `UnsupportedOperationException` and that you can extend to create real mock objects.

*Getting Started with Testing*

## UI tests

Finally, special consideration should be taken if your tests involve UI components. As you may have already known, only the main thread is allowed to alter the UI in Android. Thus a special annotation `@UIThreadTest` is used to indicate that a particular test should be run on that thread and would have the ability to alter the UI. On the other hand, if you only want to run parts of your test on the UI thread, you may use the `Activity.runOnUiThread(Runnable r)` method providing the corresponding `Runnable` containing testing instructions.

A helper class `TouchUtils` is also provided to aid in the UI test creation allowing the generation of events to send to the Views, such as:

- click
- drag
- long click
- scroll
- tap
- touch

By these means you can actually remote control you application from the tests.

## Eclipse and other IDE support

JUnit is fully supported by Eclipse and the Android ADT plugin lets you create Android testing projects. Furthermore, you can run the tests and analyze the results without leaving the IDE.

This also provides a more subtle advantage; being able to run the tests from Eclipse allows you to debug the tests that are not behaving correctly.

In the screenshot, we can see how Eclipse runs **18 tests** taking 20.008 seconds, where **0 Errors** and **0 Failures** were detected. The name of each test and its duration is also displayed. If there was a failure, the **Failure Trace** would show the related information.

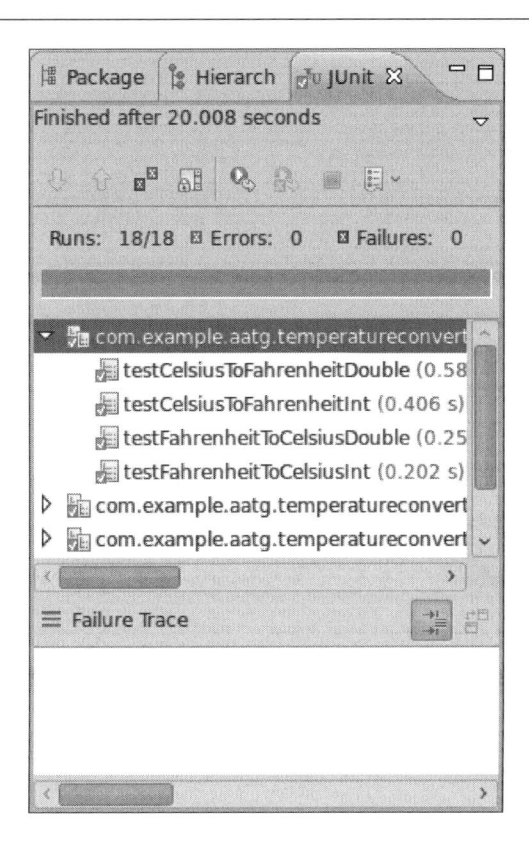

Other IDEs like ItelliJ and Netbeans have plugins integrating Android development to some degree but they are not officially supported.

Even if you are not developing in an IDE, you can find support to run the tests with **ant** (check http://ant.apache.org if you are not familiar with this tool). This setup is done by the android command using the subcommand create test-project as described by this help text:

```
$ android --help create test-project
```

```
Usage:
  android [global options] create test-project [action options]

Global options:
  -v --verbose  Verbose mode: errors, warnings and informational messages
are printed.
  -h --help     Help on a specific command.
  -s --silent   Silent mode: only errors are printed out.
```

```
Action "create test-project":
  Creates a new Android project for a test package.
Options:
  -p --path    The new project's directory [required]
  -m --main    Path to directory of the app under test, relative to the
test project directory [required]
  -n --name    Project name
```

As indicated by the help you should provide at least the path to the project (`--path`) and the path to the main project or the project under test (`--main`).

## Integration tests

Integration tests are designed to test the way individual components work jointly. Modules that have been unit tested independently are now combined together to test the integration.

Usually Android Activities require some integration with the system infrastructure to be able to run. They need the Activity lifecycle provided by the `ActivityManager`, and access to resources, filesystem, and databases.

The same criteria apply to other Android components like `Services` or `ContentProviders` that need to interact with other parts of the system to achieve their function.

In all these cases there are specialized tests provided by the Android testing framework that facilitate the creation of tests for these components.

## Functional or acceptance tests

In agile software development, functional or acceptance tests are usually created by business and Quality Assurance (QA) people and expressed in a business domain language. These are high level tests to test the completeness and correctness of a user requirement or feature. They are created ideally through collaboration between business customers, business analysts, QA, testers, and developers. However the business customers (product owners) are the primary owners of these tests.

Some frameworks and tools can help in this field, most notably FitNesse (`http://www.fitnesse.org`), which can be easily integrated, up to a point, into the Android development process and will let you create acceptance tests and check their results.

> Also check Fit, http://fit.c2.com and Slim (Simple List Invocation Method), http://fitnesse.org/FitNesse.UserGuide.SliM, as an alternative to Fit.

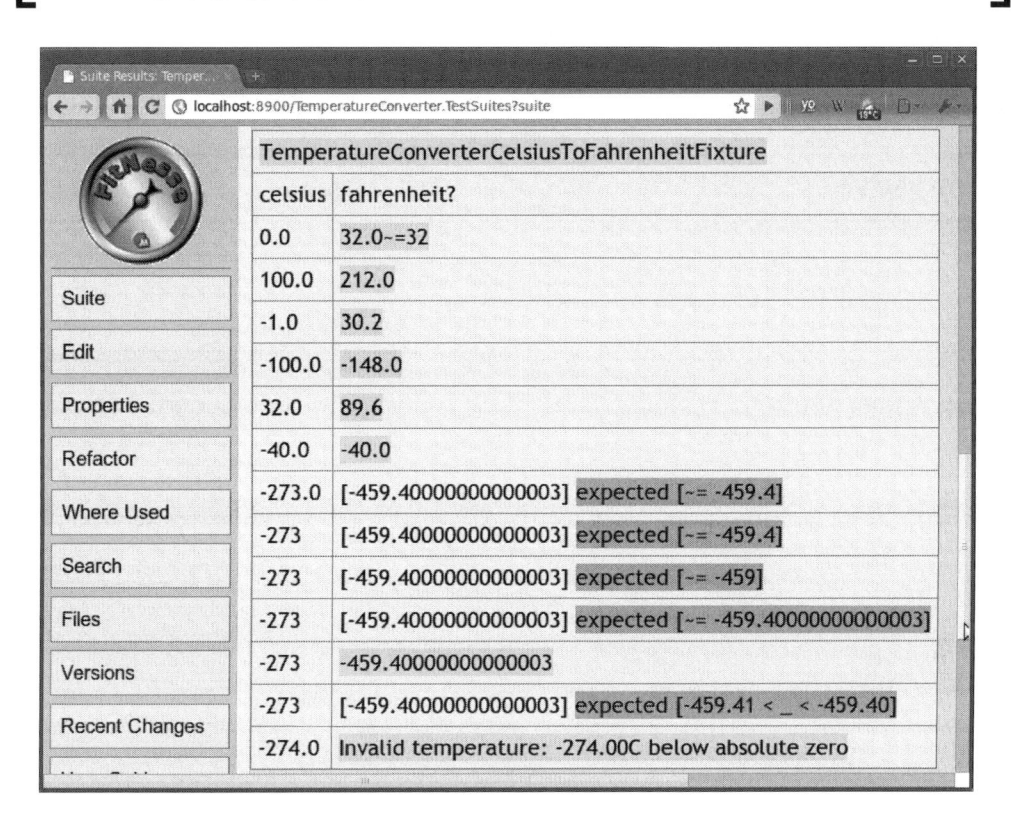

| TemperatureConverterCelsiusToFahrenheitFixture | |
|---|---|
| celsius | fahrenheit? |
| 0.0 | 32.0-=32 |
| 100.0 | 212.0 |
| -1.0 | 30.2 |
| -100.0 | -148.0 |
| 32.0 | 89.6 |
| -40.0 | -40.0 |
| -273.0 | [-459.40000000000003] expected [-= -459.4] |
| -273 | [-459.40000000000003] expected [-= -459.4] |
| -273 | [-459.40000000000003] expected [-= -459] |
| -273 | [-459.40000000000003] expected [-= -459.40000000000003] |
| -273 | -459.40000000000003 |
| -273 | [-459.40000000000003] expected [-459.41 < _ < -459.40] |
| -274.0 | Invalid temperature: -274.00C below absolute zero |

Lately, a new trend named **Behavior Driven Development** has gained some popularity and in a very brief description can be understood as the evolution of Test Driven Development. It aims to provide a common vocabulary between business and technology people in order to increase mutual understanding.

Behavior Driven Development can be expressed as a framework of activities based on three principles (more information can be found at http://behaviour-driven.org):

- Business and technology should refer to the same system in the same way
- Any system should have an identified, verifiable value to the business
- Upfront analysis, design, and planning all have a diminishing return

## Test case scenario

As an illustration of this technique here is an oversimplified example.

This scenario is:

```
Given I'm using the Temperature Converter.
When I enter 100 into Celsius field.
Then I obtain 212 in Fahrenheit field.
```

It would be translated into something similar to:

```java
@Given("I am using the Temperature Converter")
public void createTemperatureConverter() {
    // do nothing
}
@When("I enter $celsius into Celsius field")
public void setCelsius(int celsius) {
    mCelsius= celsius;
}
@Then("I obtain $fahrenheit in Fahrenheit field")
public void testCelsiusToFahrenheit(int fahrenheit) {
    assertEquals(fahrenheit,
       TemperatureConverter.celsiusToFahrenheit
          (mCelsius));
}
```

## Performance tests

Performance tests measure performance characteristics of the components in a repeatable way. If performance improvements are required by some part of the application, the best approach is to measure performance before and after some change is introduced.

As is widely known, premature optimization does more harm than good, so it is better to clearly understand the impact of your changes on the overall performance.

The introduction of the **Dalvik JIT** compiler in Android 2.2 changed some optimization patterns that were widely used in Android development. Nowadays, every recommendation about performance improvements on the Android developer's site is backed up by performance tests.

## System tests

The system is tested as a whole and the interaction between the components, software and hardware, is exercised. Normally, system tests include additional classes of tests like:

- GUI tests
- Smoke tests
- Performance tests
- Installation tests

# Android testing framework

Android provides a very advanced testing framework extending the industry standard JUnit with specific features suitable for implementing all of the testing strategies and types we mentioned before. In some cases, additional tools are needed but the integration of these tools is in most cases simple and straightforward.

The key features of the Android testing environment include:

- Android extensions to the JUnit framework that provide access to Android system objects.
- An instrumentation framework that lets tests control and examine the application.
- Mock versions of commonly used Android system objects.
- Tools for running single tests or test suites, with or without instrumentation.
- Support for managing tests and test projects in the ADT Plugin for Eclipse and at the command line.

## Instrumentation

The instrumentation framework is the foundation of the testing framework. Instrumentation controls the application under test and permits the injection of mock components required by the application to run. For example, you can create mock Contexts before the application starts and let the application use them.

*Getting Started with Testing*

All interaction of the application with the surrounding environment can be controlled using this approach. You can also isolate your application in a restricted environment to be able to predict the results, forcing the values returned by some methods or mocking persistent and unchanged data for `ContentProvider`, databases, or even the filesystem content.

A standard Android project has its tests in a correlated project that usually has the same project name but ends with **Test**. Inside this Test project, the `AndroidManifest.xml` declares the Instrumentation.

As an illustrative example, assume your project has a manifest like this:

```xml
<?xml version="1.0" encoding="utf-8"?>
<manifest xmlns:android="http://schemas.android.com/apk/res/android"
      package="com.example.aatg.sample"
      android:versionCode="1"
      android:versionName="1.0">
      <application android:icon="@drawable/icon"
            android:label="@string/app_name">
        <activity android:name=".SampleActivity"
                android:label="@string/app_name">
          <intent-filter>
            <action android:name="android.intent.action.MAIN" />
            <category android:name=
              "android.intent.category.LAUNCHER" />
          </intent-filter>
        </activity>
      </application>
    <uses-sdk android:minSdkVersion="7" />
</manifest>
```

In this case, the correlated Test project will have the following `AndroidManifest.xml`:

```xml
<?xml version="1.0" encoding="utf-8"?>
<manifest xmlns:android="http://schemas.android.com/apk/res/android"
  package="com.example.aatg.sample.test"
  android:versionCode="1" android:versionName="1.0">
  <application android:icon="@drawable/icon"
            android:label="@string/app_name">
    <uses-library android:name="android.test.runner" />
  </application>
  <uses-sdk android:minSdkVersion="7" />
  <instrumentation
    android:targetPackage="com.example.aatg.sample"
```

```
        android:name="android.test.InstrumentationTestRunner"
        android:label="Sample Tests" />
    <uses-permission android:name="
        android.permission.INJECT_EVENTS" />
</manifest>
```

Here the Instrumentation package is the same package as the main application with the `.test` suffix added.

Then the Instrumentation is declared specifying the target package and the test runner, in this case the default custom runner `android.test.InstrumentationTestRunner`.

Also notice that both, the application under test and the tests are Android applications with their corresponding APKs installed. Internally, they will be sharing the same process and thus have access to the same set of features.

When you run a test application, the **Activity Manager** (http://developer.android.com/intl/de/reference/android/app/ActivityManager.html) uses the instrumentation framework to start and control the test runner, which in turn uses instrumentation to shut down any running instances of the main application, starts the test application, and then starts the main application in the same process. This allows various aspects of the test application to work directly with the main application.

# Test targets

During the evolution of your development project your tests would be targeted to different devices. From the simplicity, flexibility, and speed of testing on an emulator to the unavoidable final testing on the specific devices you intend your application to be run on, you should be able to run on all of them.

There are also some intermediate cases like running your tests on a local **JVM** virtual machine on the development computer or on a **Dalvik** virtual machine or `Activity`, depending on the case.

Every case has its pros and cons, but the good news is that you have all of these alternatives available to run your tests.

The emulator is probably the most powerful target as you can modify almost every parameter from its configuration to simulate different conditions for your tests. Ultimately, your application should be able to handle all of these situations, so it is much better to discover the problems upfront than when the application has been delivered.

The real devices are a requirement for performance tests, as it is somewhat difficult to extrapolate performance measurements from a simulated device. You will discover the real user experience only when using the real device. Rendering, scrolling, flinging, and other cases should be tested before delivering the application.

# Summary

We have reviewed the main concepts behind testing in general and Android in particular. Having acquired this knowledge will let us start our journey and start exploiting the benefits of testing in our software development projects.

So far, we have visited the following subjects:

- We reviewed the early stages of testing on Android and mentioned some of the frameworks that created the current alternatives.
- We briefly analyzed the reasons behind testing and the whys, whats, hows, and whens of it. Furthermore, from now on we will concentrate on exploring the hows, as we can assume that you are convinced by the arguments presented.
- We enumerated the different and most common types of tests you would need in your projects, described some of the tools we can count on our testing toolbox, and provided an introductory example of a JUnit unit test to better understand what we are discussing.

We also analyzed these techniques from the Android perspective and mentioned the use of Instrumentation to run our Android tests.

Now we will start analyzing the mentioned techniques, frameworks, and tools in detail, along with examples of their usage.

# 2
# Testing on Android

Now that we have introduced the reasons and the basic concepts behind testing, it's time to put them into practice.

In this second chapter, we are covering:

- Testing on Android
- Unit testing and JUnit
- Creating an Android Test project
- Running tests

We will be creating a simple Android **main** project and its companion **test** project. The main project will be almost empty and will just highlight testing components.

From my personal experience, I suggest that this chapter is useful for new developers with no Android Testing experience. If you have some experience with Android Projects and have been using testing techniques for them, you might read this chapter as a revision or reaffirmation of the concepts.

Though not mandatory, best practices dictate that tests should live in a separate correlated project. This feature is now supported by the Android ADP plugin, but this has not always been the case. Some time ago I published an article (`http://dtmilano.blogspot.com/2008/11/android-testing-on-android-platf.html`) describing a method for manually maintaining two correlated projects—a main project and a test project.

The advantages of this decision may not be immediately evident, but among them we can count:

- Testing code is easily stripped out from a production build as it is not included in the main project and thus not in the APK

- Ease the way of running the tests in the emulator through the Instrumentation option in Dev Tools
- With large projects, deploying the main package and the tests takes less time if they are separated
- Encourages code reusability in similar projects

## JUnit

We had an overview of JUnit in the previous chapter, so no introduction is needed here. It is worth mentioning that the JUnit testing framework is the default option for Android testing projects and it is supported by Eclipse, the Android ADT plugin, and by Ant as well, in case you are not developing with an IDE.

So you are free to choose the best alternative for every case.

Most of the following examples will be based on Eclipse because is the most common option. So, let's open Eclipse and start with no preamble.

## Creating the Android main project

We will create a new Android project. This is done from Eclipse menu **File | New | Project... | Android | Android Project**.

In this particular case, we are using the following values for the required component names:

| | |
|---|---|
| Project name: | **MyFirstProject** |
| Build Target: | **Android 2.3.1** |
| Application name: | **My First Project** |
| Package name: | **com.example.aatg.myfirstproject** |
| Create Activity: | **MyFirstProjectActivity** |
| Min SDK Version: | **9** |

This is what your project creation dialog will look like after entering these values:

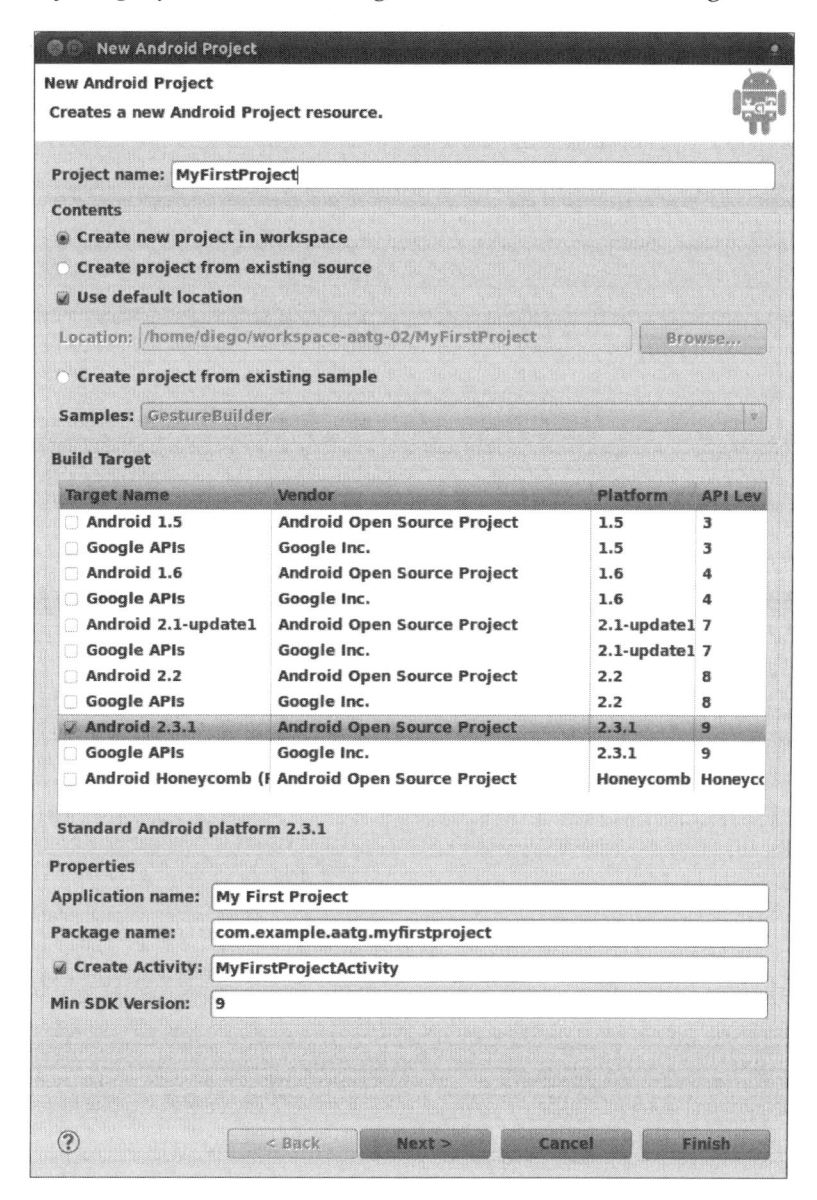

# Creating the Android test project

Press the **Next** button and the Android Test Project creation dialog will be displayed. Note that some values have been already picked according to the corresponding values selected in the main project.

*Testing on Android*

> Alternatively, to create a Test project for an existing Android project you can select the main project and then **Android Tools | Create Test Project**. Under *Test Target* select the name of the existing project and the required values will be filled in automatically.

This image shows the Android Test Project creation dialog after entering the corresponding values. All the values have been already entered for us and we should only have to click **Finish**:

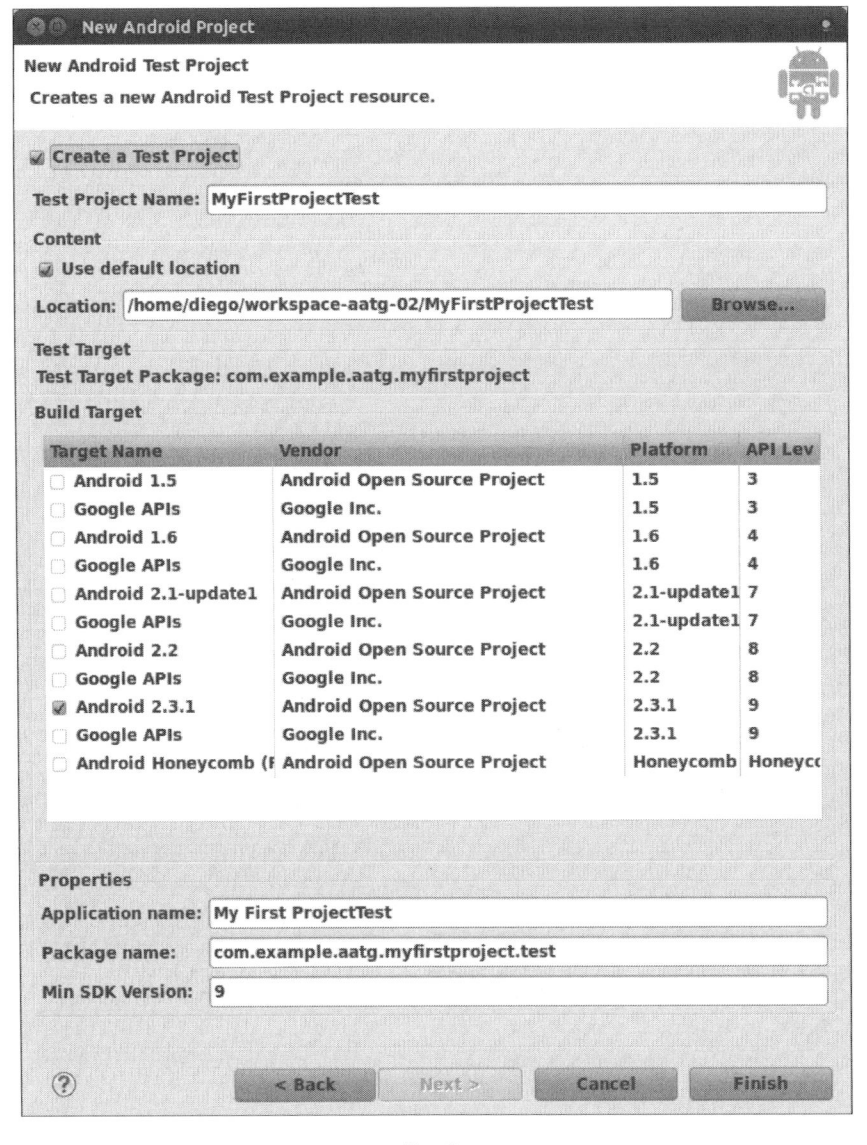

# Package explorer

After having created both projects, our Package explorer should look like the next image. We can note the existence of the two correlated projects, each with an independent set of components and project properties.

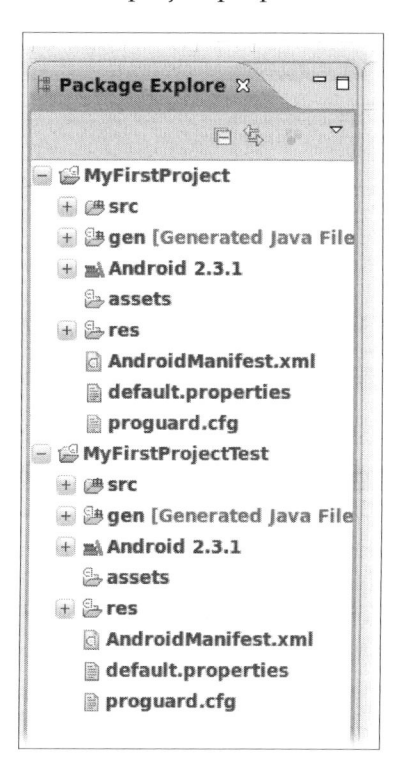

Now that we have the basic infrastructure set up, it's time for us to start adding some tests.

There's nothing to test right now, but as we are setting up the fundamentals of Test Driven Development discipline we are adding a dummy test just to get acquainted with the technique.

The `src` folder on `MyFirstProjectTest` project is the perfect place to add the tests. It is not mandatory but a good practice. The package should be the same as the corresponding package of the component being tested.

# Testing on Android

Right now, we are not concentrating on the tests but on the concepts and placement of those tests.

## Creating a test case

As described before, we are creating our test cases in the `src` folder of the Test project.

In this particular case, we are creating a unit test using JUnit TestCase. Eclipse provides a wizard to help us (**File | New... | Junit Test Case**).

We are selecting the main project's Activity as the class under test; however this is not relevant in this example.

These are the values that we should enter when we create the test case:

| | |
|---|---|
| Junit: | **Junit 3** |
| Source folder: | **MyFirstProjectTest/src** |
| Package: | **com.example.aatg.myfirstproject.test** |
| Name: | **MyFirstProjectTests** |
| Superclass: | **junit.framework.TestCase** |
| Which method stubs would you like to create? | **setUp(), tearDown(), constructor** |
| Class under test: | **com.example.aatg.myfirstproject.MyFirstProjectActivity** |

> Strictly speaking we could have left the **setUp()**, **tearDown()**, and **constructor** options unselected and this basic test we are creating would not be affected, but here we are describing the most general practices and we will find in many real life scenarios that these methods are needed.

After entering all the required values our JUnit test case creation dialog would look like this:

*Chapter 2*

![New JUnit Test Case dialog showing fields: Source folder: MyFirstProjectTest/src, Package: com.example.aatg.myfirstproject.test, Name: MyFirstProjectTests, Superclass: junit.framework.TestCase, with setUp(), tearDown(), constructor, and Generate comments checked, Class under test: com.example.aatg.myfirstproject.MyFirstProjectActivity]

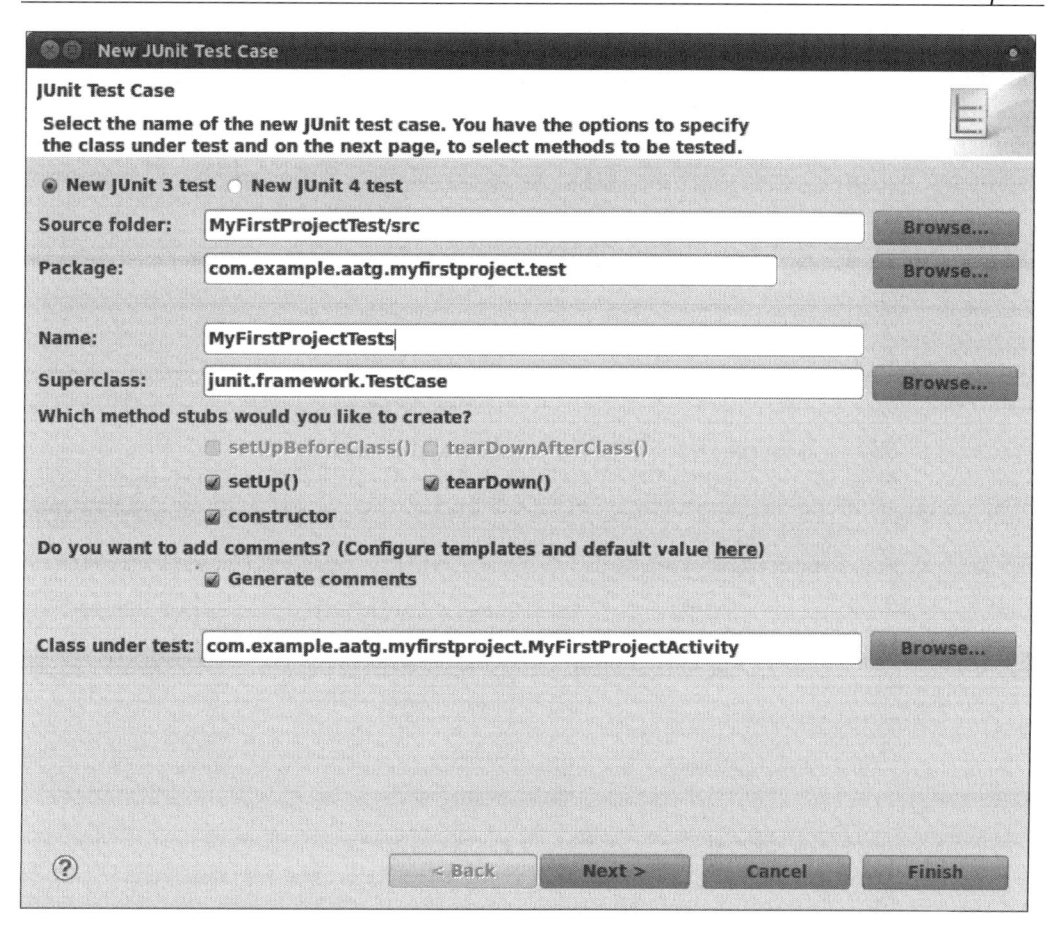

The basic infrastructure for our tests is in place; what is left is adding a dummy test to verify that everything is working as expected.

*Testing on Android*

Eclipse also provides a way of creating stubs for the test methods. After pressing **Next >** the following dialog is presented where you can choose the methods under tests you want to generate the stubs for:

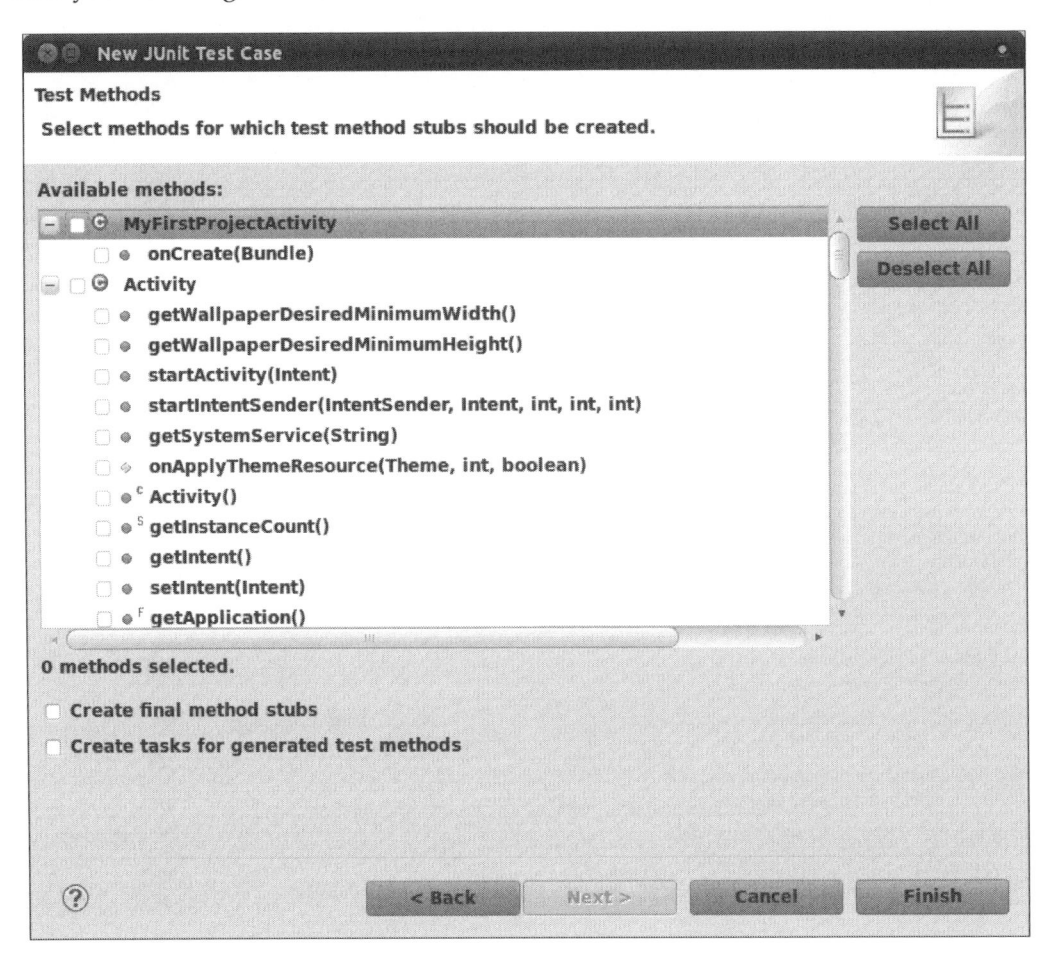

![New JUnit Test Case dialog showing Test Methods selection with available methods including MyFirstProjectActivity (onCreate(Bundle)) and Activity methods such as getWallpaperDesiredMinimumWidth(), getWallpaperDesiredMinimumHeight(), startActivity(Intent), startIntentSender(IntentSender, Intent, int, int, int), getSystemService(String), onApplyThemeResource(Theme, int, boolean), Activity(), getInstanceCount(), getIntent(), setIntent(Intent), getApplication(). Options include Select All, Deselect All, Create final method stubs, Create tasks for generated test methods. Buttons: Back, Next, Cancel, Finish.]

These stub methods may be useful in some cases but you have to consider that testing should be behavior driven rather than method driven.

We now have a test case template, so the next step is to start completing it to suit our needs. To do it, open the recently created case class and add the test `testSomething()`. As a best practice, add the tests at the end of the class.

We should have something like this:

```
/**
 *
 */
```

```java
package com.example.aatg.myfirstproject.test;

import android.test.suitebuilder.annotation.SmallTest;
import junit.framework.TestCase;
/**
 * @author diego
 *
 */
public class MyFirstProjectTests extends TestCase {
  public MyFirstProjectTests() {
    this("MyFirstProjectTests");
  }
  /**
   * @param name
   */
  public MyFirstProjectTests(String name) {
    super(name);
  }
  /* (non-Javadoc)
   * @see junit.framework.TestCase#setUp()
   */
  protected void setUp() throws Exception {
    super.setUp();
  }
  /* (non-Javadoc)
   * @see junit.framework.TestCase#tearDown()
   */
  protected void tearDown() throws Exception {
    super.tearDown();
  }
  @SmallTest
  public void testSomething() {
    fail("Not implemented yet");
  }
}
```

This test will always fail, presenting the message: **Not implemented yet**. In order to do this we are using the `fail` method from the `junit.framework.Assert` class that fails the test with the given message.

> The no-argument constructor is needed to run a specific test from the command line as explained later using `am instrumentation`.

## Special methods

The following table describes the special methods found in our test case class:

| Method | Description |
| --- | --- |
| `setUp` | Sets up the fixture. For example, opens a network connection or creates global objects that may be needed by the tests. This method is called before a test is executed. |
| | In this case we are only invoking the super method. |
| | See *Chapter 1, Getting Started with Testing* for details. |
| `tearDown` | Tears down the fixture. For example, close a network connection. This method is called after a test is executed. |
| | In this case we are only invoking the super method. |
| | See *Chapter 1, Getting Started with Testing* for details. |
| `testSomething` | A simple test. In order to be discovered by JUnit 3 using reflection, test methods should start with the word `test`. |
| | The rest of the method name should clearly identify the feature under test. |

## Test annotations

Looking carefully at the test definition you may find that we decorated the test using `@MediumTest` annotation. This is a way to organize or categorize our tests and run them separately.

There are other annotations that can be used by the tests, such as:

| Annotation | Description |
| --- | --- |
| `@SmallTest` | Marks a test that should run as part of the small tests. |
| `@MediumTest` | Marks a test that should run as part of the medium tests. |
| `@LargeTest` | Marks a test that should run as part of the large tests. |
| `@Smoke` | Marks a test that should run as part of the smoke tests. The `android.test.suitebuilder.SmokeTestSuiteBuilder` will run all tests with this annotation. |
| `@FlakyTest` | Use this annotation on `InstrumentationTestCase` class' test methods. When this is present, the test method is re-executed if the test fails. The total number of executions is specified by the tolerance and defaults to 1. This is useful for tests that may fail due to an external condition that could vary with time. |
| | For example, to specify a tolerance of 4, you would annotate your test with: `@FlakyTest(tolerance=4)`. |

| Annotation | Description |
|---|---|
| `@UIThreadTest` | Use this annotation on `InstrumentationTestCase` class' test methods. When this is present, the test method is executed on the application's main thread (or UI thread). |
| | Because instrumentation methods may not be used when this annotation is present there are other techniques if, for example, you need to modify the UI and get access to the instrumentation within the same test. |
| | In those cases you can resort to the `Activity.runOnUIThread` method allowing to create any `Runnable` and run it in the UI thread from within your test. |
| | ```
mActivity.runOnUIThread(new Runnable() {
    public void run() {
        // do somethings
    }
});
``` |
| `@Suppress` | Use this annotation on test classes or test methods that should not be included in a test suite. |
| | This annotation can be used at the class level, where none of the methods in that class are included in the test suite, or at the method level to exclude just a single method or set of methods. |

Now that we have the tests in place, it's time to run them, and that's what we are going to do next.

# Running the tests

There are several ways of running our tests, and we will analyze them here.

Additionally, as was mentioned in the previous section about annotations, tests can be grouped or categorized and run together, depending on the situation.

## Running all tests from Eclipse

This is perhaps the simplest method if you have adopted Eclipse as your development environment. This will run all the tests in the package.

Select the test project and then **Run As | Android Junit Test**.

If a suitable device or emulator is not found, one will be started automatically.
```

*Testing on Android*

Then the tests are run and the results presented inside the Eclipse DDMS perspective, which you may need to change to manually.

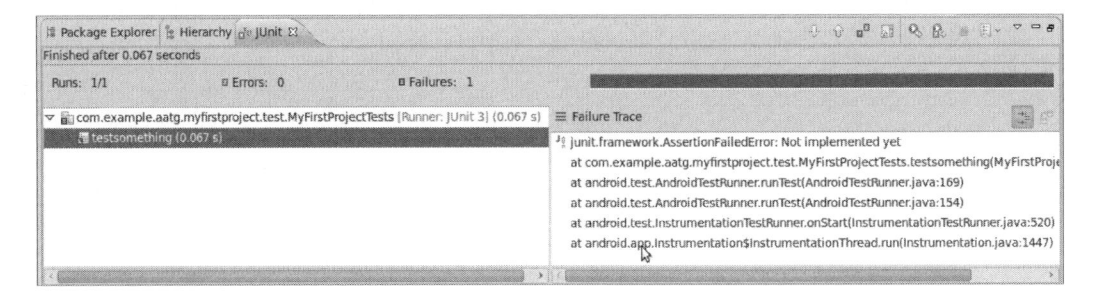

A more detailed view of the results and the messages produced during their execution can also be obtained in the LogCat view within the Eclipse DDMS perspective:

# Running a single test case from Eclipse

There is an option to run a single test case from Eclipse, should you need to.

Select the test project and then **Run As | Run Configurations**.

Then create a new configuration and under *Test*, use the following values:

| Run a single test: | **checked** |
|---|---|
| Project: | **MyFirstProjectTest** |
| Test class: | **com.example.aatg.myfirstproject.test.MyFirstProjectTests** |

When you run as usual, only this test will be executed. In our case, we have only one test, so the result will be similar to the screenshot presented earlier.

> There is a shortcut for this that you can use from within the Eclipse editor. Selecting the method name you can press *Shift+Alt+X T* or right-click on it and then choosing **Run As | JUnit Test**.

## Running from the emulator

The default system image used by the emulator has the *Dev Tools* application installed, providing several handy tools and settings. Among these tools, we can find a rather long list as is shown in this screenshot:

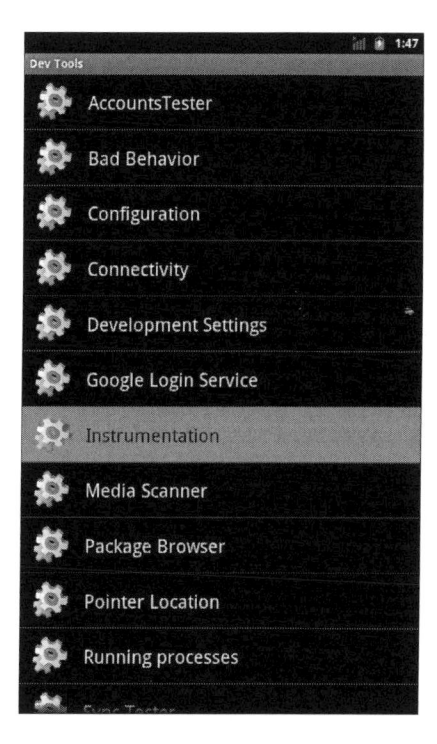

We are interested in **Instrumentation** now, which is the way to run our tests. This application lists all of the packages installed that define the `instrumentation` tag in their `AndroidManifest.xml`. By default, packages are listed using the default instrumentation which normally is `android.test.InstrumentationTestRunner` which is a problem to identify if you have more than one package list. To solve this problem you can set an optional label in the manifest, under the Instrumentation tab, as shown here:

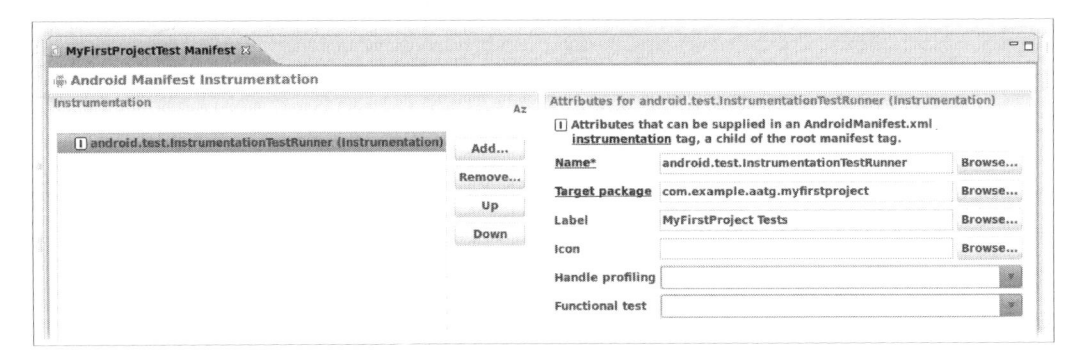

Once this is done and the Instrumentation list is re-displayed, our package will be listed under this new label and we can run the tests by selecting it:

When the tests are run in this way, the results can be seen through **LogCat** as described in the previous section.

> You can see how, as mentioned previously, if you don't set the optional Label more than one instrumentation appears under the same default label `android.test.InstrumentationTestRunner`.

## Running tests from the command line

Finally, tests can be run from the command line too. This is useful if you want to automate or script the process.

To run the tests we are using the `am instrument` command (strictly speaking the `am` command and `instrument` subcommand) which allows us to run instrumentations specifying the package name and some other options.

You may wonder what `am` stands for. It is short for **Activity Manager**, a main component of the internal Android infrastructure that is started by the **System Server** at the beginning of the boot process and is responsible for managing Activities and their life cycle. Additionally, as we can see here, it is also responsible for Activity instrumentation.

The general usage of the `am instrument` command is:

```
am instrument [flags] <COMPONENT>
        -r: print raw results (otherwise decode REPORT_KEY_STREAMRESULT)
        -e <NAME> <VALUE>: set argument <NAME> to <VALUE>
        -p <FILE>: write profiling data to <FILE>
        -w: wait for instrumentation to finish before returning
```

This table summarizes the most common options:

| Option | Description |
| --- | --- |
| `-r` | Print raw results. Useful to collect raw performance data. |
| `-e <NAME> <VALUE>` | Set arguments by name. We will examine its usage shortly. |
|  | This is a generic option argument that allows us to set `<name, value>` pairs. |
| `-p <FILE>` | Write profiling data to an external file. |
| `-w` | Wait for instrumentation to finish before exiting. Normally used in commands, although not mandatory it's very handy, as otherwise you will not be able to see the test's results. |

To invoke the `am` command we will be using the `adb shell` command or, if you already have a shell running on an emulator or device, you can issue the `am` command directly at the shell command prompt.

## Running all tests

This command line will run all tests with the exception of performance tests:

```
diego@bruce:\~$ adb shell am instrument -w com.example.aatg.myfirstproject.test/android.test.InstrumentationTestRunner

com.example.aatg.myfirstproject.test.MyFirstProjectTests:
Failure in testSomething:
junit.framework.AssertionFailedError: Not implemented yet
   at com.example.aatg.myfirstproject.test.MyFirstProjectTests.testSomething(MyFirstProjectTests.java:22)
   at java.lang.reflect.Method.invokeNative(Native Method)
   at android.test.AndroidTestRunner.runTest(AndroidTestRunner.java:169)
   at android.test.AndroidTestRunner.runTest(AndroidTestRunner.java:154)
   at android.test.InstrumentationTestRunner.onStart(InstrumentationTestRunner.java:430)
   at android.app.Instrumentation$InstrumentationThread.run(Instrumentation.java:1447)

Test results for InstrumentationTestRunner=.F
Time: 0.2

FAILURES!!!
Tests run: 1,  Failures: 1,  Errors: 0
```

## Running tests from a specific test case

To run all the tests in a specific test case, you may use:

```
diego@bruce:\~$ adb shell am instrument -w -e class com.example.aatg.myfirstproject.test.MyFirstProjectTests com.example.aatg.myfirstproject.test/android.test.InstrumentationTestRunner
```

## Running a specific test by name

Additionally we have the alternative of specifying which test we want to run in the command line:

```
diego@bruce:\~$ adb shell am instrument -w -e class com.example.aatg.
myfirstproject.test.MyFirstProjectTests\#testSomething com.example.aatg.
myfirstproject.test/android.test.InstrumentationTestRunner
```

This test cannot be run in this way unless we have a no-argument constructor in our test case — that is the reason we added it before.

## Running specific tests by category

As we mentioned before, tests can be grouped into different categories using annotations (*Test Annotations*) and you can run all tests in this category.

The following options can be added to the command line:

| | |
|---|---|
| -e unit true | Run all unit tests. These are tests that are not derived from InstrumentationTestCase (and are not performance tests). |
| -e func true | Run all functional tests. These are tests that are derived from InstrumentationTestCase. |
| -e perf true | Include performance tests. |
| -e size {small \| medium \| large} | Run small, medium, or large tests depending on the annotations added to the tests. |
| -e annotation <annotation-name> | Run tests annotated with this annotation. This option is mutually exclusive with the size option. |

In our example, we annotated the test method testSomething() with @SmallTest. So this test is considered to be in that category and thus run, eventually with other tests belonging to that same category, when we specify small as the test size.

This command line will run all the tests annotated with @SmallTest:

```
diego@bruce:\~$ adb shell am instrument -w -e size small  com.example.
aatg.myfirstproject.test/android.test.InstrumentationTestRunner
```

## Creating a custom annotation

In case you decide to sort the tests by a different criterion than their size, a custom annotation can be created and then specified in the command line.

As an example, let's say we want to arrange them according to their importance, so we create an annotation @VeryImportantTest.

# Testing on Android

```
package com.example.aatg.myfirstproject.test;
/**
 * Annotation for very important tests.
 *
 * @author diego
 *
 */
public @interface VeryImportantTest {

}
```

Following this, we can create another test and annotate it with `@VeryImportantTest`.

```
@VeryImportantTest
public void testOtherStuff() {
   fail("Not implemented yet");
}
```

So, as we mentioned before, we can include this annotation in the `am instrument` command line to run only the annotated tests:

```
diego@bruce:\~$ adb shell am instrument -w -e annotation VeryImportantTest \
com.example.aatg.myfirstproject.test/android.test.
InstrumentationTestRunner
```

## Running performance tests

We will be reviewing performance test details in *Chapter 9, Performance Testing* but here we will introduce the available options to the `am instrument` command.

To include performance tests on your test run you should add this command line option

| `-e perf true` | Include performance tests. |
|---|---|

## Dry run

Sometimes you may need to know only what tests will be run instead of actually running them.

This is the option you need to add to your command line:

| `-e log true` | Display the tests to be run instead of running them. |
|---|---|

This is useful if you are writing scripts or perhaps building other tools.

# Debugging tests

Your tests might have bugs too; you should assume that. In that case usual debugging techniques apply, for example adding messages through LogCat.

If a more sophisticated debugging technique is needed you should attach the debugger to the test runner. In order to do so, there are two main alternatives.

The first is easy — not leaving the convenience of Eclipse and not having to remember hard-to-memorize command-line options. In the latest version of the Android ADT plugin, the option **Debug As | Android JUnit Test** was added. Thus you can set a breakpoint in your tests and use it.

To toggle a breakpoint you can select the desired line in the editor and then use the menu option **Run | Toggle Line Breakpoint**. Alternatively you can slightly alter the code of your tests to wait for the debugger connection. But don't worry, this change is extremely simple. Add the following snippet to the constructor or any other test you want to debug. The place where you add it is not really relevant as the debugger would stop at breakpoints anyway. In this case, we decided to add `Debug.waitForDebugger()` to the constructor as follows:

```
public class MyFirstProjectTests extends TestCase {

  private static final boolean DEBUG = true;

  public MyFirstProjectTests(String name) {
    super(name);

    if ( DEBUG ) {
      Debug.waitForDebugger();
    }
  }
  ...
```

*Testing on Android*

When you run the tests as usual, using **Run As | Android JUnit Test**, you will probably be asked to change the perspective.

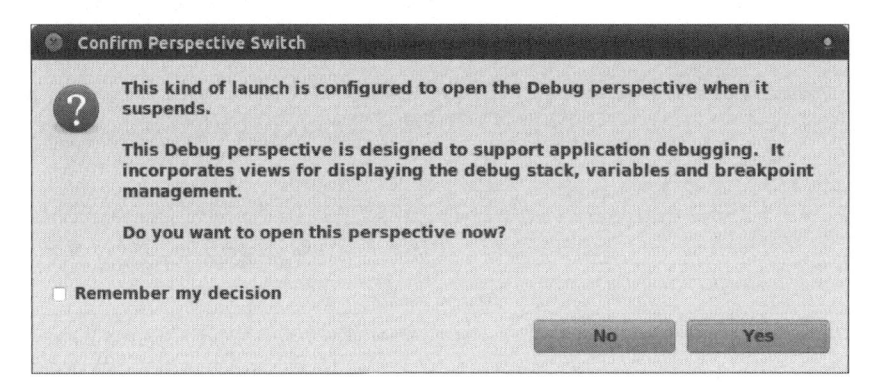

Once it is done, you will be in a standard debugging perspective and session.

Additionally if you can't or don't want to alter your tests' code, you can set breakpoints in it and pass the following option to `am instrument`.

| `-e debug true` | Attach to debugger. |

Once your tests have been started, the test runner will wait for your debugger to attach.

Execute this command line to debug the tests:

`$ adb shell am instrument -w -e debug true com.example.aatg.myfirstproject.test/android.test.InstrumentationTestRunner`

You will see this line while waiting at the first breakpoint reached:

`com.example.aatg.myfirstproject.test.MyFirstProjectTests:`

This will continue and exit normally once the debug was attached and your debugging session will be completed.

## Other command-line options

The `am instrument` command accepts other `<name, value>` pairs beside the previously mentioned ones:

| Name | Value |
| --- | --- |
| package | Fully qualified package name of one or several packages in the test application. |
| | Multiple values are separated by commas (,). |
| class | A fully qualified test case class to be executed by the test runner. |
| | Optionally this could include the test method name separated from the class name by a hash (#). |
| coverage | True |
| | Runs the EMMA code coverage and writes output to a file that can also be specified. |
| | We will dig into details about supporting EMMA code coverage for our tests in *Chapter 10, Alternative Testing Tactics*. |

## Summary

We have reviewed the main techniques and tools behind testing in Android.

The following is what we have covered in this chapter:

- Created our first Android test project as a companion for a sample Android project.
- Followed the best practice of always creating our companion test project even if initially you may think it's not needed.
- Created a simple test class to test the Activity in the project. We haven't added any useful test cases yet but adding those simple ones was intended to validate all of our infrastructure.
- We also ran this simple test from Eclipse and from the command line to understand the alternatives we have. In this process, we mentioned the Activity Manager and its command line incarnation am.
- Analyzed the most used command lines and explained their options.
- Created a custom annotation to sort our tests and demonstrated its usage.
- Running the tests and interpreting the results let us know how well our application is behaving.

In the next chapter we will start analyzing the mentioned techniques, frameworks, and tools in much greater detail and provide examples of their usage.

# 3
# Building Blocks on the Android SDK

We now know how to create test projects and run the tests. It is now time to start digging a bit deeper to find the building blocks available to create the tests.

Thus, in this third chapter, we will be covering:

- Common assertions
- View assertions
- Other assertion types
- TouchUtils, intended to test User Interfaces
- Mock objects
- Instrumentation
- TestCase class hierarchies
- Using external libraries

We will be analyzing these components and showing examples of their use when applicable. The examples in this chapter are intentionally split from the original Android project containing them to let you concentrate and focus only on the subject being presented, although the complete examples can be downloaded as explained later. Right now, we are interested in the trees and not the forest.

Along with the examples presented, we will be identifying common, reusable patterns that will help you in the creation of tests for your own projects.

*Building Blocks on the Android SDK*

# The demonstration application

We have created a very simple application to demonstrate the use of some of the tests in this chapter. The source for this application can be downloaded from `http://www.packtpub.com/support`.

The next screenshot shows this application running:

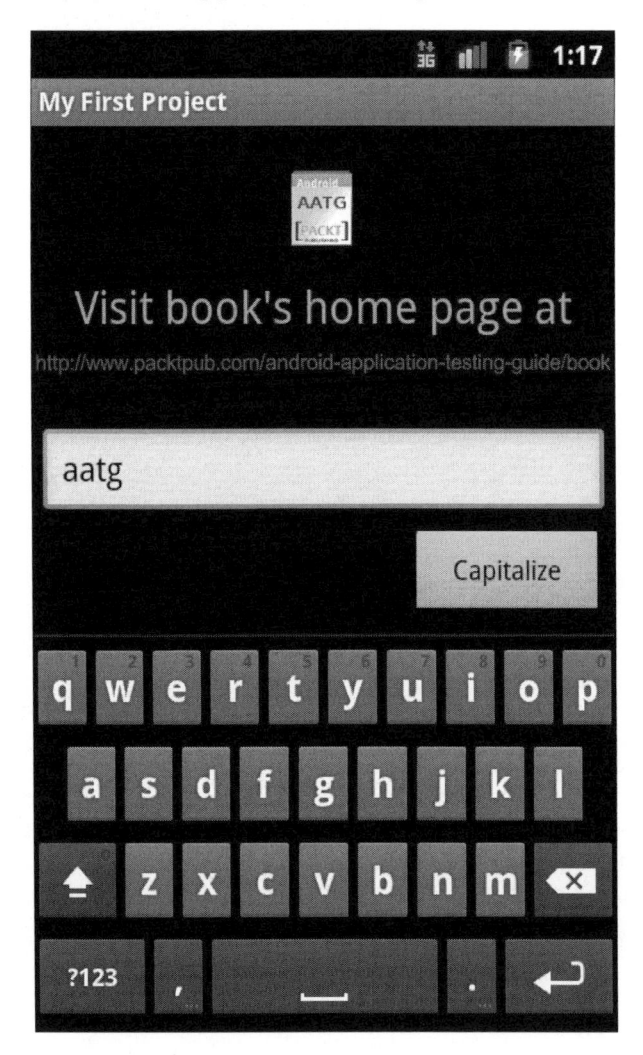

# Assertions in depth

Assertions are methods that should check for a condition that could be evaluated and throw an exception if the condition is not met, thus aborting the execution of the test.

The JUnit API includes the class `Assert`, which is the base class all of the test case classes. It holds several assertion methods useful for writing tests. These inherited methods test for a variety of conditions and are overloaded to support different parameter types. They can be grouped together in different sets, depending on the condition checked; for example:

- `assertEquals`
- `assertFalse`
- `assertNotNull`
- `assertNotSame`
- `assertNull`
- `assertSame`
- `assertTrue`
- `fail`

The condition tested is pretty obvious and easily identifiable by the method name. Perhaps the ones that deserve some attention are `assertEquals()` and `assertSame()`. The former when used on objects asserts that both objects passed as parameters are equal, calling the objects' `equals()` method. The latter asserts that both objects refer to the same object. If in some case `equals()` is not implemented by the class, then `assertEquals()` and `assertSame()` will do the same thing.

When one of these assertions fails inside a test an `AssertionFailedException` is thrown.

Occasionally, during the development process you may need to create a test that you are not implementing at that precise time. However, you want to flag that the creation of the test was postponed. We did this in *Chapter 1, Getting Started with Testing* when we added just the test method stubs. In those cases you may use the `fail` method which always fails and use a custom message indicating the condition:

```
public void testNotImplementedYet() {
   fail("Not implemented yet");
}
```

There is another common use for `fail()` that is worth mentioning. If we need to test if a method throws an exception we can surround the code with a try-catch block and force a fail if the exception was not thrown. For example:

```
public void testShouldThrowException() {
    try {
       MyFirstProjectActivity.methodThatShouldThrowException();
       fail("Exception was not thrown");
    } catch ( Exception ex ) {
```

```
        // do nothing
    }
}
```

## Custom messages

Speaking about custom messages, it is worth knowing that all `assert` methods provide an overloaded version including a custom `String` message. Should the assertion fail this custom message will be printed by the test runner instead of a default message. This custom message is extremely useful for easily identifying the failure once you are looking at the test report, so it is highly recommended as a best practice to use this version.

This is an example of a trivial test using this recommendation:

```
public void testMax() {
   final int a = 1;
   final int b = 2;
   final int expected = b;
   final int actual = Math.max(a, b);
   assertEquals("Expection " + expected + " but was " + actual,
            expected, actual);
}
```

In the example we can see another practice that would help you organize and understand your tests easily. This is the use of explicit names for variables holding the expected and actual values.

## Static imports

Though basic assertion methods are inherited from the Assert base class, some other assertions need specific imports. To improve readability of your tests there is a pattern of importing the assert methods statically from the corresponding classes. Using this pattern instead of having:

```
public void testAlignment() {
    final int margin = 0;
    ...
    android.test.ViewAsserts.assertRightAligned(
       mMessage, mCapitalize, margin);
}
```

We can simplify it by adding the static import:

```
import static android.test.ViewAsserts.assertRightAligned;
public void testAlignment() {
   final int margin = 0;
   assertRightAligned(mMessage, mCapitalize, margin);
}
```

Eclipse doesn't usually handle these static imports automatically, so if you want content assist (*Ctrl+SPACE*) to add static imports for you when you type the beginning of one of these asserts, you should add the classes to the Favorites list in Eclipse. To do this, navigate to **Window | Preferences | Java | Editor | Content Assist | Favorites | New Type**. Type in: **android.test.ViewAsserts** and then add another type: **android.test.MoreAsserts**.

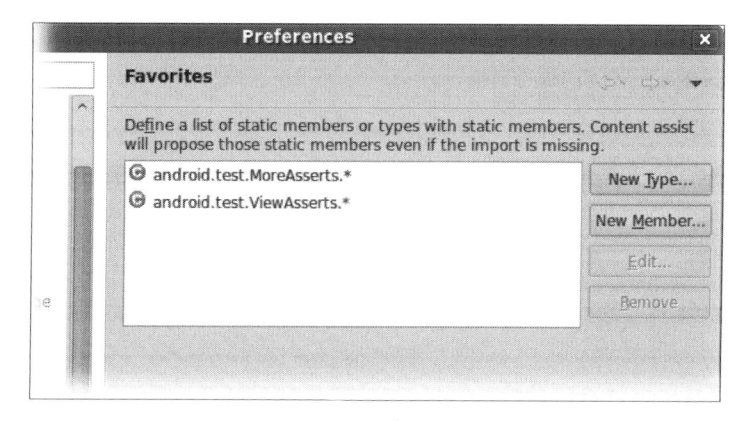

## View assertions

The assertions introduced earlier handle a variety of types as parameters but they are only intended to test simple conditions or simple objects.

For example, we have `assertEquals(short expected, short actual)` to test `short` values, `assertEquals(int expected, int actual)` to test integer values, `assertEquals(Object expected, Object actual)` to test any `Object` instance, and so on.

Usually while testing user interfaces in Android, you will face the necessity of more sophisticated methods, mainly related with `Views`. In this respect, Android provides a class with plenty of assertions in `android.test.ViewAsserts` (see http://developer.android.com/reference/android/test/ViewAsserts.html for details) that test the relationships between Views and their absolute and relative positions on the screen.

These methods are also overloaded to provide different conditions. Among the assertions, we can find:

- `assertBaselineAligned`: Asserts that two views are aligned on their baseline, that is their baselines are on the same y location.
- `assertBottomAligned`: Asserts that two views are bottom aligned, that is their bottom edges are on the same y location.
- `assertGroupContains`: Asserts that the specified group contains a specific child once and only once.
- `assertGroupIntegrity`: Asserts the specified group's integrity. The children count should be >= 0 and each child should be non-null.
- `assertGroupNotContains`: Asserts that the specified group does not contain a specific child.
- `assertHasScreenCoordinates`: Asserts that a view has a particular x and y position on the visible screen.
- `assertHorizontalCenterAligned`: Asserts that the test view is horizontally center aligned with respect to the reference view.
- `assertLeftAligned`: Asserts that two views are left aligned, that is their left edges are on the same x location. An optional margin can also be provided.
- `assertOffScreenAbove`: Asserts that the specified view is above the visible screen.
- `assertOffScreenBelow`: Asserts that the specified view is below the visible screen.
- `assertOnScreen`: Asserts that a view is on the screen.
- `assertRightAligned`: Asserts that two views are right-aligned, that is their right edges are on the same x location. An optional margin can also be specified.
- `assertTopAligned`: Asserts that two views are top-aligned, that is their top edges are on the same y location. An optional margin can also be specified.
- `assertVerticalCenterAligned`: Asserts that the test view is vertically center aligned with respect to the reference view.

The following example shows how you can use `ViewAsserts` to test the user interface layout:

```
public void testUserInterfaceLayout() {
    final int margin = 0;
    final View origin = mActivity.getWindow().getDecorView();
    assertOnScreen(origin, mMessage);
```

```
        assertOnScreen(origin, mCapitalize);
        assertRightAligned(mMessage, mCapitalize, margin);
    }
```

The `assertOnScreen` method uses an origin to start looking for the requested `View`s. In this case we are using the top-level window decor View. If for some reason you don't need to go that high in the hierarchy or if this approach is not suitable for your test, you may use another root `View` in the hierarchy; for example `View.getRootView()` which in our concrete example would be `mMessage.getRootView()`.

## Even more assertions

If the assertions reviewed previously do not seem to be enough for your tests' needs, there is yet another class included in the Android framework that covers other cases. This class is `MoreAsserts` (http://developer.android.com/reference/android/test/MoreAsserts.html).

These methods are also overloaded, to support different conditions. Among these assertions we can find:

- `assertAssignableFrom`: Asserts that an object is assignable to a class.
- `assertContainsRegex`: Asserts that an expected `Regex` matches any substring of the specified `String`. It fails with the specified message if it does not.
- `assertContainsInAnyOrder`: Asserts that the specified `Iterable` contains precisely the elements expected, but in any order.
- `assertContainsInOrder`: Asserts that the specified `Iterable` contains precisely the elements expected, in the same order.
- `assertEmpty`: Asserts that an `Iterable` is empty.
- `assertEquals` for some `Collections` not covered in JUnit asserts.
- `assertMatchesRegex`: Asserts that the specified `Regex` exactly matches the `String` and fails with the provided message if it does not.
- `assertNotContainsRegex`: Asserts that the specified `Regex` does not match any substring of the specified String, and fails with the provided message if it does.
- `assertNotEmpty`: Asserts that some `Collections` not covered in JUnit asserts are not empty.
- `assertNotMatchesRegex`: Asserts that the specified `Regex` does not exactly match the specified String, and fails with the provided message if it does.

- **checkEqualsAndHashCodeMethods**: Utility for testing `equals()` and `hashCode()` results at once. Tests that `equals()` applied to both objects matches the specified result.

This test below checks for an error during the invocation of the capitalization method called via a click on the UI button.

```
@UiThreadTest
public void testNoErrorInCapitalization() {
  final String msg = "this is a sample";
  mMessage.setText(msg);
  mCapitalize.performClick();
  final String actual = mMessage.getText().toString();
  final String notExpectedRegexp = "(?i:ERROR)";
  assertNotContainsRegex("Capitalization found error:",
    notExpectedRegexp, actual);
}
```

Note that because this is a test that modifies the user interface, we must annotate it with `@UiThreadTest`, otherwise it won't be able to alter the UI from a different thread and we will receive the following exception:

03-02 23:06:05.826: INFO/TestRunner(610): ----- begin exception -----

03-02 23:06:05.862: INFO/TestRunner(610): android.view.ViewRoot$CalledFromWrongThreadException: Only the original thread that created a view hierarchy can touch its views.

03-02 23:06:05.862: INFO/TestRunner(610):     at android.view.ViewRoot.checkThread(ViewRoot.java:2932)

[...]

03-02 23:06:05.862: INFO/TestRunner(610):     at android.app.Instrumentation$InstrumentationThread.run(Instrumentation.java:1447)

03-02 23:06:05.892: INFO/TestRunner(610): ----- end exception -----

If you are not familiar with regular expressions, invest some time and visit `http://developer.android.com/reference/java/util/regex/package-summary.html`, it will be worth it!

In this particular case, we are looking for the word "ERROR" contained in the result with a case insensitive match (setting the flag 'i' for this purpose). That is, if for some reason capitalization didn't work in our application and it contains an error message we will detect this condition with the assertion.

# The TouchUtils class

Sometimes, when testing UIs, it is helpful to simulate different kinds of touch events. These touch events can be generated in many different ways but probably `android.test.TouchUtils` is the simplest to use. This class provides reusable methods for generating touch events in test cases that are derived from `InstrumentationTestCase`.

Featured methods allow simulated interaction with the UI under test. `TouchUtils` provides the infrastructure to inject the events using the correct UI or main thread, so no special handling is needed and you don't need to annotate the test using `@UIThreadTest`.

The mentioned methods support:

- Clicking on a View and releasing it
- Tapping on a View, that is touching it and quickly releasing
- Long clicking on a View
- Dragging the screen
- Dragging Views

The following test represents a typical usage of `TouchUtils`:

```
public void testListScrolling() {
  mListView.scrollTo(0, 0);
  TouchUtils.dragQuarterScreenUp(this, mActivity);
  TouchUtils.dragQuarterScreenUp(this, mActivity);
  TouchUtils.dragQuarterScreenUp(this, mActivity);
  TouchUtils.dragQuarterScreenUp(this, mActivity);
  TouchUtils.tapView(this, mListView);

  final int expectedItemPosition = 6;
  final int actualItemPosition =
    mListView.getFirstVisiblePosition();
  assertEquals("Wrong position",
    expectedItemPosition, actualItemPosition);

  final String expected = "Anguilla";
  final String actual = mListView.getAdapter().
    getItem(expectedItemPosition).toString();
  assertEquals("Wrong content", actual, expected);
}
```

This test does the following:

1. Repositions the list at the beginning to start from a known condition.
2. Scroll the list several times.
3. Check the first visible position to see that the list was correctly scrolled.
4. Check the content of the element to verify that it is correct.

Even the most complex UIs can be tested in this way and it will help you detect a variety of conditions that could potentially affect the user experience.

# Mock Objects

We visited the Mock Objects provided by the Android testing framework in *Chapter 1, Getting Started with Testing* and evaluated the concerns regarding not using real objects in order to isolate our tests from the surrounding environment.

The next chapter deals with Test Driven Development, and if we were Test Driven Development purists we may argue about the use of mock objects and be more inclined to use real ones. Martin Fowler calls these two styles the *Classical* and *Mockist* Test Driven Development dichotomy in his great article *Mocks Aren't Stubs*. It can be read online at http://www.martinfowler.com/articles/mocksArentStubs.html.

Independent of that discussion, we are introducing here the available Mock Objects as one of the available building blocks because sometimes introducing mock objects in our tests is recommended, desirable, useful, or even unavoidable.

Android SDK provides some classes in the subpackage android.test.mock to help us in this quest:

- MockApplication: A mock implementation of the Application class. All methods are non-functional and throw UnsupportedOperationException.
- MockContentProvider: A mock implementation of ContentProvider. All methods are non-functional and throw UnsupportedOperationException.
- MockContentResolver: A mock implementation of the ContentResolver class that isolates the test code from the real content system. All methods are non-functional and throw UnsupportedOperationException.
- MockContext: A mock Context class. This can be used to inject other dependencies. All methods are non-functional and throw UnsupportedOperationException.
- MockCursor: A mock Cursor class that isolates the test code from real Cursor implementation. All methods are non-functional and throw UnsupportedOperationException.

- `MockDialogInterface`: A mock implementation of `DialogInterface` class. All methods are non-functional and throw `UnsupportedOperationException`.
- `MockPackageManager`: A mock implementation of `PackageManager` class. All methods are non-functional and throw `UnsupportedOperationException`.
- `MockResources`: A mock Resources class. All methods are non-functional and throw `UnsupportedOperationException`.

As we mentioned, all of these classes have non-functional methods that throw `UnsupportedOperationException` if used. So, if you need to use some of these methods or if you detect that your test is failing with this `Exception`, you should extend one of these base classes and provide the required functionality.

## MockContext overview

The `MockContext` class implements all methods in a non-functional way and throws `UnsupportedOperationException`. So, if you forgot to implement one of the needed methods for the test case you are handling, this exception will be thrown and you can instantly detect the situation.

This mock can be used to inject other dependencies, mocks, or monitors into the classes under test. A finer level of control can be obtained by extending this class.

Extend this class to provide your desired behavior, overriding the corresponding methods.

As we will cover next, the Android SDK provides some pre-built mock `Contexts` that are useful in some cases.

## The IsolatedContext class

In your tests you may find the need to isolate the `Activity` under test to prevent interaction with other components. This can be a complete isolation, but sometimes this isolation avoids interacting with other components and for your `Activity` to behave correctly some connection with the system is still required.

For those cases, the Android SDK provides `android.test.IsolatedContext`, a mock `Context` that prevents interaction with most of the underlying system but also satisfies the needs of interacting with other packages or components like `Services` or `ContentProviders`.

# Alternate route to file and database operations

In some cases, all we need is to be able to provide an alternate route to the file and database operations. For example, if we are testing the application on a real device, perhaps we don't want to affect existing files during our tests.

Such cases can take advantage of another class that is not part of the `android.test.mock` subpackage but of `android.test` instead: `RenamingDelegatingContext`.

This class lets us alter operations on files and databases by having a prefix that is specified in the constructor. All other operations are delegated to the delegating Context that you must specify in the constructor too.

Suppose our `Activity` under test uses some files we want to control in some way, maybe introducing specialized content or a fixture to drive our tests and we don't want to or we can't use the real files. In this case we create a `RenamingDelegatingContext` specifying a prefix; we add this prefix to the replacement file names and our unchanged `Activity` will use them instead.

For example, if our Activity tries to access a file named `birthdays.txt`, and we provide `RenamingDelegatingContext` specifying the prefix "test", then this same Activity will access the file `testbirthdays.txt` instead, when it is being tested.

# The MockContentResolver class

The `MockContentResolver` class implements all methods in a non-functional way and throws the exception `UnsupportedOperationException` if you attempt to use them. The reason for this class is to isolate tests from the real content.

Let's say your application uses a `ContentProvider` maybe from more than one `Activity`. You can create unit-tests for this `ContentProvider` using `ProviderTestCase2`, which we will be looking at shortly, and in some cases implementing a `RenamingDelegatingContext` as previously described.

But when we try to produce functional or integration tests of our Activities against the `ContentProvider`, it's not so evident what test case to use. The most obvious choice is `ActivityInstrumentationTestCase2` if your functional tests mainly simulate user experience because you may need `sendKeys()` or similar methods, which are readily available in these tests.

The first problem you may encounter then is that it's not clear where to inject a `MockContentResolver` in your test to be able to use a test database instance or database fixture with your `ContentProvider`. There's no way to inject a `MockContext` either.

This problem will be solved in *Chapter 7, Testing Recipes* where further details are provided.

## The TestCase base class

This is the base class of all other test cases in the JUnit framework. It implements the basic methods that we were analyzing in previous examples.

`TestCase` also implements the `junit.framework.Test` interface.

This is the UML class diagram of `TestCase` and the `Test` interface.

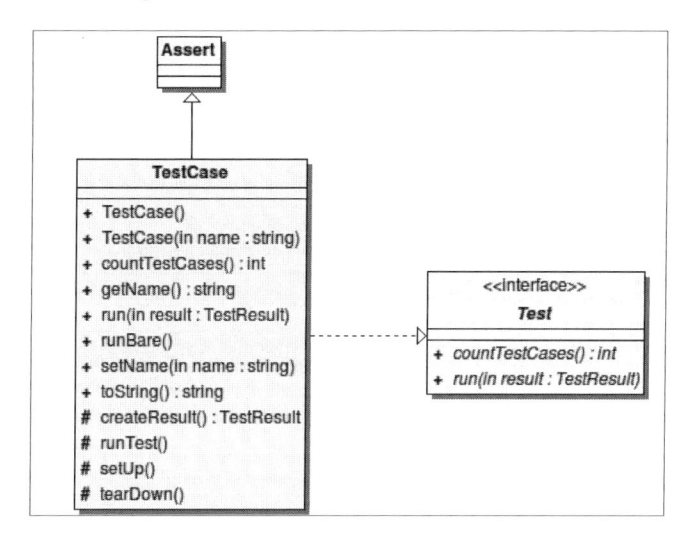

```
                    ┌─────────┐
                    │ Assert  │
                    └─────────┘
                         △
                         │
                    ┌─────────────────────────────┐
                    │         TestCase            │
                    ├─────────────────────────────┤
                    │ + TestCase()                │
                    │ + TestCase(in name : string)│
                    │ + countTestCases() : int    │      ┌────────────────────────────┐
                    │ + getName() : string        │      │       <<interface>>        │
                    │ + run(in result : TestResult)│      │           Test             │
                    │ + runBare()                 │ - - -├────────────────────────────┤
                    │ + setName(in name : string) │      │ + countTestCases() : int   │
                    │ + toString() : string       │      │ + run(in result : TestResult)│
                    │ # createResult() : TestResult│     └────────────────────────────┘
                    │ # runTest()                 │
                    │ # setUp()                   │
                    │ # tearDown()                │
                    └─────────────────────────────┘
```

Test cases should either extend `TestCase` directly or one of its descendants.

There are other methods beside the ones explained before.

## The no-argument constructor

All test cases require a default constructor because sometimes, depending on the test runner used, this is the only constructor that is invoked. It is also used for serialization.

According to the documentation, this method is not intended to be used by mere mortals without calling `setName(String name)`.

A common pattern is to use a default constant test case name in this constructor and invoke the **Given name** constructor afterwards.

```
public class MyTestCase extends TestCase {
    public MyTestCase() {
        this("MyTestCase Default Name");
    }

    public MyTestCase(String name) {
        super(name);
    }
}
```

## The given name constructor

This constructor takes a name as an argument to give to the test case. It will appear in test reports and will be helpful when you try to identify failed tests.

## The setName() method

There are some classes extending `TestCase` that don't provide a given name constructor. In such cases the only alternative is to call `setName(String name)`.

## The AndroidTestCase base class

This class can be used as a base class for general purpose Android test cases.

This is the UML class diagram of `AndroidTestCase` and the closest related classes.

```
                    ┌──────────────────────────┐
                    │ junit.framework          │
                    │        ┌────────┐        │
                    │        │ Assert │        │
                    │        └────────┘        │
                    │            △             │
                    │        ┌────────┐        │
                    │        │TestCase│        │
                    │        └────────┘        │
                    └────────────△─────────────┘
```

| AndroidTestCase |
|---|
| - mContext : Context |
| + assertActivityRequiresPermission(in packageName : string, in className : string, in permission : string) |
| + assertReadingContentUriRequiresPermission(in uri : Uri, in permission : string) |
| + assertWritingContentUriRequiresPermission(in uri : Uri, in permission : string) |
| + getContext() : Context |
| + setContext(in context : Context) |
| + testAndroidTestCaseSetupProperly() |
| # scrubClass(in testCaseClass : Class<?>) |

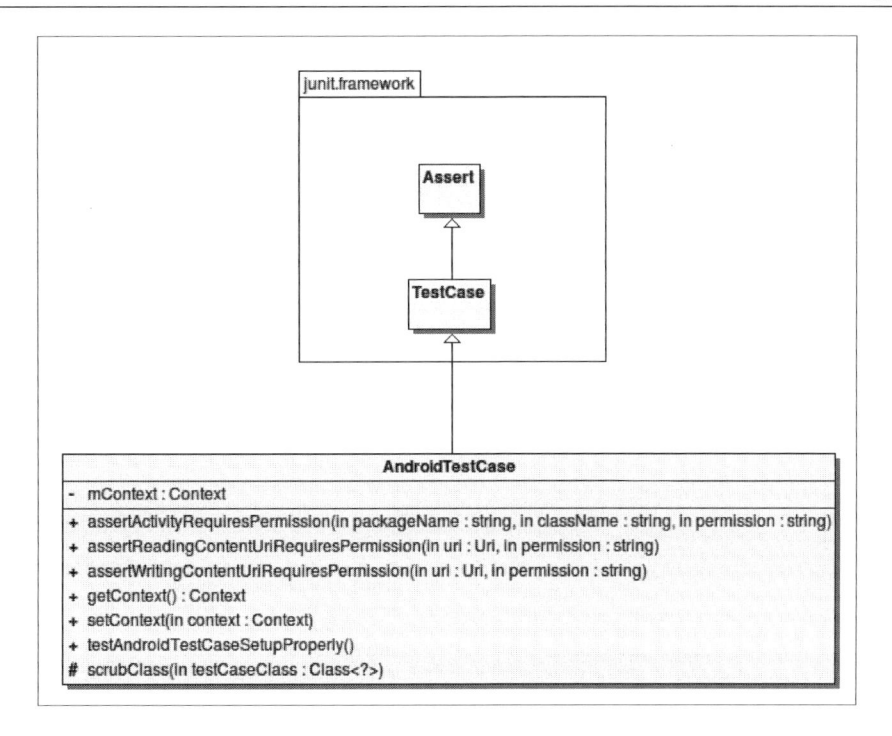

Use this class when you need access to an Activity Context like Resources, databases, or files in the filesystem. Context is stored as a field in this class conveniently named `mContext` and can be used inside the tests if needed. The `getContext()` method can be used too.

Tests based on this class can start more than one `Activity` using `Context.startActivity()`.

There are various test cases in Android SDK that extend this base class:

- `ApplicationTestCase<T extends Application>`
- `ProviderTestCase2<T extends ContentProvider>`
- `ServiceTestCase<T extends Service>`

# The assertActivityRequiresPermission() method

The signature for this method is as follows:

```
public void assertActivityRequiresPermission (String packageName,
    String className, String permission)
```

## Description

This assertion method checks that the launching of a particular `Activity` is protected by specific permission. It takes three parameters:

- `packageName`: A String indicating the package name of the Activity to launch
- `className`: A String indicating the class of the Activity to launch
- `permission`: A String with the permission to query

The `Activity` is launched and then a `SecurityException` is expected mentioning that the required permission is missing in the error message. The Activity is not handled by this test and thus an `Instrumentation` is not needed.

## Example

This test checks the requirement of the `android.Manifest.permission.WRITE_EXTERNAL_STORAGE` permission, needed to write to external storage, in the Activity `MyContactsActivity`:

```
public void testActivityPermission() {
   final String PKG = "com.example.aatg.myfirstproject";
   final String ACTIVITY =  PKG + ".MyFirstProjectActivity";
   final String PERMISSION =
       android.Manifest.permission.WRITE_EXTERNAL_STORAGE;
   assertActivityRequiresPermission(PKG, ACTIVITY, PERMISSION);
}
```

> Always use the constants describing the permissions from `android.Manifest.permission`, not the `Strings`, so if the implementation changes your code will still be valid.

# The assertReadingContentUriRequiresPermission method

The signature for this method is as follows:

```
public void assertReadingContentUriRequiresPermission (
   Uri uri, String permission)
```

## Description

This assertion method checks that reading from a specific URI requires the permission provided as a parameter.

It takes two parameters:

- `uri`: The URI that requires a permission to query
- `permission`: A String containing the permission to query

If a `SecurityException` is generated containing the specified permission, this assertion is validated.

## Example

This test tries to read contacts and verifies that the correct `SecurityException` is generated:

```
public void testReadingContacts() {
  final Uri URI = ContactsContract.AUTHORITY_URI;
  final String PERMISSION =
      android.Manifest.permission.READ_CONTACTS;
  assertReadingContentUriRequiresPermission(URI, PERMISSION);
}
```

# The assertWritingContentUriRequiresPermission() method

The signature for this method is as follows:

```
public void assertWritingContentUriRequiresPermission(
  Uri uri, String permission)
```

## Description

This assertion method checks that inserting into a specific URI requires the permission provided as a parameter.

It takes 2 parameters:

- `uri`: The URI that requires a permission to query
- `permission`: A String containing the permission to query

If a `SecurityException` containing the specified permission is generated, this assertion is validated.

## Example

This test tries to write to Contacts and verifies that the correct `SecurityException` is generated:

```
public void testWritingContacts() {
   final Uri URI = ContactsContract.AUTHORITY_URI;
   final String PERMISSION =
       android.Manifest.permission.WRITE_CONTACTS;
   assertWritingContentUriRequiresPermission(URI, PERMISSION);
}
```

# Instrumentation

Instrumentation is instantiated by the system before any of the application code is run, allowing it to monitor all of the interaction between the system and the application.

As with many other Android application components, Instrumentation implementations are described in the `AndroidManifest.xml` under the tag `<instrumentation>`. For example, if you open our tests' `AndroidManifest.xml` and look inside you will find:

```
<instrumentation
   android:targetPackage="com.example.aatg.myfirstproject"
   android:name="android.test.InstrumentationTestRunner"
   android:label="MyFirstProject Tests"/>
```

This is the Instrumentation declaration.

The `targetPackage` attribute defines the name of the package under test, `name` the name of the test runner, and `label` the text that will be displayed when this instrumentation is listed.

Please note as mentioned earlier, this declaration belongs to the test project and not to the main project.

## The ActivityMonitor inner class

As mentioned earlier, the Instrumentation class is used to monitor the interaction between the system and the application or Activities under test. The inner class `Instrumentation.ActivityMonitor` allows monitoring of a single Activity within an application.

## Example

Let's pretend that we have a `TextField` in our `Activity` that holds a URL and has its auto link property set:

```
<TextView android:layout_width="fill_parent"
   android:layout_height="wrap_content"
   android:text="@string/home"
   android:layout_gravity="center" android:gravity="center"
   android:autoLink="web" android:id="@+id/link" />
```

If we want to verify that when clicked the hyperlink is correctly followed and a Brower is invoked, we can create a test like:

```
public void testFollowLink() {
   final Instrumentation inst = getInstrumentation();
   IntentFilter intentFilter = new IntentFilter(
      Intent.ACTION_VIEW);
   intentFilter.addDataScheme("http");
   intentFilter.addCategory(Intent.CATEGORY_BROWSABLE);
   ActivityMonitor monitor = inst.addMonitor(
      intentFilter, null, false);
   assertEquals(0, monitor.getHits());
   TouchUtils.clickView(this, mLink);
   monitor.waitForActivityWithTimeout(5000);
   assertEquals(1, monitor.getHits());
   inst.removeMonitor(monitor);
}
```

Here, we:

1. Get the instrumentation.
2. Add a monitor based on an `IntentFilter`.
3. Wait for the activity.
4. Verify that the monitor hits were incremented.
5. Remove the monitor.

Using monitors we can test even the most complex interactions with the system and other Activities. This is a very powerful tool for creating integration tests.

# The InstrumentationTestCase class

The `InstrumentationTestCase` class is the direct or indirect base class for various test cases that have access to Instrumentation. This is the list of the most important direct and indirect subclasses:

- `ActivityTestCase`
- `ProviderTestCase2<T extends ContentProvider>`
- `SingleLaunchActivityTestCase<T extends Activity>`
- `SyncBaseInstrumentation`
- `ActivityInstrumentationTestCase2<T extends Activity>`
- `ActivityUnitTestCase<T extends Activity>`

This is the UML class diagram of `InstrumentationTestCase` and the closest related classes:

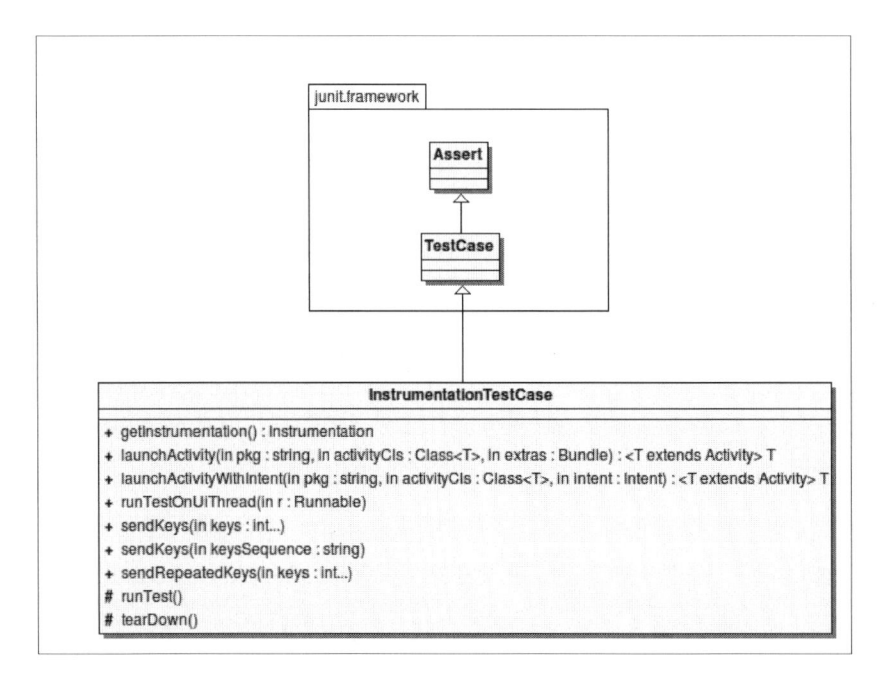

```
junit.framework
    Assert
      △
      |
    TestCase
      △
      |
InstrumentationTestCase
+ getInstrumentation() : Instrumentation
+ launchActivity(in pkg : string, in activityCls : Class<T>, in extras : Bundle) : <T extends Activity> T
+ launchActivityWithIntent(in pkg : string, in activityCls : Class<T>, in intent : Intent) : <T extends Activity> T
+ runTestOnUiThread(in r : Runnable)
+ sendKeys(in keys : int...)
+ sendKeys(in keysSequence : string)
+ sendRepeatedKeys(in keys : int...)
# runTest()
# tearDown()
```

`InstrumentationTestCase` is in the `android.test` package, not shown in the image, and extends `junit.framework.TestCase` which extends `junit.framework.Assert`.

## The launchActivity and launchActivityWithIntent method

These utility methods are used to launch Activities from the test. If the Intent is not specified using the second option, a default Intent is used:

```
public final T launchActivity(
   String pkg, Class<T> activityCls, Bundle extras)
```

> Note that the template class parameter T is used in activityCls and as the return type, limiting its use to Activities of that type.

If you need to specify a custom Intent, you can use the following code that also adds the intent parameter:

```
public final T launchActivityWithIntent(
   String pkg, Class<T> activityCls, Intent intent)
```

## The sendKeys and sendRepeatedKeys methods

When testing Activities' UI you will face the need to simulate the interaction with qwerty-based keyboards or DPAD buttons to send keys to complete fields, select shortcuts, or navigate throughout the different components.

This is what the different sendKeys and sendRepeatedKeys are for.

There is one version of sendKeys that accepts integer keys values. They can be obtained from constants defined in the KeyEvent class.

For example, we can use the sendKeys method in this way:

```
public void testSendKeyInts() {
  try {
    runTestOnUiThread(new Runnable() {
      public void run() {
        mMessage.requestFocus();
      }
    });
  } catch (Throwable e) {
    fail("Couldn't set focus");
  }
  sendKeys(KeyEvent.KEYCODE_H,
```

```
            KeyEvent.KEYCODE_E,
            KeyEvent.KEYCODE_E,
            KeyEvent.KEYCODE_E,
            KeyEvent.KEYCODE_Y,
            KeyEvent.KEYCODE_ALT_LEFT,
            KeyEvent.KEYCODE_1,
            KeyEvent.KEYCODE_DPAD_DOWN,
            KeyEvent.KEYCODE_ENTER);
        final String expected = "HEEEY!";
        final String actual = mMessage.getText().toString();
        assertEquals(expected, actual);
    }
```

Here, we are sending *H*, *E*, and *Y* letter keys, the exclamation mark, and then the *Enter* key using their integer representations to the Activity under test.

Alternatively, we can create a String concatenating the keys we desire to send discarding the KEYCODE prefix and separating them with spaces that are ultimately ignored:

```
    public void testSendKeyString() {
      try {
        runTestOnUiThread(new Runnable() {
          public void run() {
            mMessage.requestFocus();
          }
        });
      } catch (Throwable e) {
        fail("Couldn't set focus");
      }
      sendKeys("H 3*E Y ALT_LEFT 1 DPAD_DOWN ENTER");
      final String expected = "HEEEY!";
      final String actual = mMessage.getText().toString();
      assertEquals(expected, actual);
    }
```

Here, we did exactly the same as the previous test but using a `String`. Note that every key in the `String` can be prefixed by a repeating factor followed by '*' and the key to be repeated. We used 3*E in our previous example which is the same as "E E E", three times the letter *E*.

If sending repeated keys is what we need in our tests, there is also another alternative that is specifically intended for these cases:

```
    public void testSendRepeatedKeys() {
      try {
        runTestOnUiThread(new Runnable() {
          public void run() {
            mMessage.requestFocus();
          }
        });
      } catch (Throwable e) {
        fail("Couldn't set focus");
      }
      sendRepeatedKeys(1, KeyEvent.KEYCODE_H,
          3, KeyEvent.KEYCODE_E,
          1, KeyEvent.KEYCODE_Y,
          1, KeyEvent.KEYCODE_ALT_LEFT,
          1, KeyEvent.KEYCODE_1,
          1, KeyEvent.KEYCODE_DPAD_DOWN,
          1, KeyEvent.KEYCODE_ENTER);
      final String expected = "HEEEY!";
      final String actual = mMessage.getText().toString();
      assertEquals(expected, actual);
    }
```

This is the same test implemented in a different manner. Each key is preceded by the repetition number.

# The runTestOnUiThread helper method

The `runTestOnUiThread` method is a helper method for running portions of a test on the UI thread.

Alternatively, as we have discussed before, to run a test on the UI thread we can annotate it with `@UiThreadTest`.

But sometimes, we need to run only parts of the test on the UI thread because other parts of it are not suitable to run on that thread, or are using helper methods that provide the infrastructure to use that thread, like `TouchUtils` methods.

The most common pattern is changing the focus before sending keys, so the keys are correctly sent to the objective `View`:

```
    public void testCapitalizationSendingKeys() {
      final String keysSequence = "T E S T SPACE M E";
      runTestOnUiThread(new Runnable() {
```

```
      public void run() {
        mMessage.requestFocus();
      }
   });
   mInstrumentation.waitForIdleSync();

   sendKeys(keysSequence);
   TouchUtils.clickView(this, mCapitalize);
   final String expected = "test me".toUpperCase();
   final String actual = mMessage.getText().toString();
   assertEquals(expected, actual);
}
```

We request the focus for the `mMessage EditText` before waiting for the application to be idle, using `Instrumentation.waitForIdleSync()`, and then sending the key sequence to it. Afterwards, using `TouchUtils.clickView()`, we click the `Button` to finally check the content of the field after the conversion.

## The ActivityTestCase class

This is mainly a class holding common code for other test cases that access Instrumentation.

You may use this class if you are implementing specific behavior for test cases and existing alternatives don't fit your requirements.

If this is not the case, you may find the following options more suitable for your requirements:

- `ActivityInstrumentationTestCase2<T extends Activity>`
- `ActivityUnitTestCase<T extends Activity>`

This is the UML class diagram of `ActivityTestCase` and the closest related classes:

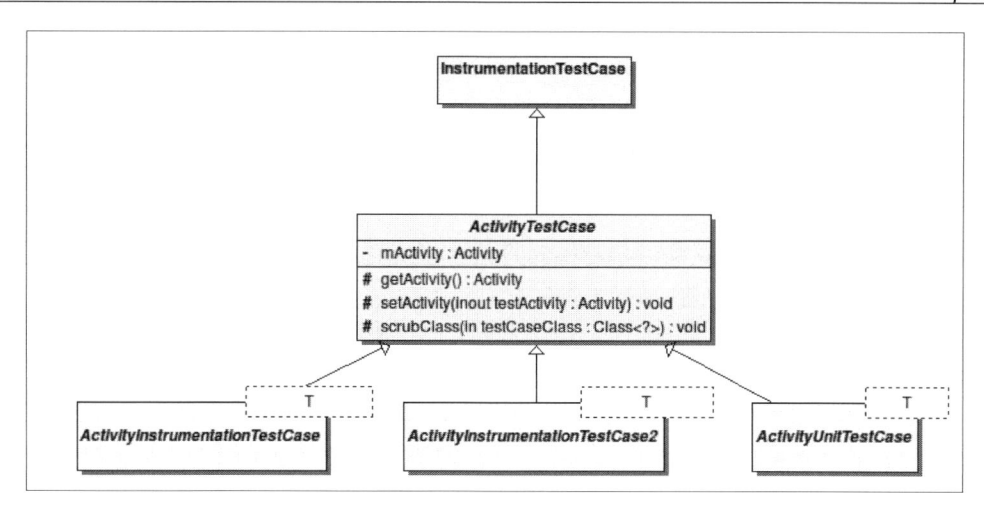

The abstract class android.testActivityTestCase extends android.test.InstrumentationTestCase and serves as a base class for other different test cases, such as android.test.ActivityInstrumentationTestCase, android.test.ActivityInstrumentationTestCase2, and android.test.ActivityUnitTestCase.

> android.test.ActivityInstrumentationTestCase is a deprecated class since Android API Level 3 (Android 1.5) and should not be used in newer projects.

## The scrubClass method

This is one of the protected methods in the class:

```
protected void scrubClass (Class<?> testCaseClass)
```

It is invoked from the tearDown() method in several test cases implementation in order to clean up class' variables that may have been instantiated as non-static inner classes avoiding the need to hold references to them.

This is in order to prevent memory leaks for large test suites.

IllegalAccessException is thrown if a problem accessing these variables is found.

# The ActivityInstrumentationTestCase2 class

This class will probably be the one you use the most in writing Android test cases. It provides functional testing of a single `Activity`.

This class has access to Instrumentation and will create the `Activity` under test using the system infrastructure by calling `InstrumentationTestCase.launchActivity()`.

This is the UML class diagram showing `ActivityInstrumentationTestCase2` and the closest related classes:

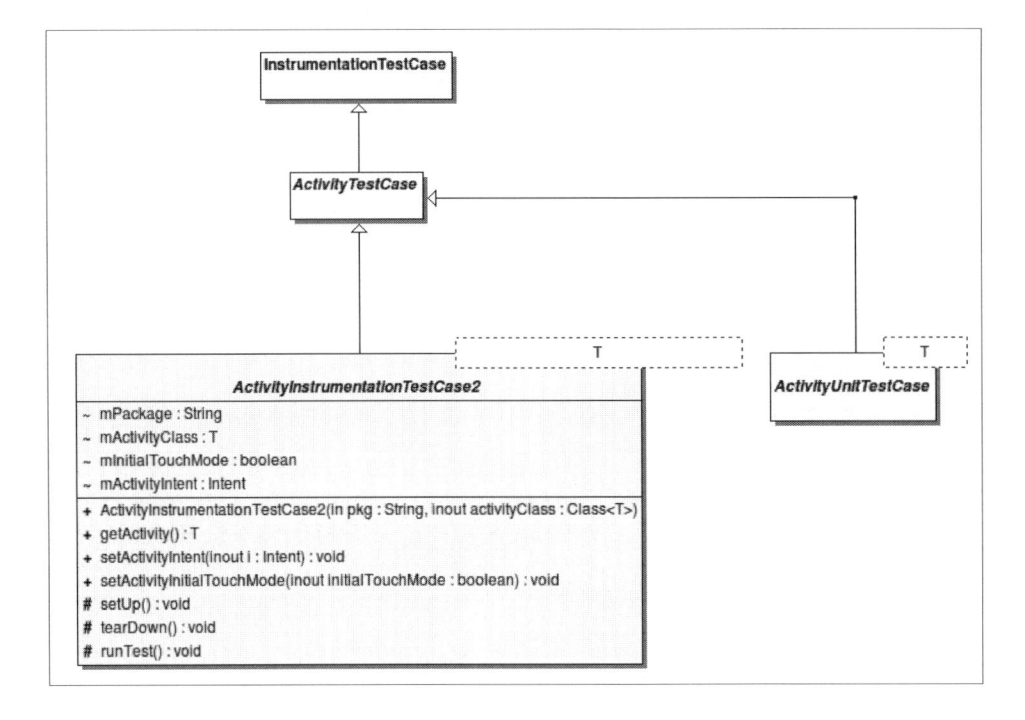

![UML class diagram showing InstrumentationTestCase, ActivityTestCase, ActivityInstrumentationTestCase2, and ActivityUnitTestCase]

The class `android.test.ActivityInstrumentationTestCase2` extends `android.test.ActivityTestCase`. This diagram also shows `ActivityUnitTestCase`, which also extends `ActivityTestCase`. Class template parameter T represents the Activity's class.

The `Activity` can then be manipulated and monitored after creation.

If you need to provide a custom Intent to start your `Activity`, before invoking `getActivity()` you may inject an Intent with `setActivityIntent(Intent intent)`.

This functional test would be very useful for testing interaction through the user interface as events can be injected to simulate user behavior.

## The constructor

There is only one public, non deprecated constructor for this class. This is:

```
ActivityInstrumentationTestCase2(Class<T> activityClass)
```

It should be invoked with an instance of the Activity class for the same Activity used as a class template parameter.

## The setUp method

As we have seen before in *Chapter 1, Getting Started with Testing* the setUp method is the best place to initialize the test case fields and other fixture components requiring initialization.

This is an example showing some of the patterns that you may find repeatedly in your test cases:

```
protected void setUp() throws Exception {
  super.setUp();
  // this must be called before getActivity()
  // disabling touch mode allows for sending key events
  setActivityInitialTouchMode(false);
  mActivity = getActivity();
  mInstrumentation = getInstrumentation();
  mLink = (TextView) mActivity.findViewById(
    com.example.aatg.myfirstproject.R.id.link);
  mMessage = (EditText) mActivity.findViewById(
    com.example.aatg.myfirstproject.R.id.message);
  mCapitalize = (Button) mActivity.findViewById(com.example.
    aatg.myfirstproject.R.id.capitalize);
}
```

We performed the following actions:

1. Invoke the super method. This is a JUnit pattern that should be followed here to ensure correct operation.

2. Disable touch mode. This should be done before the Activity is created by invoking getActivity() to have some effect. It sets the initial touch mode of the Activity under test to disabled. Touch mode is a fundamental Android UI concept and is discussed in http://developer.android.com/resources/articles/touch-mode.html.

3. Start the Activity using `getActivity()`.
4. Get the instrumentation. We have access to the Instrumentation because `ActivityInstrumentationTestCase2` extends `InstrumentationTestCase`.
5. Find the Views and set fields. In these operations, note that the R class used is from the target package, not from the tests.

## The tearDown method

Usually this method cleans up what was initialized in `setUp`.

In this example, we are only invoking the super method:

```
protected void tearDown() throws Exception {
  super.tearDown();
}
```

## The testPreconditions method

This method is used to check for some initial conditions to run our tests correctly.

Despite its name, it is not guaranteed that this test is run before other tests. However, it is a good practice to collect all of the precondition tests under this custom name.

This is an example of a `testPrecondition` test:

```
public void testPreconditions() {
  assertNotNull(mActivity);
  assertNotNull(mInstrumentation);
  assertNotNull(mLink);
  assertNotNull(mMessage);
  assertNotNull(mCapitalize);
}
```

We check only for not null values, but in this case asserting this we can also be sure that the Views were found using the specific IDs and that their types were correct, otherwise they are assigned in `setUp`.

## The ProviderTestCase2<T> class

This is a test case designed to test the `ContentProvider` classes.

This is the UML class diagram of `ProviderTestCase2` and the closest related classes:

*Chapter 3*

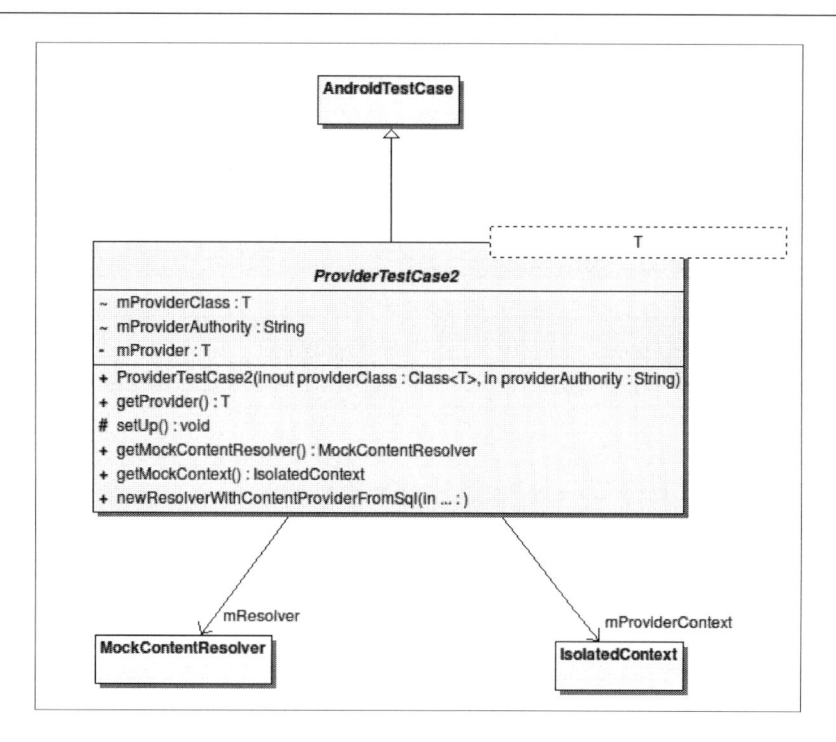

The class `android.test.ProviderTestCase2` also extends `AndroidTestCase`. Class template parameter T represents the `ContentProvider` under test. Implementation of this test uses an `IsolatedContext` and a `MockContentResolver`, mock objects that we described earlier in this chapter.

## The constructor

There is only one public, non deprecated constructor for this class. This is:

```
ProviderTestCase2(Class<T> providerClass, String providerAuthority)
```

It should be invoked with an instance of the `ContentProvider` class for the same `ContentProvider` used as a class template parameter.

The second parameter is the authority for the provider, usually defined as `AUTHORITY` constant in the `ContentProvider` class.

[ 77 ]

## Example

This is a typical example of a `ContentProvider` test:

```
public void testQuery() {
  Uri uri = Uri.withAppendedPath(
    MyProvider.CONTENT_URI, "dummy");
  final Cursor c = mProvider.query(uri, null, null, null, null);
  final int expected = 2;
  final int actual = c.getCount();
  assertEquals(expected, actual);
}
```

In this test we are expecting the query to return a `Cursor` containing 2 rows. This is just an example—use the number of rows that applies for your particular case, and asserting this condition.

Usually in the `setUp` method we obtain a reference to the provider, `mProvider` in this example, using `getProvider()`.

What is interesting to note is that because these tests are using `MockContentResolver` and `IsolatedContext`, the content of the real database is not affected and we can also run tests like this one:

```
public void testDelete() {
  Uri uri = Uri.withAppendedPath(
      MyProvider.CONTENT_URI, "dummy");
  final int actual = mProvider.delete(
      uri, "_id = ?", new String[] { "1" });
  final int expected = 1;
  assertEquals(expected, actual);
}
```

This test deletes some content of the database, but the database is restored to its initial content so as not to affect other tests.

## The ServiceTestCase<T>

This is a test case specially created to test Services.

This class, `ServiceTestCase<T>`, extends `AndroidTestCase` as is shown in this UML class diagram:

## ServiceTestCase class diagram

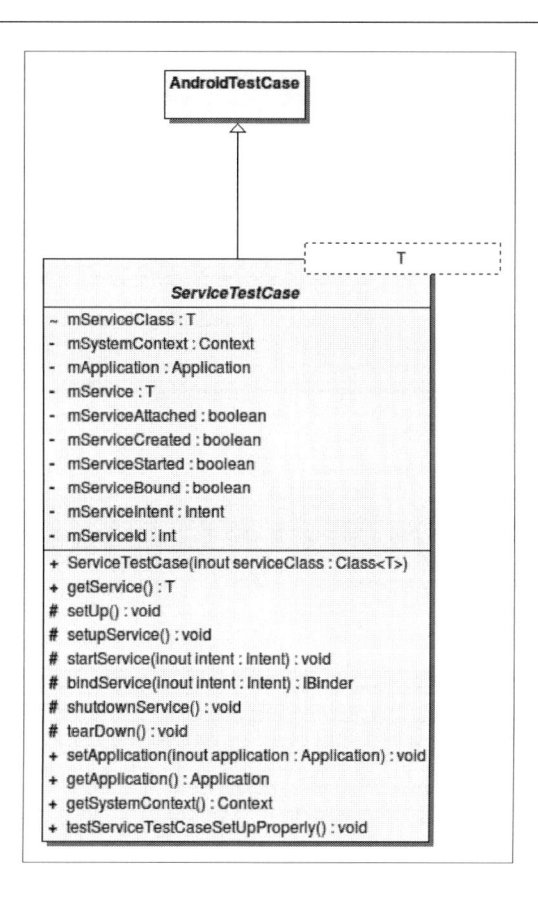

```
                    AndroidTestCase
                          △
                          |
                          |           ┌ - - ┐
                          |           ·  T  ·
                          |           └ - - ┘
                    ServiceTestCase
    ~ mServiceClass : T
    - mSystemContext : Context
    - mApplication : Application
    - mService : T
    - mServiceAttached : boolean
    - mServiceCreated : boolean
    - mServiceStarted : boolean
    - mServiceBound : boolean
    - mServiceIntent : Intent
    - mServiceId : int
    + ServiceTestCase(inout serviceClass : Class<T>)
    + getService() : T
    # setUp() : void
    # setupService() : void
    # startService(inout intent : Intent) : void
    # bindService(inout intent : Intent) : IBinder
    # shutdownService() : void
    # tearDown() : void
    + setApplication(inout application : Application) : void
    + getApplication() : Application
    + getSystemContext() : Context
    + testServiceTestCaseSetUpProperly() : void
```

Methods to exercise the service lifecycle like `setupService`, `startService`, `bindService`, and `shutDownService` are also included in this class.

## The constructor

There is only one public, non deprecated constructor for this class. This is:

    ServiceTestCase(Class<T> serviceClass)

It should be invoked with an instance of the `Service` class for the same `Service` used as a class template parameter.

# The TestSuiteBuilder.FailedToCreateTests class

The class `TestSuiteBuilder.FailedToCreateTests` is a special `TestCase` used to indicate a failure during the `build()` step.

That is, if during the test suite creation an error is detected, you will be receiving an exception like this one indicating the failure to construct the test suite:

```
01-02 06:31:26.656: INFO/TestRunner(4569): java.lang.RuntimeException: Exception during suite construction
```

```
01-02 06:31:26.656: INFO/TestRunner(4569):     at android.test.suitebuilder.TestSuiteBuilder$FailedToCreateTests.testSuiteConstructionFailed(TestSuiteBuilder.java:239)
```

```
01-02 06:31:26.656: INFO/TestRunner(4569):     at java.lang.reflect.Method.invokeNative(Native Method)
```

[...]

```
01-02 06:31:26.656: INFO/TestRunner(4569):     at android.test.InstrumentationTestRunner.onStart(InstrumentationTestRunner.java:520)
```

```
01-02 06:31:26.656: INFO/TestRunner(4569):     at android.app.Instrumentation$InstrumentationThread.run(Instrumentation.java:1447)
```

# Using external libraries in test projects

Your main Android project may require external libraries. Let's pretend that in one `Activity` we are creating objects from a class that is part of an external library. For the sake of our example, let's say the library is called `libdummy-0.0.1-SNAPSHOT.jar` and the mentioned class is `Dummy`. A dummy class that doesn't do anything is used here only to not divert your attention from the main objective which is including any library you may need, not just a particular one.

So our `Activity` would look like this:

```
package com.example.aatg.myfirstproject;

import com.example.libdummy.Dummy;

import android.app.Activity;
import android.os.Bundle;
import android.view.View;
import android.view.View.OnClickListener;
import android.widget.Button;
import android.widget.EditText;

public class MyFirstProjectActivity extends Activity {
```

```java
    private EditText mMessage;
    private Button mCapitalize;
    private Dummy mDummy;
    /** Called when the activity is first created. */
      @Override
      public void onCreate(Bundle savedInstanceState) {
        super.onCreate(savedInstanceState);
        setContentView(R.layout.main);

        mMessage = (EditText) findViewById(R.id.message);
        mCapitalize = (Button) findViewById(R.id.capitalize);

        mCapitalize.setOnClickListener(new OnClickListener() {
          public void onClick(View v) {
            mMessage.setText(mMessage.getText().toString().
              toUpperCase());
          }
        });
        mDummy = new Dummy();
      }
    public static void methodThatShouldThrowException()
    throws Exception {
      throw new Exception("This is an exception");
    }
    public Dummy getDummy() {
      return mDummy;
    }
}
```

This library should be added to the project's Java Build Path as usual as a JAR or external JAR depending on where the file is located.

Now, let's create a simple test. From our previous experience, we know that if we need to test an `Activity` we should use `ActivityInstrumentationTestCase2`, and this is precisely what we will do. Our simple test will be:

```java
public void testDummy() {
  assertNotNull(mActivity.getDummy());
}
```

Unfortunately, this test won't compile. The problem is that we are referencing a missing class. Our test project doesn't know anything about `Dummy` class or the `libdummy` library and hence we receive this error:

**The method getDummy() from the type DummyActivity refers to the missing type Dummy**.

Lets add the `libdummy` library to the test project's properties using the **Add External JARs...** button:

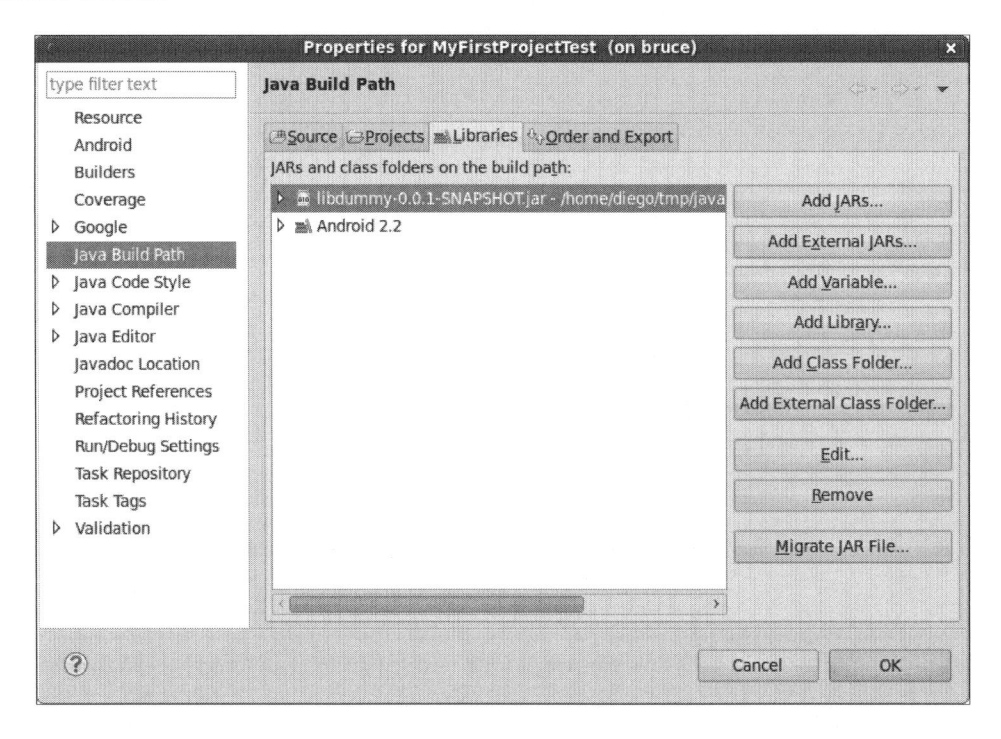

However, doing this will lead us to another error. If you run the tests, these are the errors you'll receive:

08-10 00:26:11.820: ERROR/AndroidRuntime(510): FATAL EXCEPTION: main

08-10 00:26:11.820: ERROR/AndroidRuntime(510): java.lang.IllegalAccessError: Class ref in pre-verified class resolved to unexpected implementation

...[lines removed for brevity]

08-10 00:26:11.820: ERROR/AndroidRuntime(510): at com.android.internal.os.ZygoteInit$MethodAndArgsCaller.run(ZygoteInit.java:868)

08-10 00:26:11.820: ERROR/AndroidRuntime(510):    at com.android.internal.os.ZygoteInit.main(ZygoteInit.java:626)

08-10 00:26:11.820: ERROR/AndroidRuntime(510):    at dalvik.system.NativeStart.main(Native Method)

The reason for this problem is that adding the library to both projects results in the same classes being inserted into both APKs. The tester project, however, loads classes from the tested project. The classes in the library will be loaded from the tester project but the classes in the tested project will refer to the copies in the tested project's APK. Hence the reference error.

The way to solve this problem is to export the `libdummy` entry to dependent projects and remove the JAR from the test project Java Build Path.

The following screenshot shows how to do this in the main project's properties:

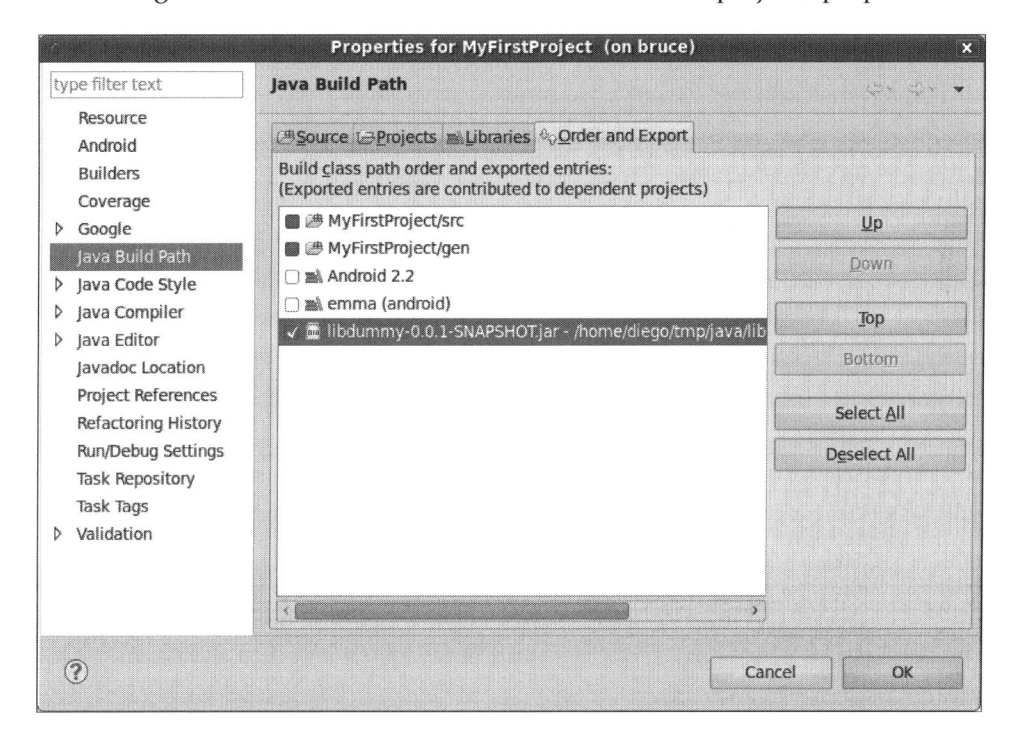

Note that `libdummy-0.0.1-SNAPSHOT.jar` is now checked in **Order and Export**.

## Summary

We investigated the most relevant building blocks and reusable patterns for creating our tests. Along this journey we:

- Used several types of assertions from the most common ones found usually in JUnit tests to the most specialized assertions found in the Android SDK to exercise application UIs
- Explained mock objects and their use in Android tests
- Exemplified the use of the different tests available in the Android SDK from unit to functional tests
- Illustrated the relationships between the most common classes using UML class diagrams to clearly understand them
- Dug into Instrumentation and different monitors available for Activities

Now that we have all the building blocks it is time to start creating more and more tests to acquire the experience needed to master the technique.

The next chapter introduces Test Driven Development using a sample project to expose all of its advantages.

# 4
# Test Driven Development

This chapter introduces the Test Driven Development discipline. We will start with a general revision and later on move to the concepts and techniques closely related to the Android platform.

This is a code intensive chapter, so be prepared to type as you read, which would be the best way to seize the examples provided.

In this chapter, we:

- Introduce and explain Test Driven Development
- Analyze its advantages
- Introduce a potential real life example
- Understand requirements by writing the tests
- Evolve through the project by applying TDD
- Get the application that fully complies with the requirements

## Getting started with TDD

Briefly, Test Driven Development is the strategy of writing tests along the development process. These test cases are written in advance of the code that is supposed to satisfy them.

A single test is added, then the code needed to satisfy the compilation of this test and finally the full set of test cases is run to verify their results.

This contrasts with other approaches to the development process where the tests are written at the end when all the coding has been done.

## Test Driven Development

Writing the tests in advance of the code that satisfies them has several advantages. First, is that the tests are written in one way or another, while if the tests are left till the end it is highly probable that they are never written. Second, developers take more responsibility for the quality of their work.

Design decisions are taken in single steps and finally the code satisfying the tests is improved by refactoring it.

This UML activity diagram depicts the Test Driven Development to help us understand the process:

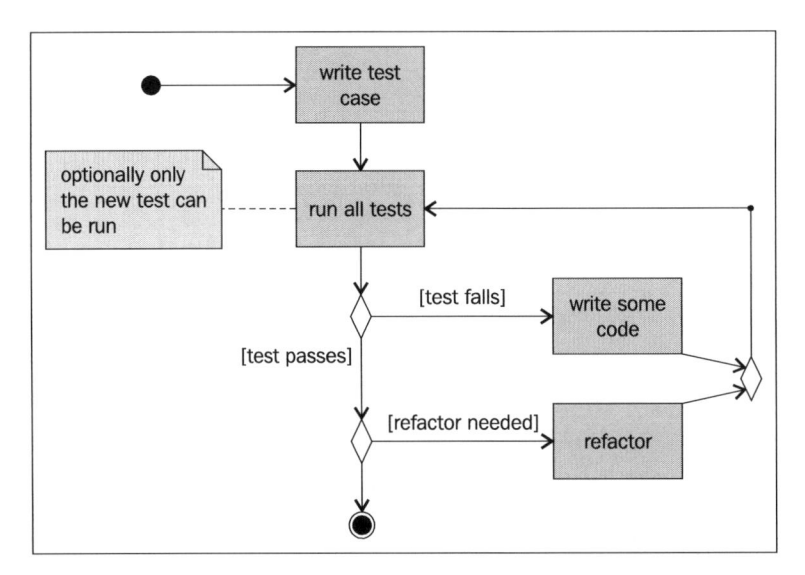

The following sections explain the individual activities depicted in this activity diagram.

## Writing a test case

We start our development process with writing a test case. This apparently simple process will put some machinery to work inside our heads. After all, it is not possible to write some code, test it or not, if we don't have a clear understanding of the problem domain and its details. Usually, this step will get you face to face with the aspects of the problem you don't understand, and you need to grasp if you want to model and write the code.

# Running all tests

Once the test is written the obvious following step is to run it, altogether with other tests we have written so far. Here, the importance of an IDE with built-in support of the testing environment is perhaps more evident than in other situations and this could cut the development time by a good fraction. It is expected that firstly, our test fails as we still haven't written any code!

To be able to complete our test, we usually write additional code and take design decisions. The additional code written is the minimum possible to get our test to compile. Consider here that not compiling is failing.

When we get the test to compile and run, if the test fails then we try to write the minimum amount of code necessary to make the test succeed. This may sound awkward at this point but the following code example in this chapter will help you understand the process.

Optionally, instead of running all tests again you can just run the newly added test first to save some time as sometimes running the tests on the emulator could be rather slow. Then run the whole test suite to verify that everything is still working properly. We don't want to add a new feature by breaking an existing one.

# Refactoring the code

When the test succeeds, we refactor the code added to keep it tidy, clean, and minimal.

We run all the tests again, to verify that our refactoring has not broken anything and if the tests are again satisfied, and no more refactoring is needed we finish our task.

Running the tests after refactoring is an incredible safety net which has been put in place by this methodology. If we made a mistake refactoring an algorithm, extracting variables, introducing parameters, changing signatures or whatever your refactoring is composed of, this testing infrastructure will detect the problem. Furthermore, if some refactoring or optimization could not be valid for every possible case we can verify it for every case used by the application and expressed as a test case.

## What is the advantage?

Personally, the main advantage I've seen so far is that you focus your destination quickly and is much difficult to divert implementing options in your software that will never be used. This implementation of unneeded features is a wasting of your precious development time and effort. And as you may already know, judiciously administering these resources may be the difference between successfully reaching the end of the project or not. Probably, Test Driven Development could not be indiscriminately applied to any project. I think that, as well as any other technique, you should use your judgment and expertise to recognize where it can be applied and where not. But keep this in mind: **there are no silver bullets**.

The other advantage is that you always have a safety net for your changes. Every time you change a piece of code, you can be absolutely sure that other parts of the system are not affected as long as there are tests verifying that the conditions haven't changed.

## Understanding the requirements

To be able to write a test about any subject, we should first understand the Subject under test.

We also mentioned that one of the advantages is that you focus your destination quickly instead of revolving around the requirements.

Translating requirements into tests and cross referencing them is perhaps the best way to understand the requirements, and be sure that there is always an implementation and verification for all of them. Also, when the requirements change (something that is very frequent in software development projects), we can change the tests verifying these requirements and then change the implementation to be sure that everything was correctly understood and mapped to code.

## Creating a sample project—the Temperature Converter

Our examples will revolve around an extremely simple Android sample project. It doesn't try to show all the fancy Android features but focuses on testing and gradually building the application from the test, applying the concepts learned before.

Let's pretend that we have received a list of requirements to develop an Android temperature converter application. Though oversimplified, we will be following the steps you normally would to develop such an application. However, in this case we will introduce the Test Driven Development techniques in the process.

# The list of requirements

Most usual than not, the list of requirements is very vague and there is a high number of details not fully covered.

As an example, let's pretend that we receive this list from the project owner:

- The application converts temperatures from Celsius to Fahrenheit and vice-versa
- The user interface presents two fields to enter the temperatures, one for Celsius other for Fahrenheit
- When one temperature is entered in one field the other one is automatically updated with the conversion
- If there are errors, they should be displayed to the user, possibly using the same fields
- Some space in the user interface should be reserved for the on screen keyboard to ease the application operation when several conversions are entered
- Entry fields should start empty
- Values entered are decimal values with two digits after the point
- Digits are right aligned
- Last entered values should be retained even after the application is paused

# User interface concept design

Let's assume that we receive this conceptual user interface design from the User Interface Design team:

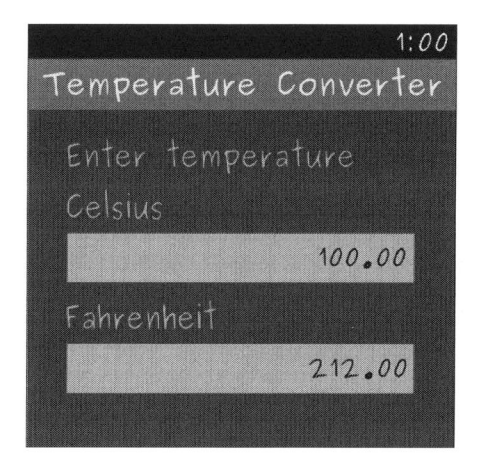

# Creating the projects

Our first step is to create the project. As we mentioned earlier, we are creating a main and a test project. The following screenshot shows the creation of the `TemperatureConverter` project (all values are typical Android project values):

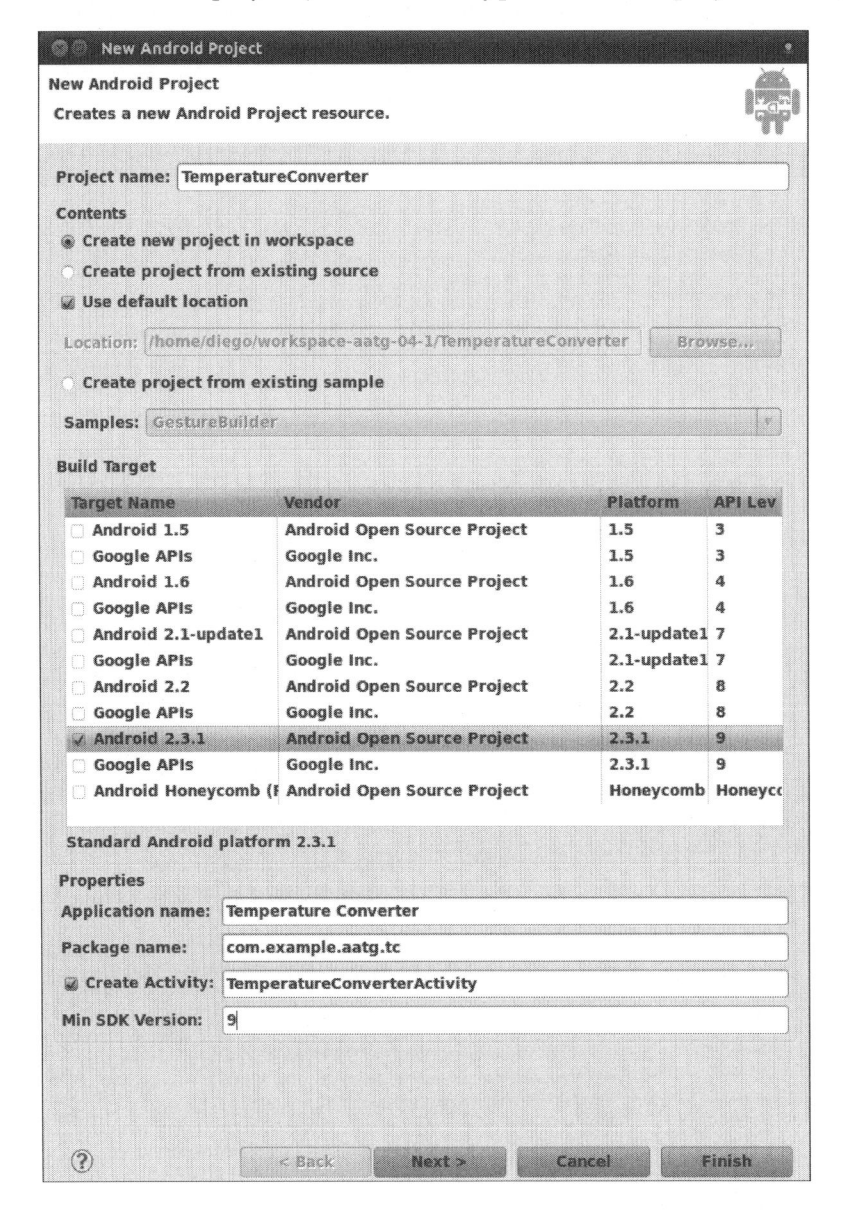

When you are ready to continue you should press the **Next >** button in order to create the related test project.

*Chapter 4*

The creation of the test project is displayed in this screenshot. All values will be selected for you based on your previous entries:

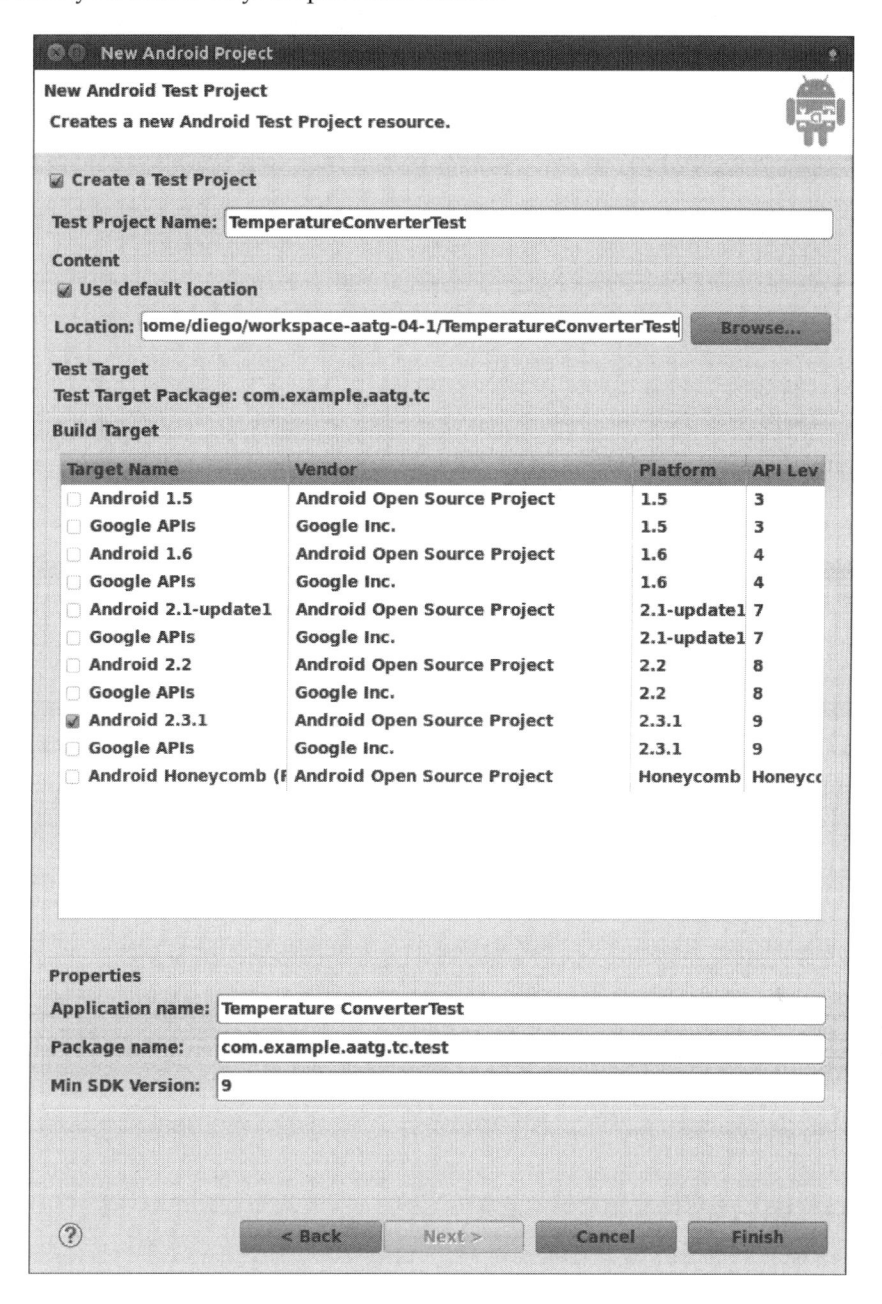

**New Android Test Project**
Creates a new Android Test Project resource.

☑ Create a Test Project

Test Project Name: TemperatureConverterTest

Content
☑ Use default location
Location: ome/diego/workspace-aatg-04-1/TemperatureConverterTest    Browse...

Test Target
Test Target Package: com.example.aatg.tc

Build Target

| Target Name | Vendor | Platform | API Lev |
|---|---|---|---|
| ☐ Android 1.5 | Android Open Source Project | 1.5 | 3 |
| ☐ Google APIs | Google Inc. | 1.5 | 3 |
| ☐ Android 1.6 | Android Open Source Project | 1.6 | 4 |
| ☐ Google APIs | Google Inc. | 1.6 | 4 |
| ☐ Android 2.1-update1 | Android Open Source Project | 2.1-update1 | 7 |
| ☐ Google APIs | Google Inc. | 2.1-update1 | 7 |
| ☐ Android 2.2 | Android Open Source Project | 2.2 | 8 |
| ☐ Google APIs | Google Inc. | 2.2 | 8 |
| ☑ Android 2.3.1 | Android Open Source Project | 2.3.1 | 9 |
| ☐ Google APIs | Google Inc. | 2.3.1 | 9 |
| ☐ Android Honeycomb (F | Android Open Source Project | Honeycomb | Honeycc |

Properties
Application name: Temperature ConverterTest
Package name: com.example.aatg.tc.test
Min SDK Version: 9

[ < Back ]  [ Next > ]  [ Cancel ]  [ Finish ]

# Creating the TemperatureConverterActivityTests project

We only have some templates in our **main project** created by the Android ADT plugin, such as:

- `TemperatureConverterActivity`
- `main.xml` layout
- `strings.xml` resources
- Other resources, like icons

Additionally, we have some templates created in our **test project**. The corresponding test packages to keep our tests separated from the main package are:

- `main.xml` layout
- `strings.xml` resources
- Other resources, like icons

> Be very cautious and don't let the template files fool you. There's little or no use of these resources in the test project so to avoid confusion, you should delete them. If later on you discover that some tests require specific resources, you can add only the needed ones.

Proceed with creating the first test by selecting the main test package name **com.example.aatg.tc.test** in Eclipse's **Package Explorer**, and then right-click on it. Select **New | JUnit Test Case**.

You should have a dialog like this:

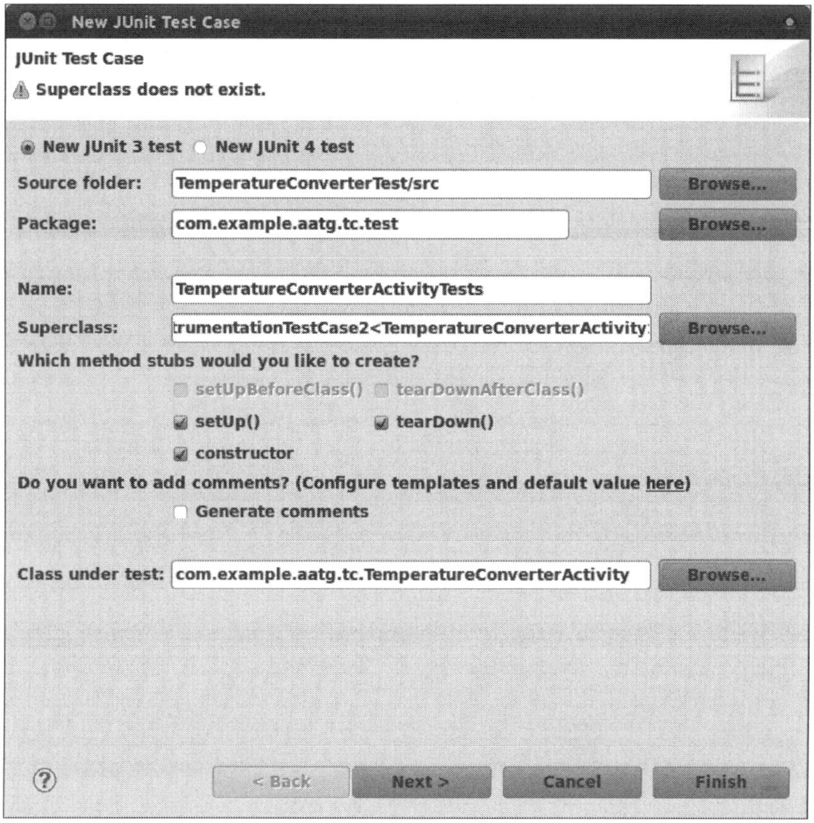


Here, you need to enter the following:

| Field | Description |
|---|---|
| **New JUnit 3 test** | JUnit 3 is the version supported by Android. Always use this option. |
| **Source folder:** | The default source folder for the tests. The default value should be fine. |
| **Package:** | The default package for the tests. This is usually the default package name for your main project followed by the subpackage test. |
| **Name:** | The name of the class for this test. The best practice here is to use the same class name of the class under test followed by the word **Tests**, in plural because most probably we will be hosting several tests in it. |

| Field | Description |
|---|---|
| **Superclass:** | We should select our superclass depending on what and how we are going to test. In *Chapter 3, Building Blocks on the Android SDK*, we reviewed the available alternatives. Use it as a reference when you try to decide what superclass to use. |
| | In this particular case and because we are testing a single `Activity` and using the system infrastructure we use `ActivityInstrumentationTestCase2`. Also note that as `ActivityInstrumentationTestCase2` is a generic class, we need the template parameter as well. This is the `Activity` under test which in our case is `TemperatureConverterActivity`. |
| | We can ignore the warning indicating that the superclass does not exist for now; we will be fixing the imports soon. |
| **Method stubs:** | Select the method stubs you want created. If at this point you are not sure what you would need, then select them all, as default stubs will be invoking their super counterparts. |
| **Do you want to add comments ?** | Generates Javadoc comments for the stub test method. |
| | Usually, unless you have changed the default template in Code Templates, the generated comments will be: |
| | `/**` |
| | `* Test method for {@link method()}.` |
| | `*/` |
| **Class under test:** | This is the class we are testing— `TemperatureConverterActivity` in this case. This is the most useful in other situations where the class under test has been implemented already and we would be able to select the list of methods we would like to test. Remember that in our case we haven't implemented the class yet so we will be presented with the only method that is in the Android ADT plugin template, which is `onCreate`. |

This situation, where the class under test has not been implemented yet and only the method created by the Android ADT is available, is better understood pressing **Next >**. Here, the list of methods available to test is presented, and in our case we don't have any methods implemented yet other than `onCreate` and the inherited methods from Activity.

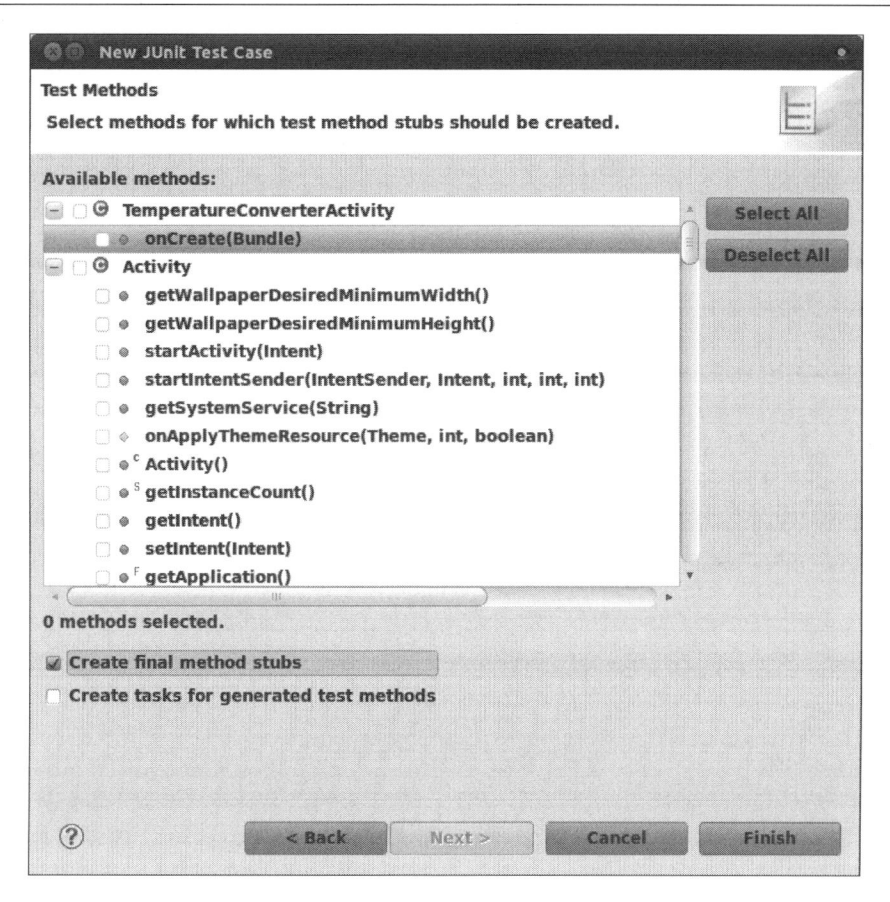

![New JUnit Test Case dialog - Test Methods page showing available methods tree with TemperatureConverterActivity and Activity nodes expanded, with checkboxes next to methods like onCreate(Bundle), getWallpaperDesiredMinimumWidth(), etc. Options at bottom: "Create final method stubs" (checked) and "Create tasks for generated test methods" (unchecked).]

This dialog has the following components:

| Field | Description |
| --- | --- |
| **Available methods:** | This is the list of all the methods we may want to test. |
| | When methods are overloaded, test names are generated accordingly to cope with the situation and parameter names are mangled into the test name. |
| **Create final method stubs** | Convenience set to add the final modifier to stub methods. |
| | The final modifier prevents these methods from being overridden by a subclass. |
| **Create tasks for generated test methods** | Creates a TODO comment in the test case. |

*Test Driven Development*

Either way, we may select `onCreate(Bundle)` to generate the `testOnCreateBundle` method for us, but we are leaving the selection list empty for now to avoid extra complexity of this simple demonstration application.

We now notice that our automatically generated class has some errors we need to fix before running. Otherwise the errors will prevent the test from running.

- First we should add the missing imports, using the shortcut *Shift+Ctrl+O*.
- Second, the problem we need to fix has been described before in *Chapter 3, Building Blocks on the Android SDK* under the section *The no-argument constructor*. As this pattern dictates, we need to implement it:

  ```
  public TemperatureConverterActivityTests() {
    this("TemperatureConverterActivityTests");
  }
  public TemperatureConverterActivityTests(String name) {
    super(TemperatureConverterActivity.class);
    setName(name);
  }
  ```

- We added the no argument constructor `TemperatureConverterActivityTests()`. From this constructor, we invoke the constructor that takes a name as a parameter.
- Finally, in this given name constructor, we invoke the super constructor and set the name.

To verify that everything has been set up in place, you may run the tests by using **Run as | Android JUnit Test**. There are no tests to run yet but at least we can verify that the infrastructure supporting our tests is already in place.

## Creating the fixture

We can start creating our test fixture by populating the `setUp` method with the elements we need in our tests. Almost unavoidable, in this case, is the use of the `Activity` under test, so let's prepare for the situation and add it to the fixture:

```
protected void setUp() throws Exception {
  super.setUp();
  mActivity = getActivity();
}
```

Let's create the `mActivity` field as well as the one proposed by Eclipse.

The `ActivityInstrumentationTestCase2.getActivity()` method has a side effect. If the `Activity` under test is not running, it is started. This may change the intention of a test if we use `getActivity()` as a simple accessor several times in a test and for some reason the `Activity` finishes or crashes before test completion. We will be inadvertently restarting the `Activity`, that is why in our tests we discourage the use of `getActivity()` in favor of having it in the fixture.

## Test preconditions

We mentioned this before and this can be identified as another pattern. It's very useful to test all the preconditions and be sure that our fixture has been created correctly.

```
public final void testPreconditions() {
   assertNotNull(mActivity);
}
```

That is, let's check that our fixture is composed by "not null" values.

We can run the tests to verify that everything is correct and green as shown in this screenshot:

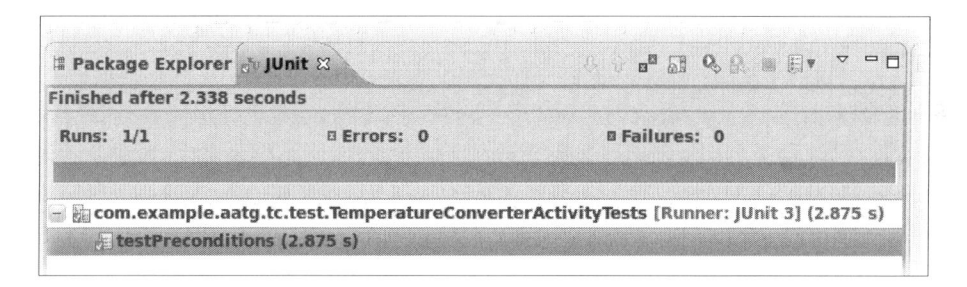

## Creating the user interface

Back to our Test Driven Development track, we need from our concise list of requirements that there be two entries for Celsius and Fahrenheit temperatures respectively. So let's add them to our test fixture.

They don't exist yet, and we haven't even started designing the user interface layout, but we know that there should be two entries like these for sure.

This is the code you should add to the `setUp()` method:

```
mCelsius = (EditText)
    mActivity.findViewById(com.example.aatg.tc.R.id.celsius);
mFahrenheit = (EditText)
    mActivity.findViewById(com.example.aatg.tc.R.id.fahrenheit);
```

*Test Driven Development*

There are some important things to notice:

- We define the fields for our fixture using `EditText` that we should import
- We use previously created `mActivity` to find the `Views` by ID
- We use the R class for the main project, not the one in the test project

## Testing the existence of the user interface components

Once we have added them to the `setUp()` method, as indicated in the previous section, we can check their existence in a specific test:

```
public final void testHasInputFields() {
  assertNotNull(mCelsius);
  assertNotNull(mFahrenheit);
}
```

We are not able to run the tests yet because we must fix some compilation problems first. We should fix the missing IDs in the R class.

Having created our test fixture that references elements and IDs in the user interface that we don't have yet, it's mandated by the Test Driven Development paradigm that we add the needed code to satisfy our tests. The first thing we should do is get it to compile at least, so if we have some tests testing unimplemented features they will fail.

## Getting the IDs defined

Our first stop would be to have the IDs for the user interface elements defined in the R class so the errors generated by referencing undefined constants `com.example.aatg.tc.R.id.celsius` and `com.example.aatg.tc.R.id.fahrenheit` go away.

You, as an experienced Android developer, know how to do it. I'll give you a refresher anyway. Open the `main.xml` layout in the layout editor and add the required user interface components to get something that resembles the design previously introduced in the section *User Interface concept design*.

```
<?xml version="1.0" encoding="utf-8"?>
<LinearLayout
    xmlns:android="http://schemas.android.com/apk/res/android"
    android:orientation="vertical"
    android:layout_width="fill_parent"
    android:layout_height="fill_parent">
```

```xml
<TextView
    android:layout_width="fill_parent"
    android:layout_height="wrap_content"
    android:text="@string/message" />
<TextView
    android:id="@+id/celsius_label"
    android:layout_width="wrap_content"
    android:layout_height="wrap_content"
    android:text="@string/celsius" />
<EditText
    android:id="@+id/celsius"
    android:layout_height="wrap_content"
    android:layout_width="wrap_content"
    android:text="EditText" />
<TextView
    android:id="@+id/fahrenheit_label"
    android:layout_width="wrap_content"
    android:layout_height="wrap_content"
    android:text="@string/fahrenheit" />
<EditText
    android:id="@+id/fahrenheit"
    android:layout_height="wrap_content"
    android:layout_width="wrap_content"
    android:text="EditText" />
</LinearLayout>
```

Doing so we get our tests to compile. Running them we get the following results:

- `testPreconditions` succeeded
- `testHasInputFields` succeeded
- Everything is green now

This clearly means that we are on track with applying TDD.

You may also have noticed that we added some decorative and non functional items to our user interface that we are not testing, mainly to keep our example as simple as possible. In a real case scenario you may want to add tests for these elements too.

## Translating requirements to tests

Tests have a double feature. They verify the correctness of our code but sometimes, and more prominently in TDD, they help us understand the design and digest what we are implementing. To be able to create the tests, we need to understand the problem we are dealing with and if we don't, we should at least have a rough understanding of the problem to allow us to handle it.

## Empty fields

From one of our requirements, we get: Entry fields should start empty.

To express this in a test we can write:

```
public final void testFieldsShouldStartEmpty() {
  assertEquals("", mCelsius.getText().toString());
  assertEquals("", mFahrenheit.getText().toString());
}
```

Here, we simply compare the initial contents of the fields against the empty string.

Not very surprisingly, we find that the test fails on execution. We forgot to clear the initial contents of the fields and they are not empty. Even though we haven't added any value to the `android:text` property of these fields, the ADT plugin layout editor adds some default values. Thus removing the default values from `android:text="@~+id/EditText01"` and `android:text="@+id/EditText02"` will force starting with empty temperature fields. These values may have been added by the ADT plugin itself or maybe by you when entering properties.

On running the test again, we find that it passes. We successfully converted one requirement to a test and validated it by obtaining the test results.

## View properties

Identically, we can verify other properties of the Views composing our layout. Among other things we can verify:

- Fields appear on the screen as expected
- Font sizes
- Margins
- Screen alignment

Let's start verifying that the fields are on the screen:

```
public final void testFieldsOnScreen() {
  final Window window = mActivity.getWindow();
  final View origin = window.getDecorView();
  assertOnScreen(origin, mCelsius);
  assertOnScreen(origin, mFahrenheit);
}
```

*Chapter 4*

As explained before, we use an assert form here: `ViewAsserts: assertOnScreen`.

> Static imports and how to add them to Eclipse's Content Assist was explained in *Chapter 3, Building Blocks on the Android SDK*. If you haven't done it before, now is the time.

The `assertOnScreen` method needs an origin to start looking for the other `Views`. In this case, because we want to start from the top most level, we use `getDecorView()`, which retrieves the top-level window decor view containing the standard window frame and decorations, and the client's content inside.

By running this test, we can ensure that the entry fields are on the screen as the UI design dictates. In some way we already knew that some Views with these specific IDs existed. That is, we made the fixture compile by adding the Views to the main layout, but we were not sure they were appearing on the screen at all. So, nothing else is needed but the sole presence of this test to ensure that the condition is not changed in the future. If we remove one of the fields for some reason, this test will tell us that it is missing and not complying with the UI design.

Following with our list of requirements, we should test that the `Views` are aligned in the layout as we expect:

```
public final void testAlignment() {
  assertLeftAligned(mCelsiusLabel, mCelsius);
  assertLeftAligned(mFahrenheitLabel, mFahrenheit);
  assertLeftAligned(mCelsius, mFahrenheit);
  assertRightAligned(mCelsius, mFahrenheit);
}
```

We continue using asserts from `ViewAssert` — in this case, `assertLeftAligned` and `assertRightAligned`. These methods verify the alignment of the specified `Views`.

The `LinearLayout` we are using by default arranges the fields in the way we are expecting them. Again, while we don't need to add anything to the layout, to satisfy the test, this will act as a guard condition.

Once we've verified that they are correctly aligned, we should verify that they are covering the whole screen width as specified by the schematic drawing. In this example, it's sufficient to verify the `LayoutParams` having the correct values:

```
public final void testCelsiusInputFieldCoverEntireScreen() {
  final int expected = LayoutParams.MATCH_PARENT;
  final LayoutParams lp = mCelsius.getLayoutParams();
  assertEquals("mCelsius layout width is not
    MATCH_PARENT", expected, lp.width);
```

```
}
public final void testFahrenheitInputFieldCoverEntireScreen() {
   final int expected = LayoutParams.MATCH_PARENT;
   final LayoutParams lp = mFahrenheit.getLayoutParams();
   assertEquals("mFahrenheit layout width is not
     MATCH_PARENT", expected, lp.width);
}
```

We used a custom message to easily identify the problem in case the test fails.

By running this test, we obtain the following message indicating that the test failed:

**junit.framework.AssertionFailedError: mCelsius layout width is not MATCH_PARENT expected:<-1> but was:<-2>**

This leads us to the layout definition. We must change `layout_width` to be `match_parent` for Celsius and Fahrenheit fields:

```
<EditText android:layout_height="wrap_content"
 android:id="@+id/celsius" android:layout_width="match_parent"
/>
```

Same for Fahrenheit—after the change is done, we repeat the cycle and by running the test again, we can verify that it is now successful.

Our method is starting to appear. We create the test to verify a condition described in the requirements. If it's not met, we change the cause of the problem and running the tests again we verify that the latest change solves the problem, and what is perhaps more important is that the change doesn't break the exiting code.

Next, let's verify that font sizes are as defined in our requirements:

```
public final void testFontSizes() {
   final float expected = 24.0f;
   assertEquals(expected, mCelsiusLabel.getTextSize());
   assertEquals(expected, mFahrenheitLabel.getTextSize());
}
```

Retrieving the font size used by the field is enough in this case.

The default font size is not `24px`, so we need to add this to our layout. It's a good practice to add the corresponding dimension to a resource file and then use it where it's needed in the layout. So, let's add `label_text_size` to `res/values/dimens.xml` with a value of `24px`. Then reference it in the `Text size` property of both labels, `celsius_label` and `fahrenheit_label`.

Now the test is passed.

Finally, let's verify that margins are interpreted as described in the user interface design:

```
public final void testMargins() {
   LinearLayout.LayoutParams lp;
   final int expected = 6;
   lp = (LinearLayout.LayoutParams) mCelsius.getLayoutParams();
   assertEquals(expected, lp.leftMargin);
   assertEquals(expected, lp.rightMargin);
   lp = (LinearLayout.LayoutParams) mFahrenheit.getLayoutParams();
   assertEquals(expected, lp.leftMargin);
   assertEquals(expected, lp.rightMargin);
}
```

This is a similar case as before. We need to add this to our layout. Let's add the margin dimension to the resource file and then use it where it's needed in the layout. Set the margin dimension in res/values/dimens.xml to a value of 6px. Then reference it in the Margin property of both fields, celsius and fahrenheit, and in the Left margin of the labels.

One more thing that is left is the verification of the justification of the entered values. We will validate input shortly to allow only the permitted values but for now let's just pay attention to the justification. The intention is to have values that are smaller than the whole field justified to the right and vertically centered:

```
public final void testJustification() {
   final int expected = Gravity.RIGHT|Gravity.CENTER_VERTICAL;
   int actual = mCelsius.getGravity();
   assertEquals(String.format("Expected 0x%02x but was 0x%02x",
      expected, actual), expected, actual);
   actual = mFahrenheit.getGravity();
   assertEquals(String.format("Expected 0x%02x but was 0x%02x",
      expected, actual), expected, actual);
}
```

Here we verify the gravity values as usual. However, we are using a custom message to help us identify the values that could be wrong. As Gravity class defines several constants whose values are better identified if expressed in hexadecimal, we are converting the values to this base in the message.

If this test is failing due to the default gravity used for the fields, then what is only left is to change it. Go to the layout definition and alter these gravity values so that the test succeeds.

This is precisely what we need to add:

```
android:gravity="right|center_vertical"
```

## Screen layout

We now want to verify that the requirement specifying that enough screen space should be reserved to display the keyboard is actually fulfilled.

We can write a test like this:

```
public final void testVirtualKeyboardSpaceReserved() {
  final int expected = 280;
  final int actual = mFahrenheit.getBottom();
  assertTrue(actual <= expected);
}
```

This verifies that the actual position of the last field in the screen, which is `mFahrenheit`, is not lower than a suggested value.

We can run the tests again verifying that everything is green again.

## Adding functionality

The user interface is in place. Now we start adding some basic functionality.

This functionality will include the code to handle the actual temperature conversion.

## Temperature conversion

From the list of requirements we can obtain this statement: When one temperature is entered in one field the other one is automatically updated with the conversion.

Following our plan we must implement this as a test to verify that the correct functionality is there. Our test would look something like this:

```
@UiThreadTest
public final void testFahrenheitToCelsiusConversion() {
  mCelsius.clear();
  mFahrenheit.clear();

  final double f = 32.5;
  mFahrenheit.requestFocus();
  mFahrenheit.setNumber(f);
  mCelsius.requestFocus();
  final double expectedC =
      TemperatureConverter.fahrenheitToCelsius(f);
  final double actualC = mCelsius.getNumber();
  final double delta = Math.abs(expectedC - actualC);
  final String msg = "" + f + "F -> " + expectedC + "C
```

```
        but was " + actualC + "C (delta " + delta + ")";
    assertTrue(msg, delta < 0.005);
}
```

Firstly, as we already know, to interact with the UI changing its values we should run the test on the UI thread and thus is annotated with `@UiThreadTest`.

Secondly, we are using a specialized class to replace `EditText` providing some convenience methods like `clear()` or `setNumber()`. This would improve our application design.

Next, we invoke a converter, named `TemperatureConverter`, a utility class providing the different methods to convert between different temperature units and using different types for the temperature values.

Finally, as we will be truncating the results to provide them in a suitable format presented in the user interface we should compare against a delta to assert the value of the conversion.

Creating the test as it is will force us to follow the planned path. Our first objective is to add the needed code to get the test to compile and then to satisfy the test's needs.

## The EditNumber class

In our main project, not in the tests one, we should create the class `EditNumber` extending `EditText` as we need to extend its functionality.

We use Eclipse's help to create this class using **File | New | Class** or its shortcut in the Toolbars.

*Test Driven Development*

This screenshot shows the window that appears after using this shortcut:

The following table describes the most important fields and their meaning in the previous screen:

| Field | Description |
| --- | --- |
| Source folder: | The source folder for the newly-created class. In this case the default location is fine. |
| Package: | The package where the new class is created. In this case the default package `com.example.aatg.tc` is fine too. |
| Name: | The name of the class. In this case we use `EditNumber`. |
| Modifiers: | Modifiers for the class. In this particular case we are creating a public class. |

| Field | Description |
|---|---|
| Superclass: | The superclass for the newly-created type. We are creating a custom `View` and extending the behavior of `EditText`, so this is precisely the class we select for the supertype. |
| | Remember to use **Browse...** to find the correct package. |
| Which method stubs would you like to create? | These are the method stubs we want Eclipse to create for us. Selecting **Constructors from superclass** and **Inherited abstract methods** would be of great help. |
| | As we are creating a custom View we should provide the constructors that are used in different situations, for example when the custom View is used inside an XML layout. |
| Do you want to add comments? | Some comments are added automatically when this option is selected. You can configure Eclipse to personalize these comments. |

Once the class is created we need to change the type of the fields first in our test:

```
public class TemperatureConverterActivityTests extends
ActivityInstrumentationTestCase2<TemperatureConverterActivity> {
    private TemperatureConverterActivity mActivity;
    private EditNumber mCelsius;
    private EditNumber mFahrenheit;
    private TextView mCelsiusLabel;
    private TextView mFahrenheitLabel;
    ...
```

Then change any cast that is present in the tests. Eclipse will help you do that.

If everything goes well, there are still two problems we need to fix before being able to compile the test:

- We still don't have the methods `clear()` and `setNumber()` in `EditNumber`
- We don't have the `TemperatureConverter` utility class

To create the methods we are using Eclipse's helpful actions. Let's choose **Create method clear() in type EditNumber**.

Same for `setNumber()` and `getNumber()`.

Finally, we must create the `TemperatureConverter` class.

*Test Driven Development*

> Be sure to create it in the main project and not in the test project.

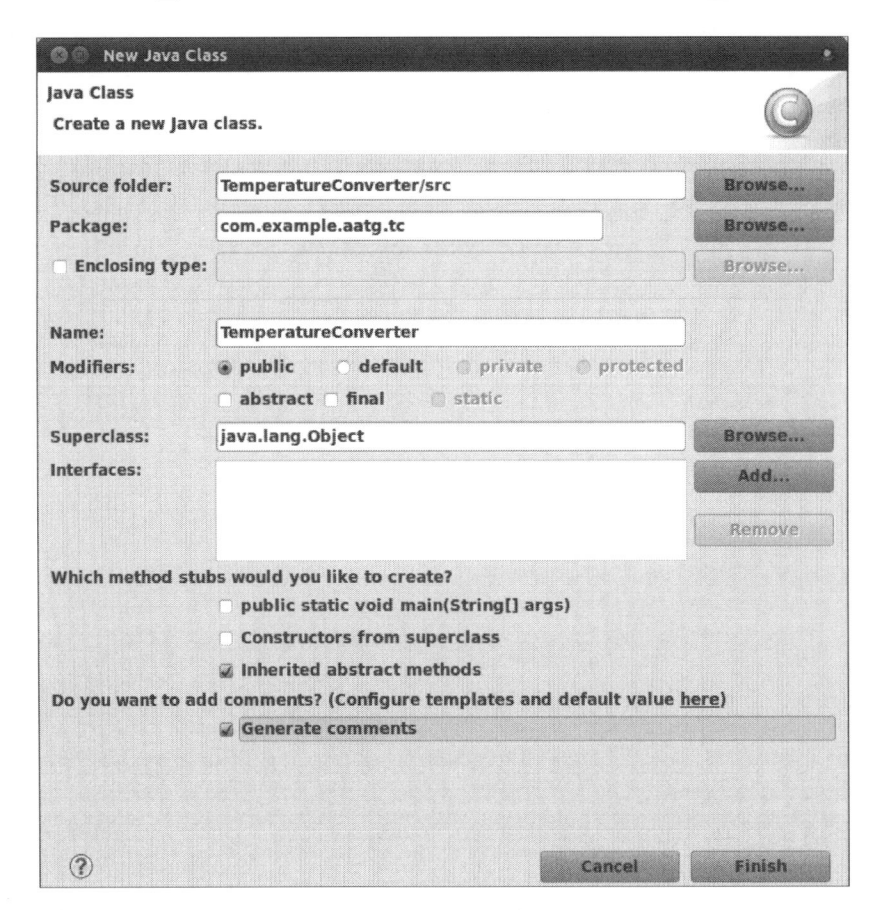

Having done this, in our test select **Create method fahrenheitToCelsius in type TemperatureConverter**.

This fixes our last problem and leads us to a test that we can now compile and run.

Surprisingly, or not, when we run the tests, they will fail with an exception:

**09-06 13:22:36.927: INFO/TestRunner(348): java.lang.ClassCastException: android.widget.EditText**

**09-06 13:22:36.927: INFO/TestRunner(348):    at com.example.aatg.tc.test.TemperatureConverterActivityTests.setUp(TemperatureConverterActivityTests.java:41)**

*Chapter 4*

**09-06 13:22:36.927: INFO/TestRunner(348):    at junit.framework.TestCase.runBare(TestCase.java:125)**

That is because we updated all of our Java files to include our newly-created `EditNumber` class but forgot to change the XMLs, and this could only be detected at runtime.

Let's proceed to update our UI definition:

```
<com.example.aatg.tc.EditNumber
  android:layout_height="wrap_content"
  android:id="@+id/celsius"
  android:layout_width="match_parent"
  android:layout_margin="@dimen/margin"
  android:gravity="right|center_vertical"

  android:saveEnabled="true" />
```

That is, we replace the original `EditText` by `com.example.aatg.tc.EditNumber` which is a `View` extending the original `EditText`.

Now we run the tests again and we discover that all tests pass.

But wait a minute, we haven't implemented any conversion or any handling of values in the new `EditNumber` class and all tests passed with no problem. Yes, they passed because we don't have enough restrictions in our system and the ones in place simply cancel themselves.

Before going further, let's analyze what just happened. Our test invoked the `mFahrenheit.setNumber(f)` method to set the temperature entered in the **Fahrenheit** field, but `setNumber()` is not implemented and it is an empty method as generated by Eclipse and does nothing at all. So the field remains empty.

Next, the value for `expectedC` — the expected temperature in Celsius is calculated invoking `TemperatureConverter.fahrenheitToCelsius(f)`, but this is also an empty method as generated by Eclipse. In this case, because Eclipse knows about the return type it returns a constant 0. So `expectedC` becomes 0.

Then the actual value for the conversion is obtained from the UI. In this case invoking `getNumber()` from `EditNumber`. But once again this method was automatically generated by Eclipse and to satisfy the restriction imposed by its signature, it must return a value that Eclipse fills with 0.

The delta value is again 0, as calculated by `Math.abs(expectedC - actualC)`.

And finally our assertion `assertTrue(msg, delta < 0.005)` is true because `delta=0` satisfies the condition, and the test passes.

*Test Driven Development*

So, is our methodology flawed as it cannot detect a simple situation like this?

No, not at all. The problem here is that we don't have enough restrictions and they are satisfied by the default values used by Eclipse to complete auto-generated methods. One alternative could be to throw exceptions at all of the auto-generated methods, something like `RuntimeException("not yet implemented")` to detect its use when not implemented. But we will be adding enough restrictions in our system to easily trap this condition.

## TemperatureConverter unit tests

It seems, from our previous experience, that the default conversion implemented by Eclipse always returns 0, so we need something more robust. Otherwise this will be only returning a valid result when the parameter takes the value of 32F.

The `TemperatureConverter` is a utility class not related with the Android infrastructure, so a standard unit test will be enough to test it.

We create our tests using Eclipse's **File | New | JUnit Test Case**, filling in some appropriate values, and selecting the method to generate a test as shown in the next screenshot.

Firstly, we create the unit test by extending `junit.framework.TestCase` and selecting `com.example.aatg.tc.TemperatureConverter` as the class under test:

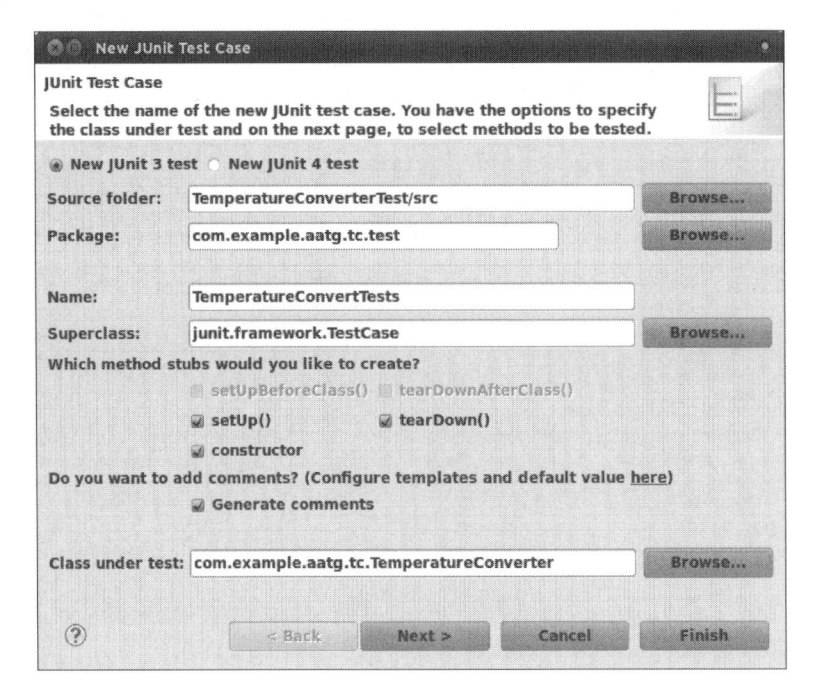

Then by pressing the **Next >** button we can obtain the list of methods we may want to test:

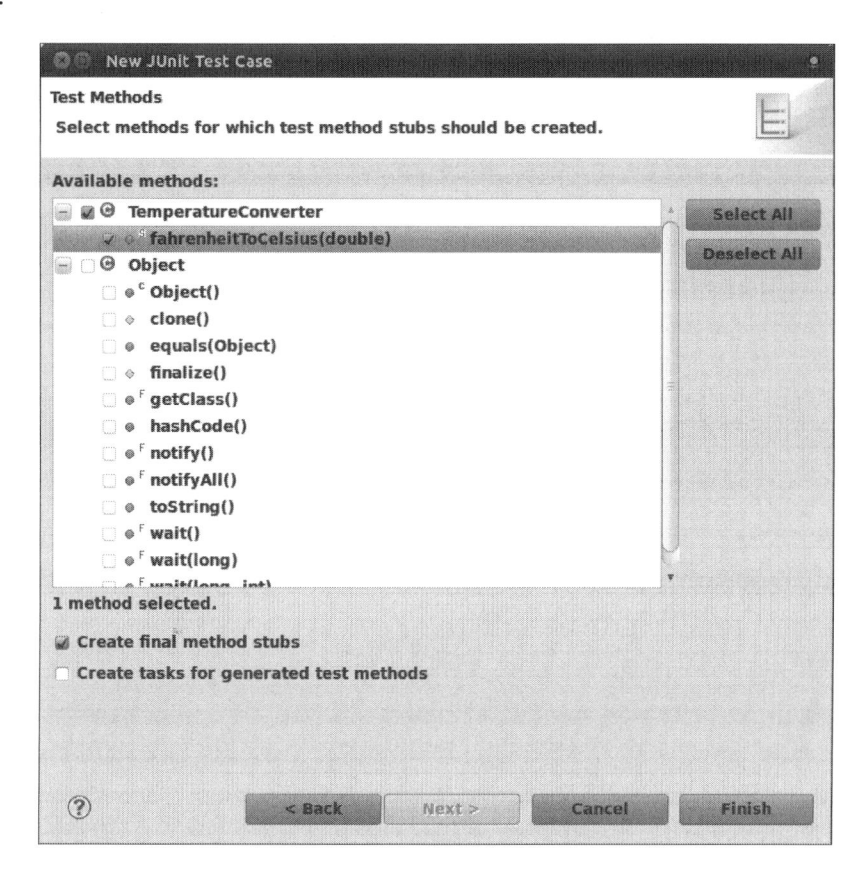

![New JUnit Test Case dialog showing Test Methods selection with fahrenheitToCelsius(double) checked under TemperatureConverter]

We have implemented only one method in `TemperatureConverter`, so it's the only one appearing in the list. Other classes implementing more methods will display all the options here.

It's good to note that even if the test method is auto-generated by Eclipse it won't pass. It will fail with the message *Not yet implemented* to remind us that something is missing.

Let's start by changing this:

```
/**
 * Test method for {@link com.example.aatg.tc.
   TemperatureConverter#fahrenheitToCelsius(double)}.
 */
public final void testFahrenheitToCelsius() {
    for (double c: conversionTableDouble.keySet()) {
```

## Test Driven Development

```
        final double f = conversionTableDouble.get(c);
        final double ca = TemperatureConverter.fahrenheitToCelsius(f);
        final double delta = Math.abs(ca - c);
        final String msg = "" + f + "F -> " + c + "C but is "
          + ca + " (delta " + delta + ")";
        assertTrue(msg, delta < 0.0001);
    }
}
```

Creating a conversion table with values for different temperature conversion we know from other sources would be a good way to drive this test.

```
    private static final HashMap<Double, Double>
      conversionTableDouble = new HashMap<Double, Double>();
static {
  // initialize (c, f) pairs
  conversionTableDouble.put(0.0, 32.0);
  conversionTableDouble.put(100.0, 212.0);
  conversionTableDouble.put(-1.0, 30.20);
  conversionTableDouble.put(-100.0, -148.0);
  conversionTableDouble.put(32.0, 89.60);
  conversionTableDouble.put(-40.0, -40.0);
  conversionTableDouble.put(-273.0, -459.40);
}
```

We may just run this test to verify that it fails, giving us this trace:

**junit.framework.AssertionFailedError: -40.0F -> -40.0C but is 0.0 (delta 40.0)**

at com.example.aatg.tc.test.TemperatureConverterTests.testFahrenheitToCelsius(TemperatureConverterTests.java:62)

at java.lang.reflect.Method.invokeNative(Native Method)

at android.test.AndroidTestRunner.runTest(AndroidTestRunner.java:169)

at android.test.AndroidTestRunner.runTest(AndroidTestRunner.java:154)

at android.test.InstrumentationTestRunner.onStart(InstrumentationTestRunner.java:520)

at android.app.Instrumentation$InstrumentationThread.run(Instrumentation.java:1447)

Well, this was something we were expecting as our conversion always returns 0. Implementing our conversion, we discover that we need some ABSOLUTE_ZERO_F constant:

```java
public class TemperatureConverter {
  public static final double ABSOLUTE_ZERO_C = -273.15d;
  public static final double ABSOLUTE_ZERO_F = -459.67d;
  private static final String ERROR_MESSAGE_BELOW_ZERO_FMT =
      "Invalid temperature: %.2f%c below absolute zero";
  public static double fahrenheitToCelsius(double f) {
    if (f < ABSOLUTE_ZERO_F) {
      throw new InvalidTemperatureException(
        String.format(ERROR_MESSAGE_BELOW_ZERO_FMT, f, 'F'));
    }
    return ((f - 32) / 1.8d);
  }
}
```

Absolute zero is the theoretical temperature at which entropy would reach its minimum value. To be able to reach this absolute zero state, according to the laws of thermodynamics, the system should be isolated from the rest of the universe. Thus it is an unreachable state. However, by international agreement, absolute zero is defined as 0K on the Kelvin scale and as -273.15°C on the Celsius scale or to -459.67°F on the Fahrenheit scale.

We are creating a custom exception, InvalidTemperatureException, to indicate a failure providing a valid temperature to the conversion method. This exception is created simply by extending RuntimeException:

```java
public class InvalidTemperatureException extends RuntimeException {
  public InvalidTemperatureException(String msg) {
    super(msg);
  }
}
```

Running the tests again we now discover that testFahrenheitToCelsiusConversion test fails, however testFahrenheitToCelsius succeeds. This tells us that now conversions are correctly handled by the converter class but there are still some problems with the UI handling this conversion.

A closer look at the failure trace reveals that there's something still returning 0 when it shouldn't.

This reminds us that we are still lacking a proper EditNumber implementation. Before proceeding to implement the mentioned methods, let's create the corresponding tests to verify what we are implementing is correct.

## The EditNumber tests

From the previous chapter, we can now determine that the best base class for our custom `View` tests is `AndroidTestCase`, as we need a mock `Context` to create the custom `View` but we don't need system infrastructure.

This is the dialog we have to complete to create the tests. In this case using `android.test.AndroidTestCase` as the base class and `com.example.aatg.tc.EditNumber` as the class under test:

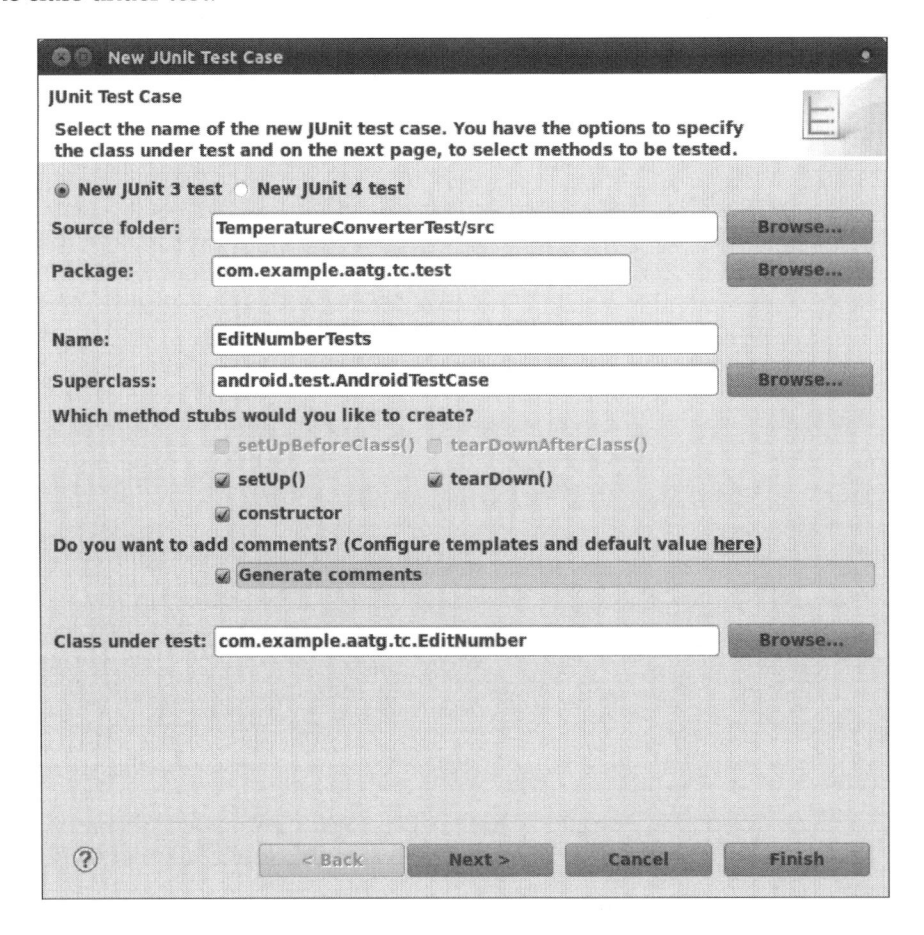

After pressing **Next >**, we select the methods for which stubs are created:

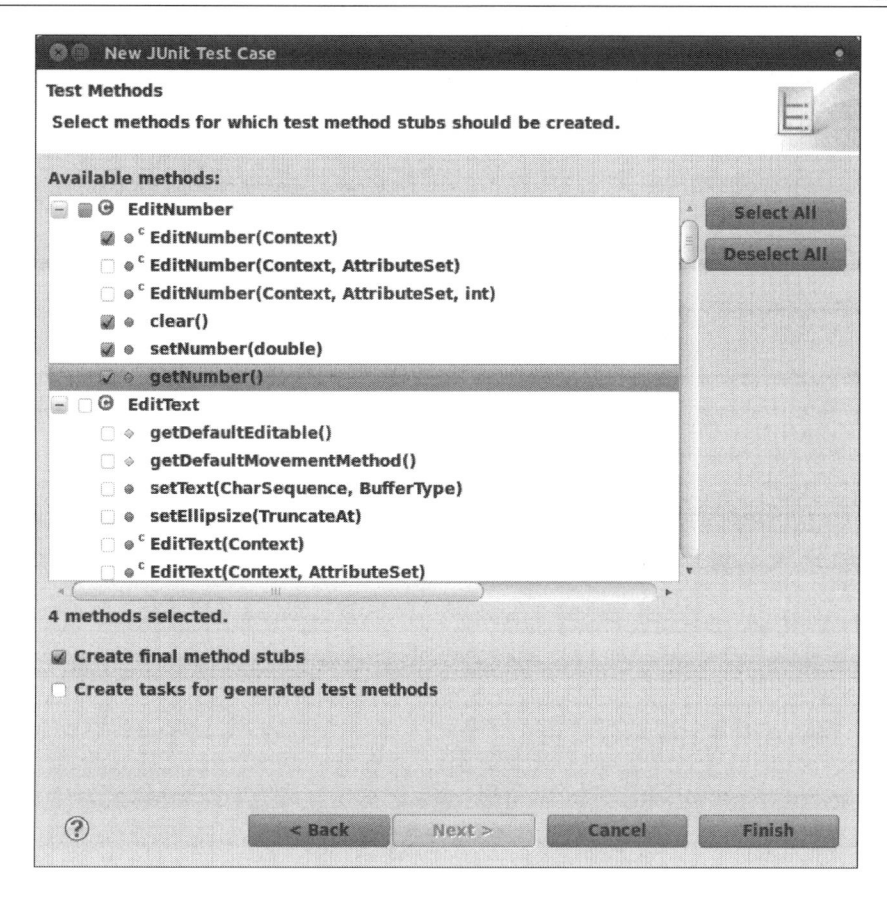

We need to update the auto-generated constructor to reflect the pattern we identified before, the given name pattern:

```
/**
 * Constructor
 */
public EditNumberTests() {
   this("EditNumberTests");
}
/**
 * @param name
 */
public EditNumberTests(String name) {
   setName(name);
}
```

## Test Driven Development

The next step is to create the fixture. In this case this is a simple `EditNumber` which we will be testing:

```
/* (non-Javadoc)
 * @see junit.framework.TestCase#setUp()
 */
protected void setUp() throws Exception {
  super.setUp();

  mEditNumber = new EditNumber(mContext);
  mEditNumber.setFocusable(true);
}
```

The mock context is obtained from the protected field mContext (http://developer.android.com/reference/android/test/AndroidTestCase.html#mContext) available in the `AndroidTestCase` class.

At the end of the test we set `mEditNumber` as a focusable `View`, that is it will be able to gain focus, as it will be participating in a bunch of tests simulating UIs that may need to request its focus explicitly.

Next, we test that the required `clear()` functionality is implemented correctly in the `testClear()` method:

```
/**
 * Test method for {@link com.example.aatg.tc.EditNumber#clear()}.
 */
public final void testClear() {
  final String value = "123.45";
  mEditNumber.setText(value);
  mEditNumber.clear();
  String expectedString = "";
  String actualString = mEditNumber.getText().toString();
  assertEquals(expectedString, actualString);
}
```

Running the test we verify that it fails:

**junit.framework.ComparisonFailure: expected:<> but was:<123.45>**

   at com.example.aatg.tc.test.EditNumberTests.testClear(EditNumberTests.java:62)

   at android.test.AndroidTestRunner.runTest(AndroidTestRunner.java:169)

   at android.test.AndroidTestRunner.runTest(AndroidTestRunner.java:154)

   at android.test.InstrumentationTestRunner.onStart(InstrumentationTestRunner.java:529) at android.app.Instrumentation$InstrumentationThread.run(Instrumentation.java:1447)

We need to implement `EditNumber.clear()` correctly.

This is a simple case, so just by adding this implementation to `EditNumber` we satisfy the test:

```
public void clear() {
   setText("");
}
```

Run the test and proceed. Now let's complete the `testSetNumber()` implementation:

```
/**
 * Test method for {@link
    com.example.aatg.tc.EditNumber#setNumber(double)}.
 */
public final void testSetNumber() {
  mEditNumber.setNumber(123.45);
  final String expected = "123.45";
  final String actual = mEditNumber.getText().toString();
  assertEquals(expected, actual);
}
```

Which fails unless we implement `EditNumber.setNumber()`, similar to this implementation:

```
private static final String DEFAULT_FORMAT = "%.2f";
public void setNumber(double f) {super.setText(
   String.format(DEFAULT_FORMAT, f));
}
```

We are using a constant, `DEFAULT_FORMAT`, to hold the desired format to convert the numbers. This can be later converted to a property that could also be specified in the `xml` layout definition of the field.

The same goes for the `testGetNumber()` and `getNumber()` pair:

```
/**
 * Test method for {@link
    com.example.aatg.tc.EditNumber#getNumber()}.
 */
public final void testGetNumber() {
  mEditNumber.setNumber(123.45);
  final double expected = 123.45;
  final double actual = mEditNumber.getNumber();
```

```
        assertEquals(expected, actual);
    }
```

And:

```
    public double getNumber() {
       Log.d("EditNumber", "getNumber() returning value
          of '" + getText().toString() + "'");
       return Double.valueOf(getText().toString());
    }
```

Surprisingly these tests succeed. But now there's a test that was passing that started to fail: `testFahrenheitToCelsiusConversion()`. The reason is that now that we have implemented `EditNumber.setNumber()` and `EditNumber.getNumber()` correctly, some values are returned differently and this test method was relying on spurious values.

This is a screenshot of the results obtained after running the tests:

If you closely analyze the case, you can discover where the problem is.

Got it ?

Our test method is expecting the conversion to be realized automatically when the focus changes, as was specified in our list of requirements: when one temperature is entered in one field the other one is automatically updated with the conversion.

Remember, we don't have buttons or anything else to convert temperature values, so the conversion is expected to be done automatically once the values are entered.

This leads us again to the `TemperatureConverterActivity` and the way it handles the conversions.

## The TemperatureChangeWatcher class

One way of implementing the required behavior of constantly updating the other temperature value once one has changed is through a `TextWatcher`. From the documentation we can understand that a `TextWatcher` is an object of a type that is attached to an `Editable`; its methods will be called when the text is changed (http://developer.android.com/intl/de/reference/android/text/TextWatcher.html).

It seems that is what we need.

*Test Driven Development*

We implement this class as an inner class of `TemperatureConverterActivity`. This is the screenshot of the New Java Class in Eclipse:

[New Java Class dialog in Eclipse with the following fields:
- Source folder: TemperatureConverter/src
- Package: com.example.aatg.tc
- Enclosing type (checked): com.example.aatg.tc.TemperatureConverterActivity
- Name: TemperatureChangedWatcher
- Modifiers: public (selected)
- Superclass: java.lang.Object
- Interfaces: android.text.TextWatcher
- Inherited abstract methods (checked)
- Generate comments (checked)]

And this is our code after some additions to the recently created class.

```
/**
 * Changes fields values when text changes applying the
    corresponding method.
 *
 */
public class TemperatureChangedWatcher implements TextWatcher {
  private final EditNumber mSource;
  private final EditNumber mDest;
  private OP mOp;
```

```java
/**
 * @param mDest
 * @param convert
 * @throws NoSuchMethodException
 * @throws SecurityException
 */
public TemperatureChangedWatcher(TemperatureConverter.OP op) {
  if ( op == OP.C2F ) {
    this.mSource = mCelsius;
    this.mDest = mFahrenheit;
  }
  else {
    this.mSource = mFahrenheit;
    this.mDest = mCelsius;
  }
  this.mOp = op;
}

/* (non-Javadoc)
 * @see android.text.TextWatcher#afterTextChanged(
     android.text.Editable)
 */
public void afterTextChanged(Editable s) {
  // TODO Auto-generated method stub

}

/* (non-Javadoc)
 * @see android.text.TextWatcher#beforeTextChanged(
     java.lang.CharSequence, int, int, int)
 */
public void beforeTextChanged(
  CharSequence s, int start, int count, int after) {
  // TODO Auto-generated method stub

}

/* (non-Javadoc)
 * @see android.text.TextWatcher#onTextChanged(
     java.lang.CharSequence, int, int, int)
 */
public void onTextChanged(CharSequence s, int start, int before,
  int count) {
  if (!mDest.hasWindowFocus() || mDest.hasFocus() || s == null )
  {
    return;
  }

  final String str = s.toString();
```

```
            if ( "".equals(str) ) {
              mDest.setText("");
              return;
            }
            try {
              final double temp = Double.parseDouble(str);
              final double result = (mOp == OP.C2F) ?
                TemperatureConverter.celsiusToFahrenheit(temp) :
                TemperatureConverter.fahrenheitToCelsius(temp);
              final String resultString = String.format("%.2f", result);
              mDest.setNumber(result);
              mDest.setSelection(resultString.length());
            } catch (NumberFormatException e) {
              // WARNING
              // this is generated while a number is entered,
              // for example just a '-'
              // so we don't want to show the error
            } catch (Exception e) {
              mSource.setError("ERROR: " + e.getLocalizedMessage());
            }
          }
        }
      }
```

We implement extending `TextWatcher` and overriding the unimplemented methods.

Because we will be using the same `TemperatureChangeWatcher` implementation for both fields, Celsius and Fahrenheit, we keep a reference to the fields used as source and destination as well as the operation needed to update their values. To specify this operation we are introducing an `enum` to the `TemperatureConverter` class.

```
      /**
       * C2F: celsiusToFahrenheit
       * F2C: fahrenheitToCelsius
       */
      public static enum OP { C2F, F2C };
```

This operation is specified in the constructor and the destination and source `EditNumber` are selected accordingly. This way we can use the same watcher for different conversions.

The method of the `TextWatcher` interface we are mainly interested in is `onTextChanged`, that will be called any time the text changes. At the beginning we avoid potential loops, checking who has focus and returning if the conditions are not met.

We also set the destination field as an empty `String` if the source is empty.

Finally, we try to set the resulting value of invoking the corresponding conversion method to set the destination field. We flag the error as necessary, avoiding showing premature errors when the conversion was invoked with a partially entered number.

We need to set the listener on the fields in `TemperatureConverterActivity.onCreate()`:

```
/** Called when the activity is first created. */
  @Override
  public void onCreate(Bundle savedInstanceState) {
      super.onCreate(savedInstanceState);
      setContentView(R.layout.main);
      mCelsius = (EditNumber) findViewById(R.id.celsius);
      mFahrenheit = (EditNumber) findViewById(R.id.fahrenheit);
      mCelsius.addTextChangedListener(
          new TemperatureChangedWatcher(OP.C2F));
      mFahrenheit.addTextChangedListener(
          new TemperatureChangedWatcher(OP.F2C));
  }
```

To be able to run the tests we should compile them. To compile we need at least to define the `celsiusToFahrenheit`, which is not yet defined.

## More TemperatureConverter tests

We need to implement `celsiusToFahrenheit` and as usual we start from the test.

This is fairly equivalent to the other conversion method `fahrenheitToCelsius` and we can use the infrastructure we devised while creating this test:

```
/**
 * Test method for {@link com.example.aatg.tc.TemperatureConverter#celsiusToFahrenheit(double)}.
 */
public final void testCelsiusToFahrenheit() {
  for (double c: conversionTableDouble.keySet()) {
    final double f = conversionTableDouble.get(c);
    final double fa = TemperatureConverter.celsiusToFahrenheit(c);
    final double delta = Math.abs(fa - f);
    final String msg = "" + c + "C -> " + f + "F but is " + fa +
      " (delta " + delta + ")";
    assertTrue(msg, delta < 0.0001);
  }
}
```

*Test Driven Development*

We use the conversion table to exercise the method through different conversions and we verify that the error is less than a predefined delta.

Then, the correspondent conversion implementation in `TemperatureConverter` class is:

```
public static double celsiusToFahrenheit(double c) {
  if (c < ABSOLUTE_ZERO_C) {
    throw new InvalidTemperatureException(
      String.format(ERROR_MESSAGE_BELOW_ZERO_FMT, c, 'C'));
  }
  return (c * 1.8d + 32);
}
```

Now all the tests are passing but we are still not testing all the common conditions. You should check if errors and exceptions are correctly generated, besides all the normal cases we created so far.

This is the test we create to check the correct generation of exceptions when a temperature below absolute zero is used in a conversion:

```
public final void testExceptionForLessThanAbsoluteZeroF() {
  try {
    TemperatureConverter.fahrenheitToCelsius(
      TemperatureConverter.ABSOLUTE_ZERO_F-1);
    fail();
  }
  catch (InvalidTemperatureException ex) {
    // do nothing
  }
}
```

In this test we decrement the absolute zero temperature to obtain an even smaller value and then we attempt the conversion. We check for the correct exception being caught and finally we assert this condition:

```
public final void testExceptionForLessThanAbsoluteZeroC() {
  try {
    TemperatureConverter.celsiusToFahrenheit(
      TemperatureConverter.ABSOLUTE_ZERO_C-1);
    fail();
  }
  catch (InvalidTemperatureException ex) {
    // do nothing
  }
}
```

In a similar manner we test for the exception being thrown when the attempted conversion involves a temperature in Celsius which is lower than the absolute zero.

## The InputFilter tests

We want to filter the input that is received by the conversion utility so no garbage reaches this point.

The `EditNumber` class already filters valid input and generates exceptions otherwise. We can verify this condition by generating some new tests in `TemperatureConverterActivityTests`. We choose this class because we are sending keys to the entry fields, just as a real user would do:

```
public void testInputFilter() throws Throwable {
  runTestOnUiThread(new Runnable() {
    @Override
    public void run() {
      mCelsius.requestFocus();
    }
  });
  final Double n = -1.234d;
  sendKeys("MINUS 1 PERIOD 2 PERIOD 3 PERIOD 4");
  Object nr = null;
  try {
    nr = mCelsius.getNumber();
  }
  catch (NumberFormatException e) {
    nr = mCelsius.getText();
  }
  final String msg = "-1.2.3.4 should be filtered to " + n +
    " but is " + nr;
  assertEquals(msg, n, nr);
}
```

This test requests the focus to the Celsius field using the pattern we have reviewed before to run parts of a test in the UI thread, and then send some keys. The keys sent are an invalid sequence containing more than one period, which is not accepted for a well formed decimal number. It is expected that when the filter is in place, this sequence will be filtered and only the valid characters reach the field. We use the possibly generated `NumberFormatException` to detect the error and then we assert that the value returned by `mCelsius.getNumber()` is what we are expecting after filtering.

*Test Driven Development*

To implement this filter, we need to add an `InputFilter` to `EditNumber`. Because this should be added to all of the constructors we create an additional method `init()` which we invoke from them. To achieve our goal we use an instance of `DigitsKeyListener` accepting digits, signs, and decimal points.

```
/**
 * Initialization.
 * Set filter.
 *
 */
private void init() {
  // DigistKeyListener.getInstance(true, true) returns an
  // instance that accepts digits, sign and decimal point
  final InputFilter[] filters = new InputFilter[]
    { DigitsKeyListener.getInstance(true, true) };
  setFilters(filters);
}
```

Then from the constructors we should invoke this method:

```
/**
 * @param context
 * @param attrs
 */
public EditNumber(Context context, AttributeSet attrs) {
  super(context, attrs);
  init();
}
```

This `init` method is factored and invoked from different constructors.

Running the tests again we can verify that all have passed and now everything is green again.

# Viewing our final application

This is our final application which satisfies all the requirements.

In the following screenshot we are showing one of these requirements, which is the detection of an attempt to convert a temperature below the absolute zero temperature in Celsius (-1000.00C):

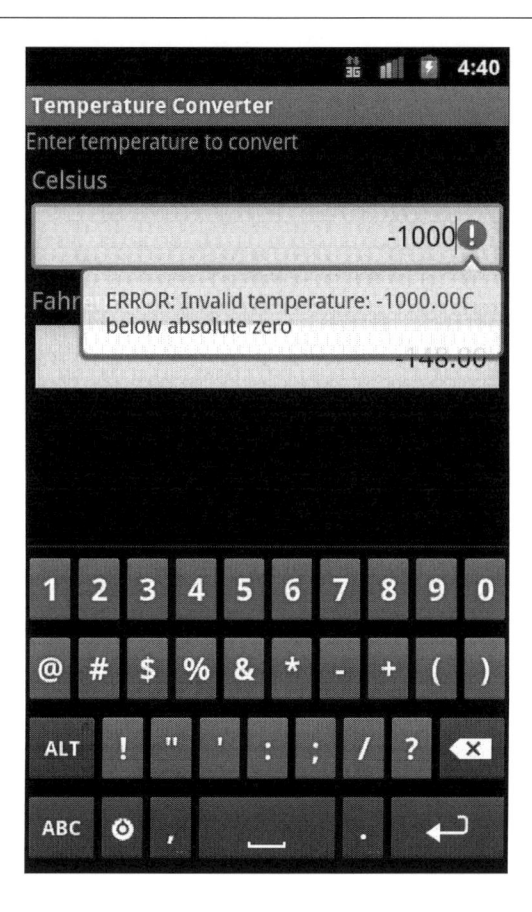

The UI respects the guidelines provided; the temperatures can be converted by entering them in the corresponding unit field.

To recap, this was the list of requirements:

- The application converts temperatures from Celsius to Fahrenheit and vice versa
- The user interface presents two fields to enter the temperatures, one for Celsius and the other for Fahrenheit
- When one temperature is entered in one field the other one is automatically updated with the conversion
- If there are errors, they should be displayed to the user, possibly using the same fields
- Some space in the user interface should be reserved for the on-screen keyboard to ease the application operation when several conversions are entered
- Entry fields should start empty

- Values entered are decimal values with two digits after the point
- Digits are right aligned

But what is perhaps more important is that we can assure that the application not only satisfies the requirements but also has no evident problems or bugs because we took every step by analyzing the test results and fixing the problems at their first appearance. This will ensure that the same bug, once discovered, will not resurface again.

# Summary

We presented Test Driven Development introducing its concepts and later on applying them step-by-step in a potential real-life problem.

We started with a concise list of requirement describing the Temperature Converter application.

Then, we implemented every test followed by the code that satisfies it. In this manner we implemented the application behavior as well as its presentation, conducting tests to verify that the UI we designed follows the specifications.

Having the tests in place lead us to analyze the different possibilities we have in running them and the next chapter will focus on the Testing Environment.

# 5
# Android Testing Environment

We built our application and a decent set of tests that we run to verify the basic aspect and behavior of the Temperature Converter application. Now it is time to provide different conditions to run these tests, other tests, or even run the application manually to understand what the user experience would be while using it.

In this chapter, we will cover:

- Creating **Android Virtual Devices (AVD)** to provide different conditions and configurations for the application
- Understanding the different configurations we can specify while creating AVDs
- How to run AVDs
- How to detach an AVD from its window to create headless emulators
- Unlocking the screen to be able to run all the tests
- Simulating real-life network conditions
- Running `monkey` to generate events to send to the application

## Creating Android Virtual Devices

To get the best opportunity of detecting problems related with the device where the application is running, you need the widest possible coverage of features and configurations.

While final and conclusive tests should always be run on real devices with the everyday increasing number of devices, it is virtually impossible that you will have one device of each to test your application. There are also device farms in the cloud to test on a variety of devices but its cost sometimes is above the average developer budget. Hopefully, Android provides a way of simulating, more or less verbatim, a great variety of features and configuration just from the convenience of the emulator and AVD configurations.

*Android Testing Environment*

> All the examples in this chapter are run from a Ubuntu 10.04 (Lucid Lynx) 64bit using **Android SDK and AVD Manager** Revision 10 and **Android SDK** with platform 2.3 (API 9) installed.

To create AVD you use `android` from the command line or even from inside Eclipse using **Window | Android SDK and AVD Manager** or its shortcut icon.

Running the command you access the **Android SDK and AVD Manager** where you press the **New...** button to create a new AVD, and this dialog box is presented:

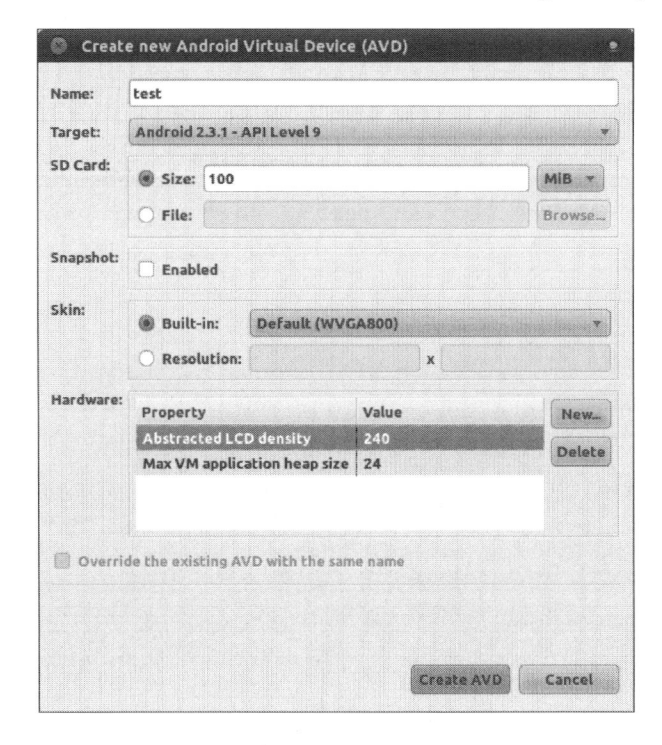

If you press **Create AVD** you finish the creation of the AVD using the default values. However if you need to support different configurations, you can specify different hardware properties by using the **New...** button.

The properties that can be set are:

| Property | Type | Description |
| --- | --- | --- |
| Camera support | boolean | Whether the device has a camera or not. |
| Cache partition size | integer | The size of the cache partition. |
| SD Card support | boolean | Whether the device supports insertion and removal of virtual SD Cards. |
| Cache partition support | boolean | Whether the cache partition is supported. Usually this partition is mounted in /cache. |
| Keyboard support | boolean | Whether the device has a physical QWERTY keyboard. |
| Audio playback support | boolean | Whether the device can play audio |
| Audio recording support | boolean | Whether the device can record audio. |
| DPAD support | boolean | Whether the device has DPAD keys. |
| Maximum vertical camera pixels | integer | The maximum vertical dimension in pixels of the virtual camera. |
| Accelerometer | boolean | Whether the device has an accelerometer. |
| GPS support | boolean | Whether the device has a GPS. |
| Device RAM size | integer | The amount of physical RAM on the device. This is expressed in megabytes. |
| Touch-screen support | boolean | Whether there is a touch screen on the device. |
| Battery support | boolean | Whether the device can run on battery. |
| GSM modem support | boolean | Whether there is a GSM modem in the device. |
| Track-ball support | boolean | Whether there is a trackball on the device. |
| Maximum horizontal camera pixels | integer | The maximum horizontal dimension in pixels of the virtual camera. |

After pressing **Start...** to start the AVD you can select other properties:

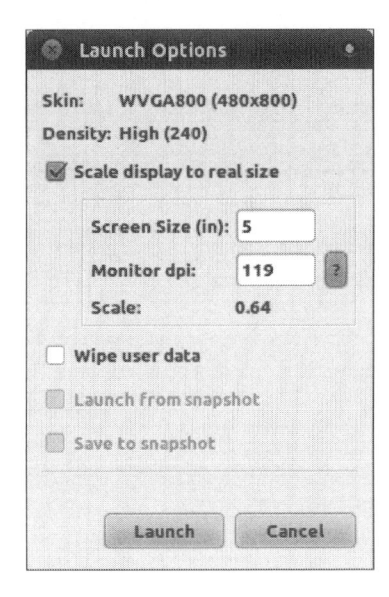

Setting the scale is also very useful to test your application in a window that resembles the size of a real device. It is a very common mistake to test your application in an AVD with a window size that is at least twice the size of a real device, and using a mouse pointer believing that everything is fine, to later realize on a physical device with a screen of 5 or 6 inches that some items on the UI are impossible to touch with your finger.

To scale the AVD screen you should also set the **Monitor dpi** to a value that corresponds to the monitor you are using.

Finally, it is also helpful to test your application under the same conditions repeatedly. To be able to test under the same conditions again and again, it is sometimes helpful to delete all the information that was entered in previous sessions. If this is the case, check **Wipe user data** to start afresh every time.

# Running AVDs from the command line

Wouldn't it be nice if we could run different AVDs from the command line and perhaps automate the way we run our tests or script them?

By freeing the AVD from its windows, open a whole new world of automation and scripting possibilities.

Well, let's explore these alternatives.

# Headless emulator

A headless emulator (its window is not displayed) comes in very handy when we run automated tests and nobody is looking at the window, or the interaction between the test runner and the application is so fast that we hardly see anything.

Anyway, it is also worth mentioning that sometimes you can't understand why some tests fail until you see the interaction on the screen, so use both alternatives with a bit of judgment.

One thing that we may have noticed running AVDs is that their communication ports are assigned at runtime, incrementing the last used port by 2 and starting with 5554. This is used to name the emulator and set its serial number, for example, the emulator using port 5554 becomes `emulator-5554`. This is very useful when we run AVDs during the development process because we don't have to pay attention to port assignment. But it can be very confusing and difficult to track which test runs on which emulator if we are running more than one simultaneously.

In those cases, we will be assigning known ports to the communication ports to keep the specific AVD under our control.

Usually, when we are running tests on more than one emulator at the same time, not only do we want to detach the window, but also avoid sound output. We will add options for this as well:

1. The command line to launch the test AVD we just created would be:

    ```
    $ emulator -avd test -no-window -no-audio -no-boot-anim -port 5580 &
    ```

2. The port must be an integer between 5554 and 5584:

    ```
    $ adb devices
    List of devices attached
    emulator-5580 device
    ```

    This shows the device in the device list.

3. The next step is to install the application and the tests:

    ```
    $ adb -s emulator-5580 install\
    TemperatureConverter/bin/TemperatureConverter.apk
    347 KB/s (16632 bytes in 0.046s)
      pkg: /data/local/tmp/TemperatureConverter.apk
    Success
    $ adb -s emulator-5580 install\
    TemperatureConverterTest/bin/TemperatureConverterTest.apk
    222 KB/s (16632 bytes in 0.072s)
    ```

```
       pkg: /data/local/tmp/TemperatureConverterTest.apk
Success
```

4. Then we can use the specified serial number to run the tests on it:

   ```
   $ adb -s emulator-5580 shell am instrument -w\
   com.example.aatg.tc.test/android.test.InstrumentationTestRunner
   
   com.example.aatg.tc.test.EditNumberTests:......
   
   com.example.aatg.tc.test.
   TemperatureConverterActivityTests:..........
   
   com.example.aatg.tc.test.TemperatureConverterTests:....
   
   Test results for InstrumentationTestRunner=..................
   
   Time: 25.295
   
   OK (20 tests)
   ```

## Disabling the keyguard

We can see the tests being run with no intervention and not requiring access to the emulator GUI.

But sometimes you may receive some errors for tests that are not failing if you run in a more standard approach, like in a standard emulator launched from Eclipse. In such cases one of the reasons is that the emulator may be locked at the first screen and we need to unlock it to be able to run tests involving the UI.

To unlock the screen you can use:

```
$ adb -s emulator-5580 emu event send EV_KEY:KEY_MENU:1 EV_KEY:KEY_MENU:0
```

The lock screen can also be disabled programmatically; however this has the disadvantage of including testing-related code in your application. This code should be removed or disabled once the application is ready to ship.

To do this, the following permission should be added to the manifest file (`AndroidManifest.xml`), and then disable the screen lock in your application under test.

To add the permission, add this element to the manifest:

```
<manifest>
...
   <uses-permission android:name="android.permission.DISABLE_KEYGUARD"/>
...
```

```
</manifest>
```

Then in the `Activity` under test you should add the following code, preferably in `onResume()`:

```
mKeyGuardManager =
       (KeyguardManager) getSystemService(KEYGUARD_SERVICE);
mLock = mKeyGuardManager.newKeyguardLock("com.example.aatg.tc");
mLock.disableKeyguard();
```

That is, get the `KeyguardManager`, then obtain the `KeyguardLock` specifying a tag, customize the package name to be able to debug who is disabling the keyguard.

Then disable the keyguard from showing using `disableKeyguard()`. If the keyguard is currently showing, it is hidden. The keyguard will be prevented from showing again until `reenableKeyguard()` is called.

# Cleaning up

On certain occasions you also need to clean up services and processes started after running some tests to prevent the results of the latter from being influenced by the ending conditions of the previous tests. In these cases, it is always better to start from a known condition freeing all the used memory, stopping services, reloading resources, and restarting processes, which is achievable by warm-booting the emulator.

```
$ adb -s emulator-5580 shell 'stop; sleep 5; start'
```

This command line opens the emulator shell for our emulator and runs the stop and start commands.

The evolution of these commands can be monitored using the `logcat` command:

```
$ adb -s emulator-5580 logcat
```

You will see messages like these:

D/AndroidRuntime( 241):

D/AndroidRuntime( 241): >>>>>>>>>>>>> AndroidRuntime START <<<<<<<<<<<<<

D/AndroidRuntime( 241): CheckJNI is ON

D/AndroidRuntime( 241): --- registering native functions ---

I/SamplingProfilerIntegration( 241): Profiler is disabled.

I/Zygote ( 241): Preloading classes...

Android Testing Environment

D/dalvikvm( 241): GC_EXPLICIT freed 816 objects / 47208 bytes in 7ms

I/ServiceManager( 28): service 'connectivity' died

I/ServiceManager( 28): service 'throttle' died

I/ServiceManager( 28): service 'accessibility' died

...

> This warm boot doesn't work well on Android 2.2 Froyo emulator but works perfectly on Android devices. A bug has been reported and you can follow its evolution at http://code.google.com/p/android/issues/detail?id=9814.

## Terminating the emulator

Once we have finished working with one of the headless emulator instances, we started using the command mentioned before. We use the following command line to kill it:

```
$ adb -s emulator-5580 emu kill
```

This will stop the emulator and free the used resources and terminate the emulator process on the host computer.

## Additional emulator configurations

Sometimes what we need to test is outside the reach of the options that can be set when the AVD is created or configured.

One of the cases could be the need to test our application under different locales. Let's say we want to test our application on a Japanese phone—an emulator with the language and country set to Japanese and Japan respectively.

We have the ability to pass these properties in the emulator command line.

The -prop command line option allows us to set any of the properties we could set:

```
$ emulator -avd test -no-window -no-audio -no-boot-anim -port 5580 -prop persist.sys.language=ja -prop persist.sys.country=JP &
```

To verify that our settings were successful, we can use the getprop command to verify them, for example:

```
$ adb -s emulator-5580 shell "getprop persist.sys.language"
```

**ja**

`$ adb -s emulator-5580 shell "getprop persist.sys.country"`

**JP**

If you want to clear all the user data after playing with the persistent settings, you can use the following command:

`$ adb -s emulator-5580 emu kill`

`$ emulator -avd test -no-window -no-audio -no-boot-anim -port 5580\ -wipe-data`

And the emulator will start afresh.

## Simulating network conditions

It is extremely important to test under different network conditions but it is neglected more often than not. This would lead to misconceptions and to believe that the application behaves differently because we use the host network which presents a different speed and latency.

The Android emulator supports network throttling, for example to support slower network speeds and higher connection latencies. This can be done in the emulator command line using the options `-netspeed <speed>` and `-netdelay <delay>`.

The complete list of supporting options is as follows:

For network speed:

| Option | Description | Speeds [kbits/s] |
|---|---|---|
| `-netspeed gsm` | GSM/CSD | up: 14.4, down: 14.4 |
| `-netspeed hscsd` | HSCSD | up: 14.4, down: 43.2 |
| `-netspeed gprs` | GPRS | up: 40.0, down: 80.0 |
| `-netspeed edge` | EDGE/EGPRS | up: 118.4, down: 236.8 |
| `-netspeed umts` | UMTS/3G | up: 128.0, down: 1920.0 |
| `-netspeed hsdpa` | HSDPA | up: 348.0, down: 14400.0 |
| `-netspeed full` | no limit | up: 0.0, down: 0.0 |
| `-netspeed <num>` | select both upload and download speed | up: as specified, down: as specified |
| `-netspeed <up>:<down>` | select individual up and down speed | up: as specified, down: as specified |

## Android Testing Environment

For latency:

| Option | Description | Delay [msec] |
|---|---|---|
| `-netdelay gprs` | GPRS | min 150, max 550 |
| `-netdelay edge` | EDGE/EGPRS | min 80, max 400 |
| `-netdelay umts` | UMTS/3G | min 35, max 200 |
| `-netdelay none` | no latency | min 0, max 0 |
| `-netdelay <num>` | select exact latency | latency as specified |
| `-netdelay <min>:<max>` | select min and max latencies | minimum and maximum latencies as specified |

The emulator, if values are not specified, uses the following default values:

- Default network speed is 'full'
- Default network latency is 'none'

This is an example of an emulator using these options to select the GSM network speed of 14.4 kbits/sec and a GPRS latency of 150 to 500 msec.

```
$ emulator -avd test -port 5580 -netspeed gsm -netdelay gprs
```

Once the emulator is running, you can verify these network settings or change them interactively using the Android console using a TELNET client:

```
$ telnet localhost 5580
```

**Trying ::1...**

**Trying 127.0.0.1...**

**Connected to localhost.**

**Escape character is '^]'.**

**Android Console: type 'help' for a list of commands**

**OK**

After we are connected we can type the following command:

```
network status
```

**Current network status:**

  **download speed:**    14400 bits/s (1.8 KB/s)

  **upload speed:**      14400 bits/s (1.8 KB/s)

minimum latency: 150 ms

maximum latency: 550 ms

OK

You can use the emulator to test applications using network services either manually or in an automated way.

In some cases this not only involves throttling the network speed but also changing the state of the GPRS connection to investigate how the application behaves and copes with these situations. To change this status we can also use the Android console in a running emulator.

For example to unregister the emulator from the network we can use:

```
$ telnet localhost 5580
```

Trying ::1...

Trying 127.0.0.1...

Connected to localhost.

Escape character is '^]'.

Android Console: type 'help' for a list of commands

OK

Next to receiving the OK subprompt, we can set the data network mode as unregistered by issuing the following command:

```
gsm data unregistered
```

OK

quit

After testing the application under this condition you can return to a connected state by using:

```
gsm data home
```

OK

To verify the status you can use:

```
gsm status
gsm voice state: home
```

```
gsm data state:   home
```

**OK**

# Additional qemu options

You may know that the Android emulator is based on an Open Source project named Qemu (`http://qemu.org`).

Qemu is a generic emulator and virtualizer. Android uses its emulator capabilities to run an OS that is made for a different architecture on a different machine as your PC or Mac. It uses dynamic translation achieving very good performance, so good that to resemble real Android devices the emulation is throttled in some cases.

Because of this you can add some qemu-specific options when you run the emulator.

For example, we may want to open the qemu console which is accessible via VNC [Virtual Network Computing], another Open Source project providing remote frame-buffer capabilities (`http://en.wikipedia.org/wiki/Virtual_Network_Computing`). In this console, we can issue some qemu-specific commands.

To do this, let's add the following options:

```
$ emulator -avd test -no-window -no-audio -no-boot-anim -port 5580\
-qemu -vnc :2 &
```

All the options following `-qemu` are passed verbatim to qemu. In this case we pass `-vnc :2`, to open the virtual display 2, which is at the port 5902 as VNC starts counting from 5900.

Using some VNC client, like Vinagre—Remote Desktop Viewer, which is provided under the GNOME desktop in most of the distributions we can open the connection to the console. Vinagre can be launched from the GNOME desktop by **Applications | Internet | Remote Desktop Viewer**.

In Microsoft Windows RealVNC can be used as the client.

Then we should open the connection to the VNC server in qemu:

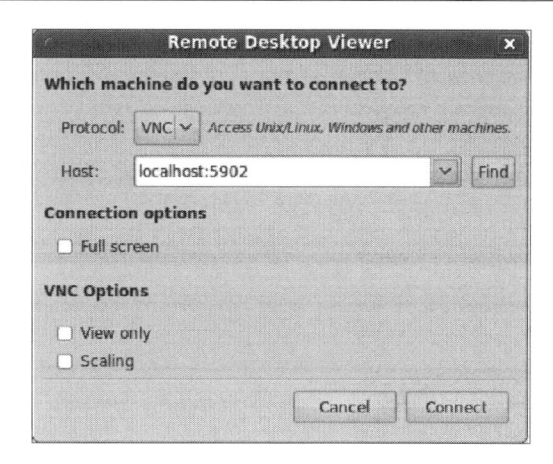

We will then be presented with the qemu console:

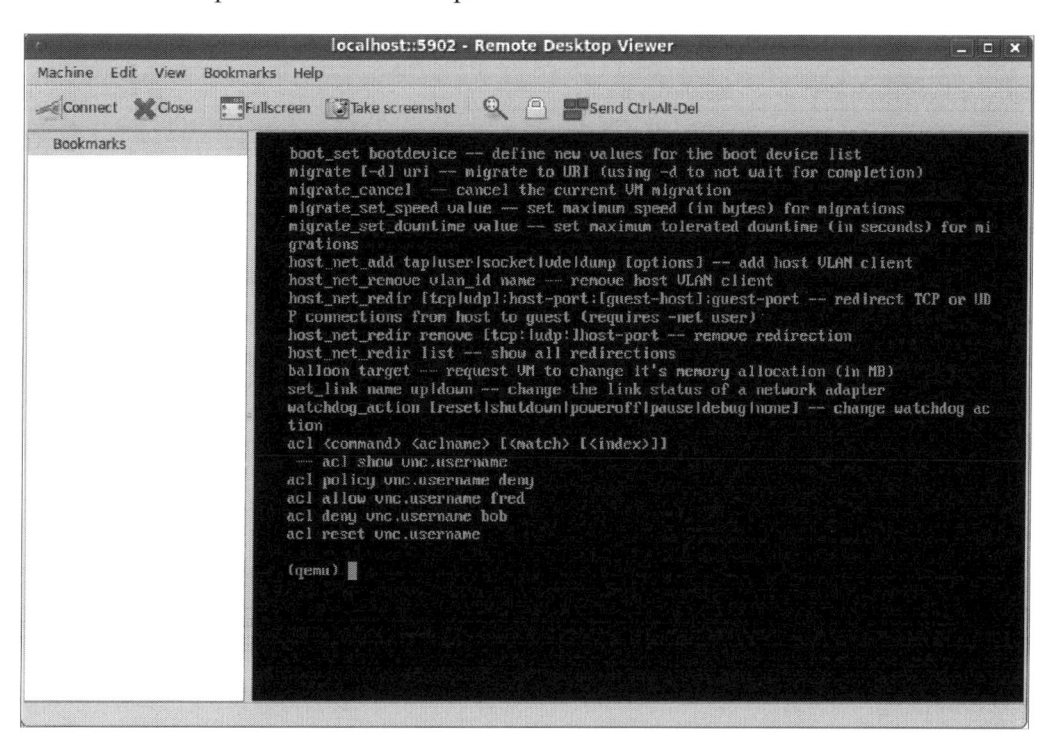

The list of internal commands can be obtained by entering the following command on the prompt:

`(qemu) help`

Android Testing Environment

The analysis of these commands is outside the scope of this book but you can find some information online on the Qemu website.

> Latest versions of the emulator, starting with Android 2.2 (Froyo), have a bug that prevents qemu options from being specified in the command line (even the help option (-qemu -h) is not working), even though they are listed in the emulator help (emulator -help) as the following:
>
> -qemu args...      pass arguments to qemu
> -qemu -h           display qemu help

## Running monkey

You may know about the infinite monkey theorem. This theorem states that a monkey hitting keys at random on a typewriter keyboard for an infinite amount of time will almost surely type a given text, such as the complete works of William Shakespeare.

The Android version of this theorem states that a monkey producing random touches on a device could crash your application in, well... much less than an infinite amount of time.

In this line, Android features a monkey application (http://developer.android.com/guide/developing/tools/monkey.html) that would generate the random events instead of a real monkey.

The simplest way to run monkey against our application to generate random events is:

```
$ adb -e shell monkey -p com.example.aatg.tc -v -v 1000
```

And you will be receiving this output:

**Events injected: 1000**

**:Dropped: keys=0 pointers=0 trackballs=0 flips=0**

**## Network stats: elapsed time=100914ms (0ms mobile, 0ms wifi, 100914ms not connected)**

**// Monkey finished**

**This displays the details of the events injected through monkey.**

The monkey will send events only to the specified package (-p), in this case com.example.aatg.tc, in a very verbose manner (-v -v). The count of events sent will be 1000.

# Client-server monkey

There is another way of running monkey. It also presents a client-server model that ultimately allows for the creation of scripts controlling what events are sent and not relying only on random generation.

Usually the port used by monkey is 1080 but you can use another one if it better suits your preferences.

`$ adb -e shell monkey -p com.example.aatg.tc --port 1080 &`

Then we need to redirect the emulator port:

`$ adb -e forward tcp:1080 tcp:1080`

Now we are ready to send events. To do it manually we can use a TELNET client:

`$ telnet localhost 1080`

**Trying ::1...**

**Trying 127.0.0.1...**

**Connected to localhost.**

**Escape character is '^]'.**

After the connection is established we can type the specific monkey command:

`tap 150 200`

**OK**

To finish this exit the telnet command.

If we need to exercise the application repeatedly, it is much more convenient to create a script with the commands we want to send. A monkey script could look like this:

```
# monkey
tap 100 180
type 123
tap 100 280
press DEL
press DEL
press DEL
press DEL
press DEL
press DEL
press DEL
press DEL
type -460.3
```

*Android Testing Environment*

The events and its parameters are defined here.

After having started the Temperature Converter application we can run this script to exercise the user interface. To start the application you can use the emulator window and click on its launcher icon or use the command line, which is the only alternative if the emulator is headless, as follows:

```
$ adb shell am start -n com.example.aatg.tc/.TemperatureConverterActivity
```

This is informed in the log by this line:

**Starting: Intent { cmp=com.example.aatg.tc/.TemperatureConverterActivity }**

Once the application has started you can send the events using the script and the `netcat` utility:

```
$ nc localhost 1080 < monkey.txt
```

This will send the events contained in the script file to the emulator. These are the following events:

- touch and select the Celsius field
- type 123
- touch and select the Fahrenheit field
- delete its content
- type -460.3

In this manner simple scripts consisting of touch events and key presses can be created.

# Test scripting with monkeyrunner

The possibilities of monkey are fairly limited and the lack of flow control restricts its use to very simple cases.

To circumvent these limitations a new project was created, named monkeyrunner (`http://developer.android.com/guide/developing/tools/monkeyrunner_concepts.html`). Notwithstanding that the name is almost the same and leads to not a small amount of confusion, they are not related in any way.

Monkeyrunner, which is already included in the latest versions of the Android SDK, is in its initial stages and nowadays its use is quite limited but its future could be bright. It is a tool providing an API for writing scripts that externally control an Android device or emulator.

Monkeyrunner is built on top of Jython (http://www.jython.org/), a version of Python (http://www.python.org/) programming language which is designed to run on the Java(tm) Platform.

According to its documentation, monkeyrunner tool provides these unique features for Android testing. These are just the highlights of the complete list of features, examples and reference documentation that can be obtained from the monkeyrunner home page (http://developer.android.com/guide/developing/tools/monkeyrunner_concepts.html):

- **Multiple device control**: The monkeyrunner API can apply one or more test suites across multiple devices or emulators. You can physically attach all the devices or start up all the emulators (or both) at once, connect to each one in turn programmatically, and then run one or more tests. You can also start up an emulator configuration programmatically, run one or more tests, and then shut down the emulator.
- **Functional testing**: monkeyrunner can run an automated start-to-finish test of an Android application. You provide input values with keystrokes or touch events, and view the results as screenshots.
- **Regression testing**: monkeyrunner can test application stability by running an application and comparing its output screenshots to a set of screenshots that are known to be correct.
- **Extensible automation**: Since monkeyrunner is an API toolkit, you can develop an entire system of Python-based modules and programs for controlling Android devices. Besides using the monkeyrunner API itself, you can use the standard Python OS and subprocess modules to call Android tools such as Android Debug Bridge.
- You can also add your own classes to the monkeyrunner API. This is described in more detail in the online documentation under Extending monkeyrunner with plugins.

## Getting test screenshots

Currently, one of the most evident uses of monkeyrunner is getting screenshots of the application under test to be further analyzed or compared.

These screenshots can be obtained with the help of the following steps:

1. Importing the needed modules.
2. Creating the connection with the device.
3. Checking for errors.

## Android Testing Environment

4. Starting the `TemperatureConverter` activity.
5. Adding some delay.
6. Typing '123'
7. Adding some delay to allow for the events to be processed.
8. Obtaining the screenshots and saving it to a file.
9. Pressing **BACK** to exit the Activity.

The following is the code for the script needed to perform the above mentioned steps:

```
#! /usr/bin/env monkeyrunner
'''
Created on 2011-03-12

@author: diego
'''
import sys

# Imports the monkeyrunner modules used by this program
from com.android.monkeyrunner import MonkeyRunner, MonkeyDevice, MonkeyImage

# Connects to the current device, returning a MonkeyDevice object
device = MonkeyRunner.waitForConnection()

if not device:
    print >> sys.stderr, "Couldn't get connection"
    sys.exit(1)

device.startActivity(component='com.example.aatg.tc/.TemperatureConverterActivity')

MonkeyRunner.sleep(3.0)

device.type("123")

# Takes a screenshot
MonkeyRunner.sleep(3.0)
result = device.takeSnapshot()

# Writes the screenshot to a file
result.writeToFile('/tmp/device.png','png')

device.press('KEYCODE_BACK', 'DOWN_AND_UP')
```

Once this script runs, you will find the screenshot of `TemperatureConverter` in /tmp/device.png.

# Record and playback

If you need something simpler probably there is no need to manually create these scripts. To simplify the process, the script monkey_recorder.py, which is included in the Android source repository in the sdk project (http://android.git.kernel.org/?p=platform/sdk.git;a=summary), can be used to record event descriptions that are later interpreted by another script called monkey_playback.py.

Run monkey_recorder.py from the command line and you will be presented with this UI:

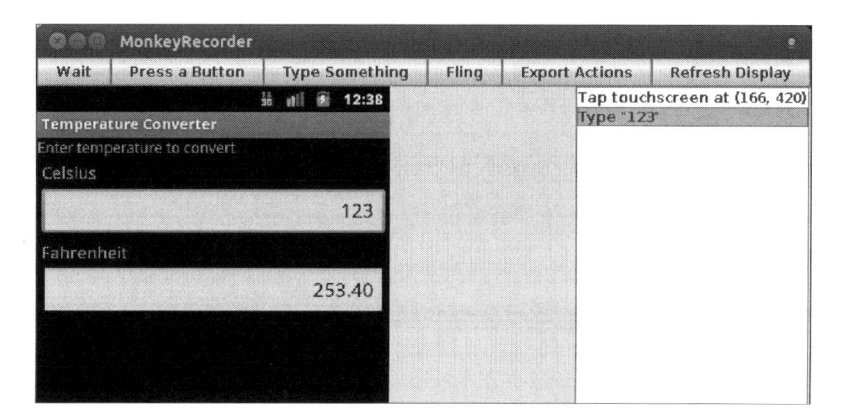

This interface has a toolbar with buttons to insert different commands in the recorded script:

| Button | Description |
|---|---|
| Wait | How many seconds to wait. This number is requested by a dialog box. |
| Press a Button | Sends a MENU, HOME, or SEARCH button. Press, Down, or Up event. |
| Type Something | Sends a string. |
| Fling | Sends a fling event in the specified direction, distance, and number of steps. |
| Export Actions | Saves the script. |
| Refresh Display | Refreshes the copy of the screenshot that is displayed. |

Once the script is completed, save it, let's say as script.mr and then you can re-run it by using this command line:

```
$ monkey_playback.py script.mr
```

Now all the events will be replayed.

## Summary

In this chapter we covered all the alternatives we have to expose our application and its tests to a wide range of conditions and configurations, ranging from different screen sizes, the availability of devices such as cameras or keyboards, to simulating real life network conditions to detect problems in our application.

We also analyzed all of the options we have to be able to control emulators remotely when they are detached from its windows. This prepares the foundation for Continuous Integration that we will be visiting in *Chapter 8, Continuous Integration*, and relies on the ability to automatically run all the test suites and having the ability to configure, start, and stop the emulator will be necessary.

At the end, some scripting alternatives were introduced and examples to get you started were provided.

The next chapter will introduce Behavior Driven Development—a technique that makes use of a common vocabulary to express the tests permitting the inclusion of business people in the software development project.

# 6
# Behavior Driven Development

Behavior Driven Development can be understood as the evolution and confluence of Test Driven Development and Acceptance Testing. Both techniques were discussed in previous chapters, so you may want to look back at *Chapter 1, Getting Started with Testing* and *Chapter 4, Test Driven Development* before proceeding.

Behavior Driven Development introduces some new concepts, such as the use of a common vocabulary to describe the tests and the inclusion of business participants in the software development project. And some people still believe that it is only Test Driven Development done right.

We have visited Test Driven Development before and we focused on converting low level requirements into tests that could drive our development process. Behavior Driven Development forces us to concentrate on higher level requirements and on using a specific vocabulary we can express these requirements in a way that can be further analyzed or evaluated.

We will explore these concepts so that you can make your own conclusions.

## Brief history

Behavior Driven Development was a term introduced by Dan North back in 2003 to describe a technique that focuses on collaboration between developers and other stakeholders by using a process usually called **outside-in** software development. Its primary goal is to satisfy the business needs of the client.

Behavior Driven Development grew out of a thought experiment based on **Neuro Linguistic Programming (NLP)** techniques.

The primary idea is that the words used to describe a thought severely influence that thought to the point that we seem to think in the language we speak.

There is empirical proof of the fact that subjects in memory tests are more likely to remember a specific color if their mother language has a specific word for that color. So if we have a specific language to describe our requirements, it would probably influence the way we think about them and hence improve the way we write them.

Therefore, the words used by Behavior Driven Development were carefully selected to influence the way you think about the specification of features. They are closely related to the notion of cause-effect and follow this concept to describe a feature starting from a known state, applying some process, and expecting some results.

These words are described in the next section.

# Given, when, then

**Given/When/Then** words are the common vocabulary that spans the divide between business and technology, and as described at `http://behaviour-driven.org/` they can also be referred to as the ubiquitous language of Behavior Driven Development. The framework is based on three core principles that we reproduce here verbatim:

- Business and Technology should refer to the same system in the same way
- Any system should have an identified, verifiable value to the business
- Up-front analysis, design, and planning all have a diminishing return

Behavior Driven Development relies on the use of this specific vocabulary. Additionally, the format in which requirements are expressed is predetermined allowing tools to interpret and execute them.

- **Given**, is to describe the initial state before external stimuli is received.
- **When**, is to describe the key action the user performs.
- **Then**, is to analyze the results of the actions. To be observable the actions performed should have some kind of outcome.

# FitNesse

FitNesse is a software development collaboration tool. Strictly speaking FitNesse is a set of tools, described as follows:

- As a software testing tool, FitNesse is a lightweight, open source framework that allows teams to collaborate
- It is also a Wiki where you can easily create and edit pages and share information
- FitNesse is also a web server so it doesn't require additional configuration or administrative privileges to set up or configure

Download the FitNesse distribution from `http://fitnesse.org/`. The distribution is a JAR file that installs itself on first run. Throughout these examples we used FitNesse release 20100303 but newer versions should also work.

## Running FitNesse from the command line

By default when FitNesse runs it listens on port 80, so to run unprivileged you should change the port on the command line. In this example we use `8900`:

```
$ java -jar fitnesse.jar -p 8900
```

This is the output obtained when we run the command:

**FitNesse (v20100303) Started...**

port:             8900

root page:        fitnesse.wiki.FileSystemPage at ./FitNesseRoot

logger:           none

authenticator:    fitnesse.authentication.PromiscuousAuthenticator

html page factory: fitnesse.html.HtmlPageFactory

page version expiration set to 14 days.

Once running, you can direct your browser to the local FitNesse server home page and you will be presented with this content:

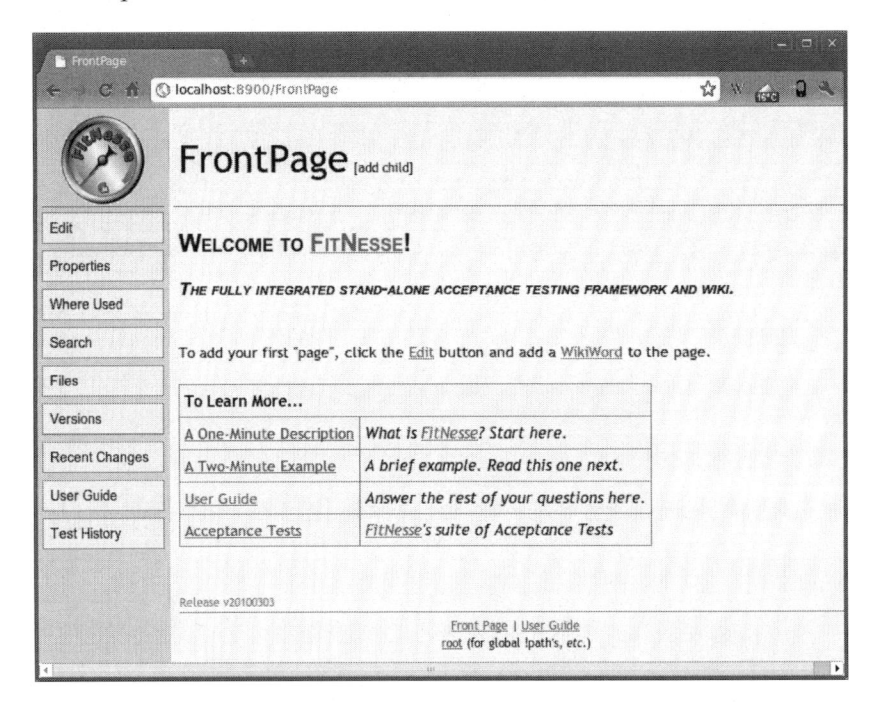

## Creating a TemperatureConverterTests subwiki

Once FitNesse is up and running, we can start by creating a subwiki to organize our tests.

You may already be familiar with the wiki concept. If not, a wiki is a website that allows page editing and creation by its users. This editing process is done from within the browser and uses a markup language that greatly simplifies the process.

> You can find out more about wikis in what could perhaps be the most famous wiki: http://en.wikipedia.org/wiki/Wiki.

Though this subwiki organization is not mandatory, it is highly recommended, especially if you plan to use FitNesse for acceptance testing on multiple projects.

One of the most simplified processes is hyperlink creation which is done only by using *CamelCase* or *WikiWords*; that is a word that starts with a capital letter and has at least one more capital letter in it. This WikiWord will be converted into a hyperlink to a page with that name.

To create the **TemperatureConverterTests** subwiki, we simply press the **Edit** button below the FitNesse logo to edit the home page, adding the following:

```
| '''My Tests''' |
| TemperatureConverterTests | ''Temperature Converter Tests'' |
```

This adds a new table to the page, by using the "|" markup as the first character and to delimit the columns.

Then a wiki page `TemperatureConverterTests` will be created and we also add a column with a descriptive comment about the tests. This comment is turned into italics by surrounding it by double single quotes ('').

Press **Save** and the page will be modified.

Once the page is displayed we can verify that `TemperatureConverterTests` is now followed by **[?]** (question mark) because the page has not been created yet and will be created when we click on it.

We can add some comments to clearly identify this newly-created front page of the subwiki.

```
!contents -R2 -g -p -f -h
This is the !-TemperatureConverterTests SubWiki-!.
```

Here, the text `TemperatureConverterTests SubWiki` is escaped using !- and -! to prevent it from being converted to another page link.

**Save** again.

## Adding child pages to the subwiki

Now we add a new child page by using the **[add child]** link that appears next to the page title.

There are different options for creating the child page, and we can select:

- **Normal**, for a normal wiki page
- **Test**, a page that contains tests
- **Suite**, a page containing other tests composing a suite
- **Default**, a default page

## Behavior Driven Development

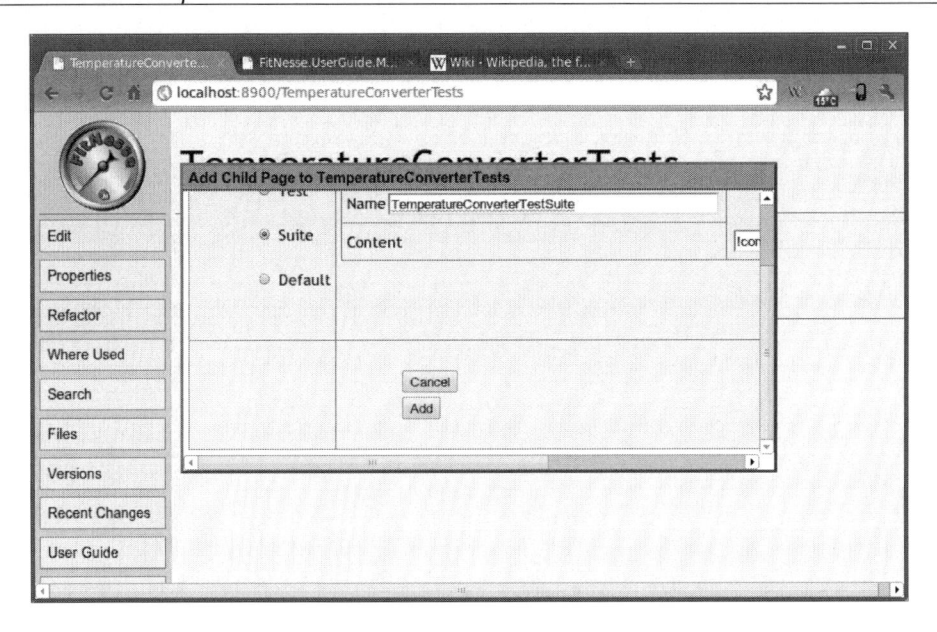

These are the values to use:

| Field | Value |
|---|---|
| Type of page: | Suite |
| Name: | TemperatureConverterTestSuite |
| Content: | !contents |

After pressing **Add**, this page is created and automatically added as a link to the subwiki.

Let's follow this newly-created link to reach the test suite page.

Once you're here, add another child using the **[add child]** link. This time, let's add a Test page and name it **TemperatureConverterCelsiusToFahrenheitFixture** as this will contain our fixture.

These are the values to use:

| Field | Value |
|---|---|
| Type of page: | Test |
| Name: | TemperatureConverterCelsiusToFahrenheitFixture |
| Content: | !contents |

Click on **Add** to finish the operation.

# Adding the acceptance test fixture

Up until now, we were only creating wiki pages. Nothing exciting about that! But now we will be adding our acceptance test fixture directly to the page. Be sure of navigating to the newly added page, **TemperatureConverterCelsiusToFahrenheitFixture**, click on **Edit** as usual, and add the following:

```
!contents

!|TemperatureConverterCelsiusToFahrenheitFixture            |
|celsius|fahrenheit?                                        |
|0.0    |~= 32                                              |
|100.0  |212.0                                              |
|-1.0   |30.2                                               |
|-100.0 |-148.0                                             |
|32.0   |89.6                                               |
|-40.0  |-40.0                                              |
|-273.0 |~= -459.4                                          |
|-273   |~= -459.4                                          |
|-273   |~= -459                                            |
|-273   |~= -459.40000000000003                             |
|-273   |-459.40000000000003                                |
|-273   |-459.41 < _ < -459.40                              |
|-274.0 |Invalid temperature: -274.00C below absolute zero|
```

This table defines several items for our text feature:

- `TemperatureConverterCelsiusToFahrenheitFixture`: This is the table title and the test fixture name.
- `celsius`: This is the column name for the value we are providing as input to the test.
- `fahrenheit?`: This is the column name for the value expected as the result of the conversion. The question mark indicates that this is a result value.
- `~=`: This indicates that the result is approximately this value.
- `< _ <`: This indicates that the expected value is within this range.
- Invalid temperature: -274.00C below absolute zero, is the value expected by the failed conversion.

Save this content by clicking on **Save**.

*Behavior Driven Development*

## Adding the supporting test classes

If we just press the **Test** button, which is below the FitNesse logo (see the next screenshot for details), we will receive an error. In some way this is expected because we haven't created the supporting test fixture yet. This is a very simple class that invokes the `TemperatureConverter` methods.

FitNesse supports two different test systems:

- **fit**: This is the older of the two methods, and uses HTML, parsed just prior to the fixture being called.
- **slim**: This is newer, all the table processing is done inside FitNesse, within slim runners.

Further information about these test systems can be found at `http://fitnesse.org/FitNesse.UserGuide.TestSystems`.

In this example we are using slim, which is selected by setting the variable `TEST_SYSTEM` within the same page as:

```
!define TEST_SYSTEM {slim}
```

To create the slim test fixture we simply create a new package, named `com.example.aatg.tc.test.fitnesse.fixture`, in our existing Android test project `TemperatureConverterTest`. We will be creating the fixture inside this package.

Next, we have to create the `TemperatureConverterCelsiusToFahrenheitFixture` class that we defined in our acceptance test table:

```
package com.example.aatg.tc.test.fitnesse.fixture;
import com.example.aatg.tc.TemperatureConverter;
public class TemperatureConverterCelsiusToFahrenheitFixture {
  private double celsius;
  public void setCelsius(double celsius) {
    this.celsius = celsius;
  }
  public String fahrenheit() throws Exception {
    try {
      return String.valueOf(
        TemperatureConverter.celsiusToFahrenheit(celsius));
    }
    catch (RuntimeException e) {
      return e.getLocalizedMessage();
    }
  }
}
```

This fixture should delegate on real code and not do anything by itself. We decided to return `String` from `fahrenheit` so we can return the `Exception` message in the same method.

In the test page we should also define the import statement used by the tests:

```
|import|
|com.example.aatg.tc.test.fitnesse.fixture|
```

> Note that in the next variable you should change the paths to the ones appropriate to your system and the classpath to locate the classes.

```
!path /opt/fitnesse/fitnesse.jar:/home/diego/aatg/TemperatureConverter/bin/:/home/diego/aatg/TemperatureConverterTest/bin/
```

> This should be adapted to your system paths.

After finishing these steps we can click on the **Test** button to run the tests and the page will reflect the results:

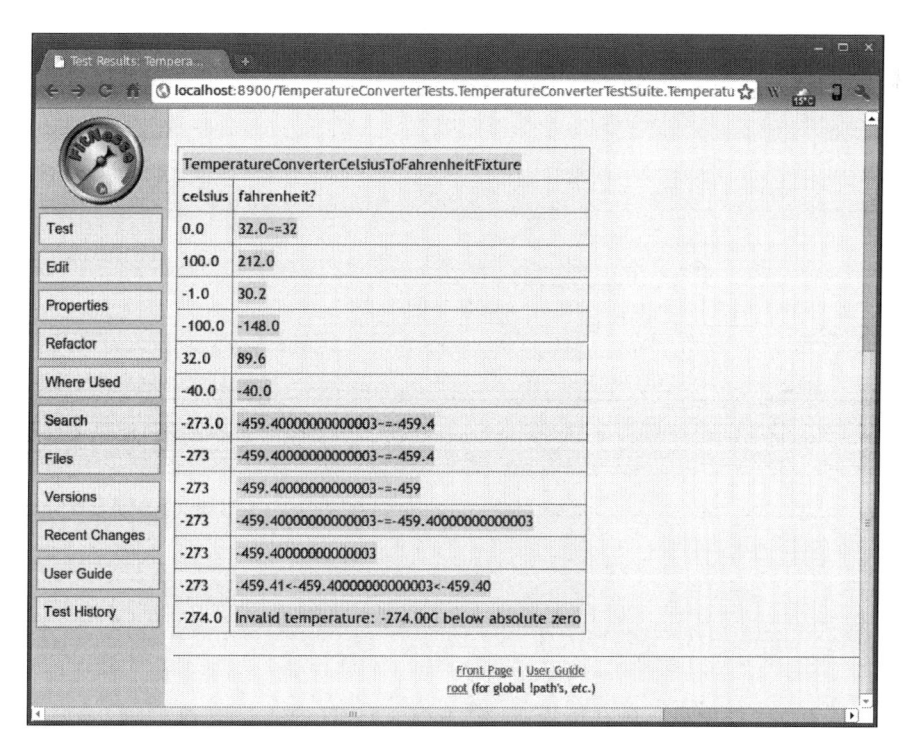

| TemperatureConverterCelsiusToFahrenheitFixture | |
|---|---|
| celsius | fahrenheit? |
| 0.0 | 32.0-=32 |
| 100.0 | 212.0 |
| -1.0 | 30.2 |
| -100.0 | -148.0 |
| 32.0 | 89.6 |
| -40.0 | -40.0 |
| -273.0 | -459.40000000000003-=-459.4 |
| -273 | -459.40000000000003-=-459.4 |
| -273 | -459.40000000000003-=-459 |
| -273 | -459.40000000000003-=-459.40000000000003 |
| -273 | -459.40000000000003 |
| -273 | -459.41<-459.40000000000003<-459.40 |
| -274.0 | invalid temperature: -274.00C below absolute zero |

*Behavior Driven Development*

We can easily identify every test that succeeded by their green color and failed ones by their red color. In this example, we don't have any failure so everything is green.

FitNesse has another useful feature which is the **Test History**. All the test runs and a specific number of results are saved for a period of time so that you can review the results later on and compare the results, and thus analyze the evolution of your changes.

This feature is accessed by clicking **Test History** at the bottom of the list of options on the left pane.

In the following image we can see the results for the last 4 test runs, where 3 failed and 1 succeeded. Also by clicking on the "+" (plus) or "-" (minus) signs, you can expand or collapse the view to show or hide detailed information about the test run.

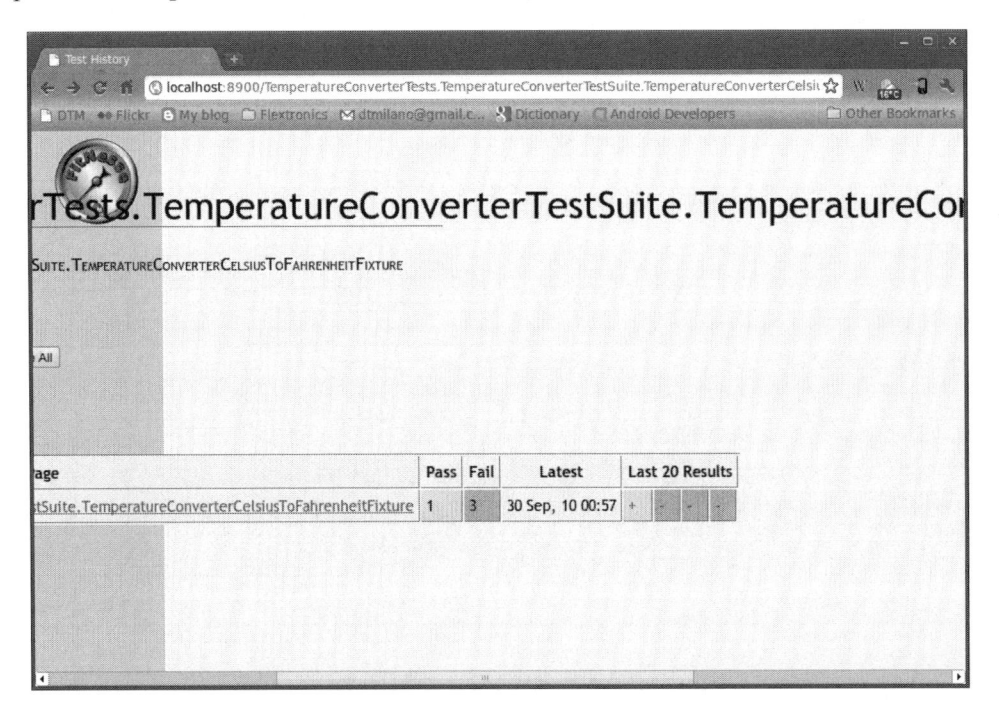

# GivWenZen

GivWenZen is a framework that builds upon FitNesse and Slim to allow the user to exploit the Behavior Driven Development technique of expressing the tests using the **Given-When-Then** vocabulary to describe tests. These test descriptions are also created using the FitNesse wiki facility of expressing the tests as plain text contained in tables in a wiki page.

The idea is pretty simple and straightforward and follows up what we have been doing with FitNesse, but this time instead of writing acceptance tests giving a table of values we will use the three Behavior Driven Development magic words **Given-When-Then** to describe our scenarios.

Firstly, let's install GivWenZen. Download the full distribution from its download list page at `http://code.google.com/p/givwenzen/downloads/list` and follow the instructions on its website. We used givwenzen 1.0.1 in these examples but newer versions should work as well.

The GivWenZen full distribution includes all the dependencies needed, including FitNesse, so if you have FitNesse running from previous examples it is better to stop it or you must use a different port for GivWenZen.

Upon startup, point your browser to the home page and you will find a familiar FitNesse front page. You can take some time to explore the examples included.

## Creating the test scenario

Let's create a simple scenario for our Temperature Converter to understand things better.

In plain tests, our scenario would be:

*Given* I'm using the Temperature Converter, *When* I enter 100 into Celsius field, *Then* I obtain 212 in the Fahrenheit field.

And it is directly translated into a GivWenZen scenario by adding this to a wiki page:

```
-|script|
 |given |I'm using the !-TemperatureConverter-!|
 |when  |I enter 100 into Celsius field         |
 |then  |I obtain 212 in Fahrenheit field       |
```

The translation is straightforward. The table title must be `script`, and in this case it is preceded by a dash (-) to hide it. Then each of the **Give-When-Then** scenarios is placed in a column and the predicate in the other column.

Before running this script, when the whole page is executed, we need to initialize GivWenZen by running yet another script. In this case it would be:

```
|script                   |
|start|giv wen zen for slim|
```

We need to initialize the classpath and add the corresponding imports before the script that starts GivWenZen. Usually this is done in one of the **SetUp** pages, which are executed before running every test script, but for the sake of simplicity we are adding the initialization to this same page:

```
!define TEST_SYSTEM {slim}
!path ./target/classes/main
!path ./target/classes/examples
!path ./lib/commons-logging.jar
!path ./lib/fitnesse.jar
!path ./lib/log4j-1.2.9.jar
!path ./lib/slf4j-simple-1.5.6.jar
!path ./lib/slf4j-api-1.5.6.jar
!path ./lib/javassist.jar
!path ./lib/google-collect-1.0-rc4.jar
!path ./lib/dom4j-1.6.1.jar
!path ./lib/commons-vfs-1.0.jar
!path ./lib/clover-2.6.1.jar
!path /home/diego/workspace/TemperatureConverter/bin
!path /home/diego/workspace/TemperatureConverterTest/bin
```

If you just run the test here by clicking the **Test** button, you will receive the following message:

**__EXCEPTION__:org.givwenzen.DomainStepNotFoundException:**

You need a step class with an annotated method matching this pattern: "I'm using the TemperatureConverter".

Typical causes of this error are:

- `StepClass` is missing the `@DomainSteps` annotation
- `StepMethod` is missing the `@DomainStep` annotation
- The step method annotation has a regular expression that is not matching the current test step

This, and the other exception messages are very helpful in implementing the steps class, however you should add some behavior.

The step class should be placed in the package or subpackage of `bdd.steps`, or your own custom package if defined.

For example:

```
@DomainSteps
public class StepClass {
  @DomainStep("I'm using the TemperatureConverter")
  public void domainStep() {
    // TODO implement step
  } }
```

In our particular case this will be the implementation of the StepClass:

```
package bdd.steps.tc;
import org.givwenzen.annotations.DomainStep;
import org.givwenzen.annotations.DomainSteps;
import com.example.aatg.tc.TemperatureConverter;
@DomainSteps
public class TemperatureConverterSteps {
  private static final String CELSIUS = "Celsius";
  private static final String FAHRENHEIT = "Fahrenheit";
  private static final String ANY_TEMPERATURE =
    "([-+]?\\d+(?:\\.\\d+)?)";
  private static final String UNIT = "(C|F)";
  private static final String UNIT_NAME =
    "(" + CELSIUS + "|" + FAHRENHEIT + ")";
  private static final double DELTA = 0.01d;
  private double mValue = Double.NaN;
  @DomainStep("I(?: a|')m using the TemperatureConverter")
  public void createTemperatureConverter() {
    // do nothing
  }
  @DomainStep("I enter " + ANY_TEMPERATURE + " into "
    + UNIT_NAME + " field")
  public void setField(double value, String unitName) {
    mValue = value;
  }
    @DomainStep("I obtain " + ANY_TEMPERATURE + " in "
      + UNIT_NAME + " field")
    public boolean verifyConversion(double value, String unitName) {
      try {
        final double t = (FAHRENHEIT.compareTo(unitName) == 0) ?
          getFahrenheit() : getCelsius();
        return (Math.abs(t-value) < DELTA);
      }
      catch (RuntimeException ex) {
        return false;
      }
    }
```

```
    @DomainStep("Celsius")
    public double getCelsius() {
        return TemperatureConverter.fahrenheitToCelsius(mValue);
    }
    @DomainStep("Fahrenheit")
    public double getFahrenheit() {
        return TemperatureConverter.celsiusToFahrenheit(mValue);
    }
}
```

In this example, we are using a subpackage of `bdd.steps` because, by default, this is the package hierarchy GivWenZen searches for steps implementations. Otherwise, extra configuration is needed.

Classes implementing steps should be annotated by `@DomainSteps` and the step's methods annotated by `@DomainStep`. The latter receives a regular expression String as a parameter. This regular expression is used by GivWenZen to match the steps.

For example, in our scenario we have defined this step:

```
I enter 100 into Celsius field
```

Our annotation is:

```
@DomainStep("I enter " + ANY_TEMPERATURE + " into "
    + UNIT_NAME + " field")
```

This will match, and the regular expression group values defined by `ANY_TEMPERATURE` and `UNIT_NAME` will be obtained and provided to the method as its argument's value and `unitName`:

```
public void setField(double value, String unitName)
```

Recall that in a previous chapter, I recommended reviewing regular expressions because they could be useful. Well this is probably one of these places where they are extremely useful. In `ANY_TEMPERATURE` we are matching every possible temperature value with the optional sign and decimal point. Consequently `UNIT` and `UNIT_NAME` match the unit symbol or its name; that is Celsius or Fahrenheit.

These regular expressions are used in the construction of the `@DomainStep` annotation parameters. Groups, delimited by "()" parenthesis in these regular expressions are converted into method parameters. This is how `setField()` obtains its parameters.

Then we have a `verifyConversion()` method that returns true or false depending on whether the actual conversion is within a `DELTA` value of the expected one.

Finally, we have some methods that actually invoke the conversion methods in the `TemperatureConverter` class.

On running the tests once again, all the tests pass. We can confirm this by analyzing the output message:

**Assertions: 2 right, 0 wrong, 0 ignored, 0 exceptions.**

Notice that we are receiving the results for 2 assertions as one is for the invocation of the GivWenZen initialization script we added to the page and the other is for our scenario.

We should not only create scenarios for normal situations but cover exceptional conditions as well. Say, in plain text, our scenario is something like this:

> *Given* I'm using the Temperature Converter, *When* I enter -274 into Celsius field, *Then* I obtain 'Invalid temperature: -274.00C below absolute zero' exception.

It can be translated into a GivWenZen table like the following:

```
-|script|
|given|I am using the !-TemperatureConverter-!           |
|when |I enter -274 into Celsius field                   |
|then |I obtain 'Invalid temperature: -274.00C below absolute zero' exception|
```

And by adding a supporting step method, we will be able to run it. The step method can be implemented like this:

```
@DomainStep("I obtain '(Invalid temperature: " + ANY_TEMPERATURE
    + UNIT + " below absolute zero)' exception")
public boolean verifyException(String message,
    String value, String unit) {
  try {
    if ( "C".compareTo(unit) == 0 ) {
      getFahrenheit();
    }
    else {
      getCelsius();
    }
  }
  catch (RuntimeException ex) {
    return ex.getMessage().contains(message);
  }
  return false;
}
```

This method obtains the exception message, temperature value, and unit from the regular expression. Then this is compared against the actual exception message to verify that it matches.

Additionally, we can create other scenarios which, in this situation, will be supported by the existing steps methods. These scenarios could be:

```
-|script|
|given |I'm using the !-TemperatureConverter-!        |
|when  |I enter -100 into Celsius field               |
|then  |I obtain -148 in Fahrenheit field             |
-|script|
|given |I'm using the !-TemperatureConverter-!        |
|when  |I enter -100 into Fahrenheit field            |
|then  |I obtain -73.33 in Celsius field              |
|show  |then                          |Celsius        |
-|script|
|given|I'm using the !-TemperatureConverter-!         |
|when  |I enter -460 into Fahrenheit field            |
|then  |I obtain 'Invalid temperature: -460.00F below absolute zero' exception|
```

Because GivWenZen is based on FitNesse, we are free to combine both approaches and include the tests from our previous session in the same suite. Doing so, we can run the entire suite from the suite page obtaining the overall results.

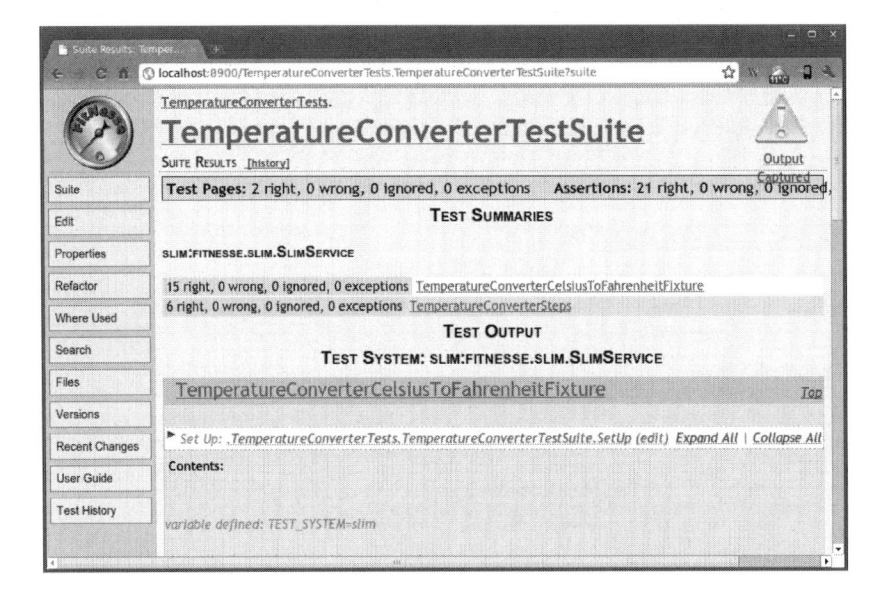

# Summary

In this chapter we covered Behavior Driven Development as an evolution of Test Driven Development which we examined in previous chapters.

We discussed the origin and driving forces behind Behavior Driven development. We analyzed the concepts serving as the foundations, explored the Given-When-Then vocabulary idea, and introduced FitNesse and Slim as helpful tools in deploying tests.

We presented GivWenZen, a tool based on FitNesse that gives us the ability to create scenarios and test them.

We introduced these techniques and tools to our sample Android project. However, we are still limited to test subjects that are testable under the JVM avoiding the use of Android-specific classes and mainly the User Interface. We will be exploring some alternatives to overcome this limitation in *Chapter 10, Alternative Testing Tactics*.

The next chapter presents practical examples of different common situations that you will encounter, applying all the disciplines and techniques discussed so far.

# 7
# Testing Recipes

This chapter provides practical examples of different common situations that you will encounter by applying the disciplines and techniques described in the previous chapters. The examples are presented in a Cookbook style so you can adapt and use them for your projects.

The following are the topics that will be covered in this chapter:

- Android Unit tests
- Testing activities and applications
- Testing databases and ContentProviders
- Testing local and remote services
- Testing UIs
- Testing exceptions
- Testing parsers
- Testing for memory leaks

After this chapter you will have a reference to apply testing to your projects and to know what to do in every situation.

## Android Unit tests

There are some cases where you really need to test parts of the application in isolation with little connection to the underlying system. In such cases we have to select a base class that is high enough in the hierarchy to remove some of the dependencies but not high enough for us to be responsible for some of the basic infrastructure.

The candidate base class in this case is possibly `AndroidTestCase`. This example has been taken from the **Android CTS** test suite (http://source.android.com/compatibility/cts-intro.html):

# Testing Recipes

```
/*
 * Copyright (C) 2009 The Android Open Source Project
 *
 * Licensed under the Apache License, Version 2.0 (the "License");
 * you may not use this file except in compliance with the License.
 * You may obtain a copy of the License at
 *
 *      http://www.apache.org/licenses/LICENSE-2.0
 *
 * Unless required by applicable law or agreed to in writing,
 * software distributed under the License is distributed on an
 * "AS IS" BASIS, WITHOUT WARRANTIES OR CONDITIONS OF ANY KIND,
 * either express or implied.
 * See the License for the specific language governing permissions
 * and limitations under the License.
 */
package com.android.cts.appaccessdata;

import java.io.FileInputStream;
import java.io.FileNotFoundException;
import java.io.IOException;

import android.test.AndroidTestCase;

/**
 * Test that another app's private data cannot be accessed.
 *
 * Assumes that {@link APP_WITH_DATA_PKG} has already created
   the private data.
 */
public class AccessPrivateDataTest extends AndroidTestCase {
    /**
     * The Android package name of the application that owns
       the private data
     */
    private static final String APP_WITH_DATA_PKG =
      "com.android.cts.appwithdata";
```

Up to here we have:

- The standard Android Open Source Project copyright.
- The package definition. This test lives in `com.android.cts.appaccessdata`.
- Some imports.

- The definition of `AccessPrivateDataTest`, which extends `AndroidTestCase` because it's a unit test that doesn't require the system infrastructure. In this particular case we could have also used `TestCase` directly, because we are not accessing Context.

- The definition of the constant `APP_WITH_DATA_PKG`, indicating the package name of the application containing the private data we are trying to access:

    ```
    /**
     * Name of private file to access. This must match the name
     * of the file created by
     * {@link APP_WITH_DATA_PKG}.
     */
    private static final String PRIVATE_FILE_NAME =
      "private_file.txt";

    /**
     * Tests that another app's private file cannot be accessed
     * @throws IOException
     */
    public void testAccessPrivateData() throws IOException {
      try {
        // construct the absolute file path to the app's
          private file
        String privateFilePath = String.format(
          "/data/data/%s/%s", APP_WITH_DATA_PKG,
          PRIVATE_FILE_NAME);
        FileInputStream inputStream = new
          FileInputStream(privateFilePath);
        inputStream.read();
        inputStream.close();
        fail("Was able to access another app's private data");
      } catch (FileNotFoundException e) {
        // expected
      } catch (SecurityException e) {
        // also valid
      }
    }
    ```

In this second part, we have:

- The definition of `PRIVATE_FILE_NAME`, containing the name of the file we will try to access

- The test method `testAccessPrivateData`, which actually exercises the feature

This test method, `testAccessPrivateData()`, tests the access to other packages' private data and fails if this is possible. To achieve this, the expected exceptions are caught and if this doesn't happen `fail()` is invoked with a custom message.

# Testing activities and applications

This section shows some examples of activities and applications tests. They cover some common cases that you will find in your day-to-day testing and you can adapt them to suit your specific needs.

# Applications and preferences

In Android parlance, application refers to a base class used when it is needed to maintain a global application state. This is usually utilized for dealing with shared preferences. We expect that tests altering these preferences' values don't affect the behavior of the real application. Imagine the tests deleting user account information for an application storing these values as shared preferences. It doesn't sound like a good idea. So what we really need is the ability to mock a `Context` that also mocks the access to the `SharedPreferences`.

Our first attempt could be to use `RenamingDelegatingContext`, but unfortunately, it does not mock `SharedPreferences`, although it is close because it mocks database and filesystem access. So, first we need to create a specialized mock `Context` that also mocks the latter.

# The RenamingMockContext class

Let's create the specialized `Context`. The class `RenamingDelegatingContext` is a very good point to start from because as we mentioned before, database and filesystem access will be mocked. The problem is how to mock `SharedPreferences` access.

Remember that `RenamingDelegatingContext` as its name suggests, delegates everything to a `Context`. So the root of our problem lies in this `Context`. Because it is a mock `Context` as well, `MockContext` seems to be the correct base class. As you may remember, in *Chapter 3, Building Blocks on the Android SDK*, we looked at the mock object and we noted that `MockContext` can only be used to inject other dependencies and all methods are non-functional and throw `UnsupportedOperationException`. However, this is also a feature we can use to our advantage in detecting the minimum set of methods that needs to be implemented in a case like this. So let's start creating an empty `MockContext` to whom the other `Context`, that we can name `RenamingMockContext`, delegates:

```java
    private static class RenamingMockContext extends
      RenamingDelegatingContext {
      private static final String PREFIX = "test.";
      public RenamingMockContext(Context context) {
        super(new DelegatedMockContext(context), PREFIX);
      }
      private static class DelegatedMockContext extends MockContext {
        public DelegatedMockContext(Context context) {
          // TODO Auto-generated constructor stub
        }
      }
    }
```

We created a mock `Context`, `RenamingMockContext`, that delegates to another empty `MockContext`, `DelegatedMockContext`, and uses a renaming prefix.

## The TemperatureConverterApplicationTests class

We have the `RenamingMockContext`, now we need a test that uses it. Because we will be testing an application, the base class for the test would be `ApplicationTestCase`. This test case provides a framework in which you can test application classes in a controlled environment. It provides basic support for the lifecycle of an application, and hooks by which you can inject various dependencies and control the environment in which your application is tested. We can inject the `RenamingMockContext` before the `Application` is created using the `setContext()` method.

Our `TemperatureConverter` application, which we started in *Chapter 4, Test Driven Development*, will be storing the decimal places as a shared preference. Consequently we will be creating a test to set the decimal places and then retrieving it to verify its value:

```java
    public class TemperatureConverterApplicationTests extends
        ApplicationTestCase<TemperatureConverterApplication> {
      private TemperatureConverterApplication mApplication;
      public TemperatureConverterApplicationTests() {
        this("TemperatureConverterApplicationTests");
      }
      public TemperatureConverterApplicationTests(String name) {
        super(TemperatureConverterApplication.class);
        setName(name);
      }
      @Override
      protected void setUp() throws Exception {
```

# Testing Recipes

```
      super.setUp();
      final RenamingMockContext mockContext = new
        RenamingMockContext(getContext());
      setContext(mockContext);
      createApplication();
      mApplication = getApplication();
    }

    @Override
    protected void tearDown() throws Exception {
      super.tearDown();
    }

    public final void testPreconditions() {
      assertNotNull(mApplication);
    }

    public final void testSetDecimalPlaces() {
      final int expected = 3;
      mApplication.setDecimalPlaces(expected);
      assertEquals(expected, mApplication.getDecimalPlaces());
    }
  }
```

We extend `ApplicationTestCase` using the `TemperatureConverterApplication` template parameter. Soon, we will be creating the class extending `Application`.

Then we use the **Given name constructor** pattern that we discussed in *Chapter 3, Building Blocks on the Android SDK*.

In the `setUp()` method we create the mock context and set the context for this test using `setContext()` method; we create the application using `createApplication()` and finally hold a reference to it as it will be used frequently in our tests.

Regarding our tests, using the **Test preconditions** pattern that we reviewed previously, we check that the recently created application is not null.

Lastly is the test that actually tests for the required behavior setting the decimal places, retrieving it, and verifying its value.

Our first objective is to get these tests to compile. Later we will focus on the success of these tests. To get it to compile, we need to create the class `TemperatureConverterApplication` and the getter and setter for decimal places, that ultimately should use `SharedPreferences` to store and retrieve the specific preference:

```
    /**
     * Copyright (C) 2010-2011 Diego Torres Milano
     */
```

```
package com.example.aatg.tc;
import android.app.Application;
/**
 * @author diego
 *
 */
public class TemperatureConverterApplication extends
Application {
  /**
   *
   */
  public TemperatureConverterApplication() {
    // TODO Auto-generated constructor stub
  }
  public void setDecimalPlaces(int expected) {
    // TODO Auto-generated method stub
  }
  public Object getDecimalPlaces() {
    // TODO Auto-generated method stub
    return null;
  }
}
```

Running the tests we obtain a failure related to the fact that we are not storing the decimal places anywhere. We can implement this using `SharedPreferences` in this way:

```
/**
 * Copyright (C) 2010-2011 Diego Torres Milano
 */
package com.example.aatg.tc;

import android.app.Application;
import android.content.SharedPreferences;
import android.content.SharedPreferences.Editor;
import android.preference.PreferenceManager;
/**
 * @author diego
 *
 */
public class TemperatureConverterApplication extends Application {
  private static final String TAG =
    "TemperatureConverterApplication";
```

# Testing Recipes

```java
        public static final int DECIMAL_PLACES_DEFAULT = 2;
        public static final String DECIMAL_PLACES = "decimalPlaces";
    private SharedPreferences mSharedPreferences;
    /**
     *
     */
    public TemperatureConverterApplication() {
      // TODO Auto-generated constructor stub
    }
    @Override
    public void onCreate() {
      super.onCreate();
      mSharedPreferences =
        PreferenceManager.getDefaultSharedPreferences(this);
    }
    public void setDecimalPlaces(int d) {
      final Editor editor = mSharedPreferences.edit();
      editor.putString(DECIMAL_PLACES, Integer.toString(d));
      editor.commit();
    }
    public int getDecimalPlaces() {
      return Integer.parseInt(
        mSharedPreferences.getString(DECIMAL_PLACES,
          Integer.toString(DECIMAL_PLACES_DEFAULT)));
    }
}
```

If we complete these steps, compile and run the tests, we discover that they fail with an `UnsupportedOperationException` in `MockContext.getPackageName()`.

We change `DelegateMockContext` to override `getPackageName()`, delegating to the original context passed as a parameter to the constructor:

```java
      private static class RenamingMockContext extends
      RenamingDelegatingContext {
        /**
         * The renaming prefix.
         */
        private static final String PREFIX = "test.";
        public RenamingMockContext(Context context) {
          super(new DelegatedMockContext(context), PREFIX);
        }
        private static class DelegatedMockContext extends MockContext {
```

```
    private Context mDelegatedContext;
    public DelegatedMockContext(Context context) {
       mDelegatedContext = context;
    }
    @Override
    public String getPackageName() {
       return mDelegatedContext.getPackageName();
    }
}
```

Running the tests again, this time we obtain a different, though somewhat expected, `UnsupportedOperationException`. This exception is received while invoking `getSharedPreferences()`. Thus, the next step is to override this method in `DelegatedMockContext`:

```
    @Override
    public SharedPreferences getSharedPreferences(
       String name, int mode) {
       return mDelegatedContext.getSharedPreferences(
          PREFIX + name, mode);
    }
```

Any time that a `SharedPreference` is requested, this method will invoke the delegating context, adding the prefix for the name. The original `SharedPreferences` used by the application are unchanged.

We can verify this behavior by furnishing the `TemperatureConverterApplication` class with the previously mentioned methods, then storing some value in the shared preferences, running the tests, and eventually verifying that this value was not affected by running the tests.

# Testing activities

The next example shows how an activity can be tested in complete isolation using `ActivityUnitTestCase<Activity>` base class as opposed to `ActivityInstrumentationTestCase2<Activity>`. This method requires more care and attention but also provides a greater flexibility and control over the `Activity` under test. This kind of test is intended for testing general `Activity` behavior and not an `Activity` instance's interaction with other system components or UI related tests.

*Testing Recipes*

We are taking this example from the ApiDemos sample application (http://developer.android.com/resources/samples/ApiDemos/index.html) that is provided as an SDK companion. This sample is somewhat long so we have split it into several code snippets to improve its readability:

```
/*
 * Copyright (C) 2008 The Android Open Source Project
 *
 * Licensed under the Apache License, Version 2.0 (the "License");
 * you may not use this file except in compliance with the License.
 * You may obtain a copy of the License at
 *
 *      http://www.apache.org/licenses/LICENSE-2.0
 *
 * Unless required by applicable law or agreed to in writing,
 * software distributed under the License is distributed on an
 * "AS IS" BASIS,
 * WITHOUT WARRANTIES OR CONDITIONS OF ANY KIND, either express or
 * implied.
 * See the License for the specific language governing permissions
 * and limitations under the License.
 */
package com.example.android.apis.app;

import com.example.android.apis.R;
import com.example.android.apis.view.Focus2ActivityTest;

import android.content.Context;
import android.content.Intent;
import android.test.ActivityUnitTestCase;
import android.test.suitebuilder.annotation.MediumTest;
import android.widget.Button;
```

This first code snippet has nothing more than the required copyrights and imports:

```
/**
 * This demonstrates completely isolated "unit test" of an Activity
 * class.
 *
 * <p>This model for testing creates the entire Activity (
 * like {@link Focus2ActivityTest}) but does
 * not attach it to the system (for example, it cannot launch another
 * Activity).
 * It allows you to inject additional behaviors via the
 * {@link android.test.ActivityUnitTestCase#setActivityContext(
 * Context)} and
```

```
 * {@link android.test.ActivityUnitTestCase#setApplication(
 * android.app.Application)} methods.
 * It also allows you to more carefully test your Activity's
 * performance
 * Writing unit tests in this manner requires more care and
 * attention, but allows you to test
 * very specific behaviors, and can also be an easier way
 * to test error conditions.
 *
 * <p>Because ActivityUnitTestCase creates the Activity
 * under test completely outside of
 * the usual system, tests of layout and point-click UI
 * interaction are much less useful
 * in this configuration.  It's more useful here to concentrate
 * on tests that involve the
 * underlying data model, internal business logic, or exercising
 * your Activity's life cycle.
 *
 * <p>See {@link com.example.android.apis.AllTests} for
 * documentation on running
 * all tests and individual tests in this application.
 */
public class ForwardingTest extends
   ActivityUnitTestCase<Forwarding> {

  private Intent mStartIntent;
  private Button mButton;

  public ForwardingTest() {
    super(Forwarding.class);
  }
```

This second snippet includes the test case definition extending `ActivityUnitTestCase<Forwarding>` as we mentioned earlier as a unit test for an Activity class. This activity under test will be disconnected from the system so it is only intended to test internal aspects of it and not its interaction with other components.

The no-argument constructor is also defined here as we mentioned in previous examples:

```
@Override
protected void setUp() throws Exception {
    super.setUp();

    // In setUp, you can create any shared test data,
    // or set up mock components to inject
    // into your Activity.  But do not call startActivity()
```

```
            // until the actual test methods.
            mStartIntent = new Intent(Intent.ACTION_MAIN);
    }
```

This `setUp()` method follows the pattern of invoking the super method and initializes the field with the Intent used to start the Activity. In this case we are saving the `Intent` as member `mStartIntent`:

```
    /**
     * The name 'test preconditions' is a convention to
     * signal that if this
     * test doesn't pass, the test case was not set up
     * properly and it might
     * explain any and all failures in other tests.
     * This is not guaranteed
     * to run before other tests, as junit uses reflection
     * to find the tests.
     */
    @MediumTest
    public void testPreconditions() {
        startActivity(mStartIntent, null, null);
        mButton = (Button) getActivity().findViewById(R.id.go);

        assertNotNull(getActivity());
        assertNotNull(mButton);
    }
```

This defines the `testPreconditions()` method that we also explained before. As noted in the method's comment, remember that this name is just a convention and no execution order is guaranteed:

```
    /**
     * This test demonstrates examining the way that activity calls
     * startActivity() to launch
     * other activities.
     */
    @MediumTest
    public void testSubLaunch() {
        Forwarding activity = startActivity(
            mStartIntent, null, null);
        mButton = (Button) activity.findViewById(R.id.go);

        // This test confirms that when you click the button,
        // the activity attempts to open
        // another activity (by calling startActivity) and
        // close itself (by calling finish()).
        mButton.performClick();
```

*Chapter 7*

```
        assertNotNull(getStartedActivityIntent());
        assertTrue(isFinishCalled());
    }
```

This test performs a click on the "go" button of the Forwarding Activity. The `onClickListener` of that button invokes `startActivity()` with an `Intent` defining the component as the `ForwardTarget` class, thus this is the `Activity` that will be started.

After performing this action we verify that the `Intent` used to launch the new `Activity` is not null and that `finish()` was called on our `Activity`.

Once the activity under test is started using `startActivity(mStartIntent, null, null)`, the components are verified to assure that they are as expected. In order to do that, the recently started activity is verified for "not null" using an assertion on `getActivity()` and then the button that was obtained by `findViewById()` is also verified for a "not null" value:

```
    /**
     * This test demonstrates ways to exercise the Activity's
     * life cycle.
     */
    @MediumTest
    public void testLifeCycleCreate() {
      Forwarding activity = startActivity(
        mStartIntent, null, null);

      // At this point, onCreate() has been called, but nothing else
      // Complete the startup of the activity
      getInstrumentation().callActivityOnStart(activity);
      getInstrumentation().callActivityOnResume(activity);

      // At this point you could test for various configuration
      // aspects, or you could
      // use a Mock Context to confirm that your activity has made
      // certain calls to the system
      // and set itself up properly.

      getInstrumentation().callActivityOnPause(activity);

      // At this point you could confirm that the activity has
      // paused properly, as if it is
      // no longer the topmost activity on screen.

      getInstrumentation().callActivityOnStop(activity);

      // At this point, you could confirm that the activity has
      // shut itself down appropriately,
      // or you could use a Mock Context to confirm that your
      // activity has released any system
```

[ 179 ]

*Testing Recipes*

```
            // resources it should no longer be holding.
            // ActivityUnitTestCase.tearDown(), which is always
            // automatically called, will take care
            // of calling onDestroy().
        }
    }
```

This is perhaps the most interesting test method in this test case. This test case demonstrates how to exercise the `Activity` lifecycle. After starting the `Activity`, `onCreate()` was automatically called, and we then exercise other lifecycle methods by invoking them manually. To be able to invoke these methods we use the `Intrumentation` of this test.

Finally, we don't manually invoke `onDestroy()` as it will be invoked for us in `tearDown()`.

Next, we have the `testSubLaunch()` test. This test checks for various conditions after starting the `Activity` under test using `startActivity(mStartIntent, null, null)`. The `Button` is obtained using `findViewById()` and then it is pressed issuing `performClick()`. The action when this button is touched is to launch a new `Activity` and this is precisely the condition that is checked, asserting that `getStartedActivityIntent()` returns "not null". The latter method returns the Intent that was used if the `Activity` under tests invoked `startActivity(Intent)` or `startActivityForResult(Intent, int)`. The last step is to verify that `finish()` was called if the other `Activity` was launched and we do that by verifying the return value of `isFinishCalled()`, which returns true if one of the finish methods (`finish()`, `finishFromChild(Activity)`, or `finishActivity(int)`) were called in the `Activity` under test.

It's time to exercise the `Activity` lifecycle for which the `testLifeCycleCreate()` method is used. This method starts the `Activity` in the same way as the previously analyzed test.

After that, the activity is started, its `onCreate()` method is called, and the `Instrumentation` is used to invoke other lifecycle methods like `getInstrumentation().callActivityOnStart(activity)` and `getInstrumentation().callActivityOnResume(activity)` to complete the `Activity` under test start up.

The `Activity` is now completely started and its time to test for the aspects we are interested in. Once this is achieved, we can follow other steps in the lifecycle. Note that this sample test does not test for anything special here.

To finish the lifecycle, we will call `getInstrumentation().callActivityOnPause(activity)` and `getInstrumentation().callActivityOnStop(activity)`. As it's mentioned in the method's comments, we don't have to worry about calling `onDestory()` as it will be automatically called by `tearDown()`.

If you want to run the tests, once you have the `ApiDemos.apk` and its tests installed onto a device or emulator, you can run this command line:

```
$ adb -e shell am instrument -w -e class com.example.android.apis.
app.ForwardingTest com.example.android.apis.tests/android.test.
InstrumentationTestRunner
```

The output is as follows:

**com.example.android.apis.app.ForwardingTest:...**

**Test results for InstrumentationTestRunner=...**

**Time: 0.614**


**OK (3 tests)**

This test represents a skeleton you can reuse to test your `Activities` in isolation and to test lifecycle related cases. The injection of mock object could also facilitate testing other aspects of the `Activity` such as accessing system resources.

# Testing files, databases, and ContentProviders

Some test cases have the need to exercise databases or ContentProviders operations, and soon comes the need to mock these operations. For example, if we are testing an application on a real device, we don't want to interfere with the normal operation of applications on such devices, mainly when we change values that may be shared by more than one application.

Such cases can take advantage of another mock class that is not a part of `android.test.mock` package but of `android.test` instead, namely `RenamingDelegatingContext`.

This class lets us mock file and database operations. A prefix supplied in the constructor is used to modify the target of these operations. All other operations are delegated to the delegating `Context` that you must specify in the constructor too.

## Testing Recipes

Suppose our `Activity` under test uses some files or databases that we want to control in some way, maybe to introduce specialized content to drive our tests, and we don't want to, or we cannot use real files or database. In such cases we create `RenamingDelegatingContext` specifying a prefix. We provide mock files using this prefix and introduce any content we need to drive our tests, and the `Activity` under test could you use them with no alteration.

The advantage of keeping our `Activity` unchanged, that is not modifying it to read from a different source, is that this assures all tests are valid. If we introduce a change only intended for our tests, we will not be able to assure that under real conditions, the `Activity` behaves the same.

To demonstrate this case, we will create an extremely simple `Activity`.

The activity `MockContextExampleActivity` displays the content of a file inside `TextView`. What we intend to demonstrate is how it displays different content during normal operation of `Activity` as compared to when it is under test:

```java
package com.example.aatg.mockcontextexample;

import android.app.Activity;
import android.graphics.Color;
import android.os.Bundle;
import android.widget.TextView;

import java.io.FileInputStream;

public class MockContextExampleActivity extends Activity {
    public final static String FILE_NAME = "myfile.txt";

    private TextView mTv;

    /** Called when the activity is first created. */
    @Override
    public void onCreate(Bundle savedInstanceState) {
        super.onCreate(savedInstanceState);
        setContentView(R.layout.main);

        mTv = (TextView) findViewById(R.id.TextView01);
        final byte[] buffer = new byte[1024];

        try {
            final FileInputStream fis = openFileInput(FILE_NAME);
            final int n = fis.read(buffer);
            mTv.setText(new String(buffer, 0, n-1));
        } catch (Exception e) {
            mTv.setText(e.toString());
            mTv.setTextColor(Color.RED);
        }
```

```
        }
        public String getText() {
            return mTv.getText().toString();
        }
    }
}
```

This is our simple `Activity`. It reads the content of the `myfile.txt` file and displays it on a `TextView`. It also displays any error that may occur.

We need some content for this file. Probably the easiest way of creating the files is as shown:

```
$ adb shell echo "This is real data" \> \
   /data/data/com.example.aatg.mockcontextexample/files/myfile.txt

$ adb shell echo "This is *MOCK* data" \> \
   /data/data/com.example.aatg.mockcontextexample/files/test.myfile.txt
```

We created two different files, one named `myfile.txt` and the other `test.myfile.txt`, with different content. The latter indicates that it is a mock content.

The following code demonstrates the use of this mock data in our activity tests:

```
package com.example.aatg.mockcontextexample.test;

import com.example.aatg.mockcontextexample.
   MockContextExampleActivity;

import android.content.Intent;
import android.test.ActivityUnitTestCase;
import android.test.RenamingDelegatingContext;

public class MockContextExampleTest extends ActivityUnitTestCase<MockContextExampleActivity> {
    private static final String PREFIX = "test.";
    private RenamingDelegatingContext mMockContext;

    public MockContextExampleTest() {
        super(MockContextExampleActivity.class);
    }

    protected void setUp() throws Exception {
        super.setUp();
        mMockContext = new RenamingDelegatingContext(
            getInstrumentation().getTargetContext(), PREFIX);
        mMockContext.makeExistingFilesAndDbsAccessible();
    }

    protected void tearDown() throws Exception {
        super.tearDown();
```

## Testing Recipes

```
    }
    public void testSampleTextDisplayed() {
        setActivityContext(mMockContext);
        startActivity(new Intent(), null, null);
        final MockContextExampleActivity activity = getActivity();
        assertNotNull(activity);
        String text = activity.getText();
        assertEquals("This is *MOCK* data", text);
    }
}
```

The class `MockContextExampleTest` extends `ActivityUnitTestCase` because we are looking for isolated testing of `MockContextExampleActivity` and because we are going to inject a mocked context; in this case the injected context is a `RenamingDelegatinContext` as a dependency.

Our fixture consists of the mock context, `mMockContext`, the `RenamingDelegatingContext` using the target context obtained by `.getInstrumentation().getTargetContext()`. Note that the context where the instrumentation is run is different than the context of the `Activity` under test.

Here a fundamental step follows—since we want to make the existing files and databases accessible to this test we have to invoke `makeExistingFilesAndDbsAccessible()`.

Then, our test named `testSampleTextDisplayed()` injects the mock context using `setActivityContext()`.

> You must invoke `setActivityContext()` to inject a mock context **before** you start the Activity under test by invoking `startActivity()`.

Then the `Activity` is started by `startActivity()` using an `Intent` just created.

The `Activity` under test is obtained using `getActivity()` and it is verified for a "not null" value.

We obtain the text value held by the `TextView` by using a getter we added to the `Activity`.

Finally, the text value obtained is checked against the `String` "*This is MOCK* data*". It is important here to notice that the value used for this test is the test file content not the real file content.

## The BrowserProvider tests

These tests are taken from the Android Open Source Project (AOSP). Source code can be obtained as a component of the Browser.git project at http://android.git.kernel.org/?p=platform/packages/apps/Browser.git. They are intended to test some aspects of the Browser Bookmarks content provider, BrowserProvider, which is part of the standard Browser included with the Android platform.

```
/*
 * Copyright (C) 2010 The Android Open Source Project
 *
 * Licensed under the Apache License, Version 2.0 (the "License");
 * you may not use this file except in compliance with the License.
 * You may obtain a copy of the License at
 *
 *      http://www.apache.org/licenses/LICENSE-2.0
 *
 * Unless required by applicable law or agreed to in writing,
 * software
 * distributed under the License is distributed on an "AS IS" BASIS,
 * WITHOUT WARRANTIES OR CONDITIONS OF ANY KIND, either express
 * or implied.
 * See the License for the specific language governing permissions
 * and limitations under the License.
 */
package com.android.browser;

import android.app.SearchManager;
import android.content.ContentValues;
import android.database.Cursor;
import android.net.Uri;
import android.test.AndroidTestCase;
import android.test.suitebuilder.annotation.MediumTest;

import java.util.ArrayList;
import java.util.Arrays;
```

This first code snippet has nothing more than the required copyrights and imports:

```
/**
 * Unit tests for {@link BrowserProvider}.
 */
@MediumTest
public class BrowserProviderTests extends AndroidTestCase {
    private ArrayList<Uri> mDeleteUris;

    @Override
```

## Testing Recipes

```java
    protected void setUp() throws Exception {
        mDeleteUris = new ArrayList<Uri>();
        super.setUp();
    }

    @Override
    protected void tearDown() throws Exception {
        for (Uri uri : mDeleteUris) {
            deleteUri(uri);
        }
        super.tearDown();
    }
```

This second snippet includes the test case definition extending `AndroidTestCase`. The class `BrowserProviderTests` extends `AndroidTestCase` because a `Context` is needed to access provider content.

The fixture created in the `setUp()` method creates an `ArrayList` of `Uris` that is used to keep track of the inserted `Uris` to be deleted in the `tearDown()` method. Perhaps we could have saved all this hassle using a mock content provider, maintaining the isolation between our tests and the system. Anyway, `tearDown()` iterates over this list and deletes the stored `Uris`.

There is no need to override the constructor here as `AndroidTestCase` is not a parameterized class and we don't need to do anything special in it:

```java
    public void testHasDefaultBookmarks() {
        Cursor c = getBookmarksSuggest("");
        try {
            assertTrue("No default bookmarks", c.getCount() > 0);
        } finally {
            c.close();
        }
    }

    public void testPartialFirstTitleWord() {
        assertInsertQuery("http://www.example.com/rasdfe",
          "nfgjra sdfywe", "nfgj");
    }

    public void testFullFirstTitleWord() {
        assertInsertQuery("http://www.example.com/",
          "nfgjra dfger", "nfgjra");
    }

    public void testFullFirstTitleWordPartialSecond() {
        assertInsertQuery("http://www.example.com/",
          "nfgjra dfger", "nfgjra df");
```

```
    }
    public void testFullTitle() {
        assertInsertQuery("http://www.example.com/",
          "nfgjra dfger", "nfgjra dfger");
    }
```

The next test, `testHasDefaultBookmarks()`, is a test for the default bookmarks. Upon startup a cursor iterates over the default bookmarks obtained by invoking `getBookmarksSuggest("")`, which returns the bookmarks unfiltered; that is why the query parameter is "".

Then, `testPartialFirstTitleWord()`, `testFullFirstTitleWord()`, `testFullFirstTitleWordPartialSecond()`, and `testFullTitle()` test for the insertion of bookmarks. To achieve this they invoke `assertInsertQuery()` using the bookmarked `Url`, its title, and the query. The method `assertInsertQuery()` adds the bookmarks to the bookmark provider, inserting the `Url` issued as a parameter with the specified title. The `Uri` returned is verified to be not null and not exactly the same as the default one. Finally the `Uri` is inserted in the list of `Uri` instances to be deleted in `testDown()`:

```
    // Not implemented in BrowserProvider
    //    public void testFullSecondTitleWord() {
    //        assertInsertQuery("http://www.example.com/rasdfe",
    //          "nfgjra sdfywe", "sdfywe");
    //    }
    public void testFullTitleJapanese() {
        String title = "\u30ae\u30e3\u30e9\u30ea\u30fc\
          u30fcGoogle\u691c\u7d22";
        assertInsertQuery("http://www.example.com/sdaga",
          title, title);
    }
    public void testPartialTitleJapanese() {
        String title = "\u30ae\u30e3\u30e9\u30ea\u30fc\
          u30fcGoogle\u691c\u7d22";
        String query = "\u30ae\u30e3\u30e9\u30ea\u30fc";
        assertInsertQuery("http://www.example.com/sdaga",
          title, query);
    }
    // Test for http://b/issue?id=2152749
    public void testSoundmarkTitleJapanese() {
        String title = "\u30ae\u30e3\u30e9\u30ea\u30fc\
          u30fcGoogle\u691c\u7d22";
        String query = "\u30ad\u30e3\u30e9\u30ea\u30fc";
        assertInsertQuery("http://www.example.com/sdaga",
          title, query);
    }
```

*Testing Recipes*

These tests are similar to the tests presented before, but in this case they use Japanese titles and queries. It is recommended to test the application's components under different conditions like in this case where other languages with different character sets are used.

We have several tests that are intended to verify the utilization of this bookmark provider for other locales and languages than just English. These particular cases cover the Japanese language utilization in bookmark titles. The tests `testFullTitleJapanese()`, `testPartialTitleJapanese()`, and `testSoundmarkTitleJapanese()` are the Japanese versions of the tests introduced before using Unicode characters:

```
//
// Utilities
//

private void assertInsertQuery(String url, String title,
  String query) {
    addBookmark(url, title);
    assertQueryReturns(url, title, query);
}

private void assertQueryReturns(String url, String title,
  String query) {
    Cursor c = getBookmarksSuggest(query);
    try {
        assertTrue(title + " not matched by " + query,
            c.getCount() > 0);
        assertTrue("More than one result for " + query,
            c.getCount() == 1);
        while (c.moveToNext()) {
            String text1 = getCol(c,
                SearchManager.SUGGEST_COLUMN_TEXT_1);
            assertNotNull(text1);
            assertEquals("Bad title", title, text1);
            String text2 = getCol(c,
                SearchManager.SUGGEST_COLUMN_TEXT_2);
            assertNotNull(text2);
            String data = getCol(c,
                SearchManager.SUGGEST_COLUMN_INTENT_DATA);
            assertNotNull(data);
            assertEquals("Bad URL", url, data);
        }
    } finally {
        c.close();
    }
}
```

```java
        private Cursor getBookmarksSuggest(String query) {
            Uri suggestUri = Uri.parse(
              "content://browser/bookmarks/search_suggest_query");
            String[] selectionArgs = { query };
            Cursor c = getContext().getContentResolver().query(
              suggestUri, null, "url LIKE ?",selectionArgs, null);
            assertNotNull(c);
            return c;
        }
        private void addBookmark(String url, String title) {
            Uri uri = insertBookmark(url, title);
            assertNotNull(uri);
            assertFalse(
              android.provider.Browser.BOOKMARKS_URI.equals(uri));
            mDeleteUris.add(uri);
        }
        private Uri insertBookmark(String url, String title) {
            ContentValues values = new ContentValues();
            values.put("title", title);
            values.put("url", url);
            values.put("visits", 0);
            values.put("date", 0);
            values.put("created", 0);
            values.put("bookmark", 1);
            return getContext().getContentResolver().insert(
              android.provider.Browser.BOOKMARKS_URI, values);
        }
        private void deleteUri(Uri uri) {
            int count = getContext().getContentResolver().
              delete(uri, null, null);
            assertEquals("Failed to delete " + uri, 1, count);
        }
        private static String getCol(Cursor c, String name) {
            int col = c.getColumnIndex(name);
            String msg = "Column " + name + " not found, columns: "
              + Arrays.toString(c.getColumnNames());
            assertTrue(msg, col >= 0);
            return c.getString(col);
        }
    }
}
```

Several utility methods follow. These are the utilities used in the tests. We briefly looked at `assertInsertQuery()` before, so now let's look at the other methods as well.

*Testing Recipes*

The method `assertInsertQuery()` invokes `assertQueryReturns(url, title, query)`, after `addBookmark()`, to verify that the `Cursor` returned by `getBookmarksSuggest(query)` contains the expected data. This expectation can be summarized as:

- Number of rows returned by the query is greater than 0
- Number of rows returned by the query is equal to 1
- The title in the returned row is not null
- The title returned by the query is exactly the same as the method parameter
- The second line for the suggestion is not null
- The URL returned by the query is not null
- This URL matches exactly the URL issued as the method parameter

This is a simplified Activity Diagram that will help us understand the relationship among these methods:

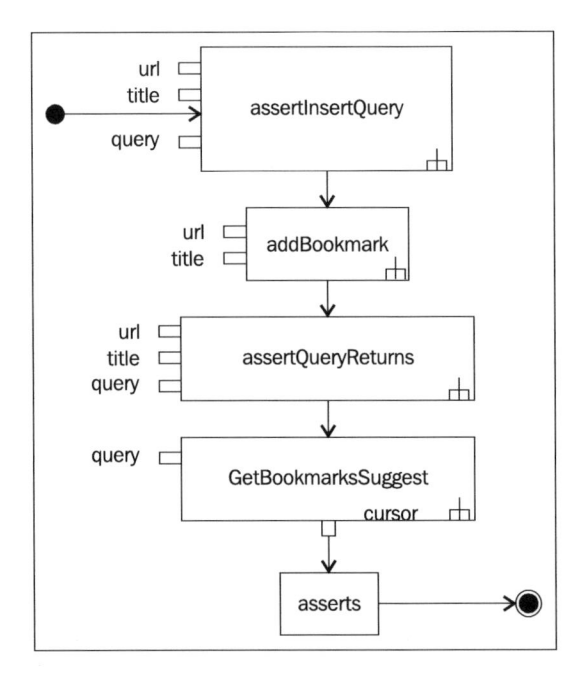

These tests follow the basic structure described before and are depicted in the UML activity diagram. Firstly, `assertInsertQuery()` is invoked which in turns invokes `addBookmark()` and `assertQueryReturns()`. Then, `getBookmarksSuggest()` is called and finally the asserts to validate the conditions we are testing. The most outstanding thing here is the utilization of asserts in these utility methods, which helps us test conditions along the way.

This strategy provides an interesting pattern to follow in our tests. Some of the utility methods that we need to create to complete our tests can also carry their own verification of several conditions and improve our test quality.

Creating assert methods in our classes allows us to introduce domain-specific testing language that can be reused when testing other parts of the system.

# Testing exceptions

We have mentioned this before. In *Chapter 1, Getting Started* with *Testing* we stated that you should test for exceptions and wrong values instead of just testing positive cases.

We have also presented this test before but here we are digging deeper into it:

```
public final void testExceptionForLessThanAbsoluteZeroF() {
  try {
    TemperatureConverter.fahrenheitToCelsius(
      TemperatureConverter.ABSOLUTE_ZERO_F-1);
    fail();
  }
  catch (InvalidTemperatureException ex) {
    // do nothing
  }
}
public final void testExceptionForLessThanAbsoluteZeroC() {
  try {
    TemperatureConverter.celsiusToFahrenheit(
      TemperatureConverter.ABSOLUTE_ZERO_C-1);
    fail();
  }
  catch (InvalidTemperatureException ex) {
    // do nothing
  }
}
```

Every time we have a method that is supposed to generate an exception, we should test this condition. The best way of doing it is by invoking the method inside a try-catch block, catching the expected `Exception`, and failing otherwise. In this precise case we test for `InvalidTemperature`:

```
public void testLifeCycleCreate() {
    Forwarding activity = startActivity(mStartIntent,
      null, null);
    // At this point, onCreate() has been called,
```

# Testing Recipes

```
        // but nothing else
        // Complete the startup of the activity
        getInstrumentation().callActivityOnStart(activity);
        getInstrumentation().callActivityOnResume(activity);

        // At this point you could test for various
        // configuration aspects, or you could
        // use a Mock Context to confirm that your activity has made
        // certain calls to the system and set itself up properly.
        getInstrumentation().callActivityOnPause(activity);

        // At this point you could confirm that the activity has
        // paused properly, as if it is
        // no longer the topmost activity on screen.
        getInstrumentation().callActivityOnStop(activity);

        // At this point, you could confirm that the activity
        // has shut itself down appropriately,
        // or you could use a Mock Context to confirm that your
        // activity has released any system
        // resources it should no longer be holding.

        // ActivityUnitTestCase.tearDown(), which is always
        // automatically called, will take care
        // of calling onDestroy().
    }
```

## Testing local and remote services

This test is also from a ApiDemos sample application (http://developer.android.com/resources/samples/ApiDemos/index.html).

The idea is to extend the `ServiceTestCase<Service>` class to test a service in a controlled environment:

```
    /*
     * Copyright (C) 2008 The Android Open Source Project
     *
     * Licensed under the Apache License, Version 2.0 (the "License");
     * you may not use this file except in compliance with the License.
     * You may obtain a copy of the License at
     *
     *      http://www.apache.org/licenses/LICENSE-2.0
     *
     * Unless required by applicable law or agreed to in writing,
     * software
     * distributed under the License is distributed on an "AS IS" BASIS,
```

```
 * WITHOUT WARRANTIES OR CONDITIONS OF ANY KIND, either express or
 * implied.
 * See the License for the specific language governing permissions
 * and limitations under the License.
 */
package com.example.android.apis.app;

import android.app.Notification;
import android.app.NotificationManager;
import android.content.Context;
import android.content.Intent;
import android.os.Handler;
import android.os.IBinder;
import android.test.MoreAsserts;
import android.test.ServiceTestCase;
import android.test.suitebuilder.annotation.MediumTest;
import android.test.suitebuilder.annotation.SmallTest;
```

This first code snippet has nothing more than the required copyrights and imports:

```
/**
 * This is a simple framework for a test of a Service.
 * See {@link android.test.ServiceTestCase
 * ServiceTestCase} for more information on how to write and
 * extend service tests.
 *
 * To run this test, you can type:
 * adb shell am instrument -w \
 *   -e class com.example.android.apis.app.LocalServiceTest \
 *   com.example.android.apis.tests/android.test.
 *     InstrumentationTestRunner
 */
public class LocalServiceTest extends ServiceTestCase<LocalService> {
    public LocalServiceTest() {
      super(LocalService.class);
    }
```

Then, we are using the no argument constructor as we did before, invoking the super constructor using the service class `LocalService`:

```
    @Override
    protected void setUp() throws Exception {
        super.setUp();
    }
```

Now we are using the pattern of invoking the super methods in `setUp()` and `tearDown()`.

We are not setting up any specific fixture in this test so we are just invoking super methods:

```
/**
 * The name 'test preconditions' is a convention to signal that
 * if this
 * test doesn't pass, the test case was not set up properly and
 * it might
 * explain any and all failures in other tests.  This is not
 * guaranteed to run before other tests, as junit uses
 * reflection to find the tests.
 */
@SmallTest
public void testPreconditions() {
}
```

We now have an empty `testPreconditions()`. We don't need any preconditions tested here:

```
/**
 * Test basic startup/shutdown of Service
 */
@SmallTest
public void testStartable() {
    Intent startIntent = new Intent();
    startIntent.setClass(getContext(), LocalService.class);
    startService(startIntent);
}
/**
 * Test binding to service
 */
@MediumTest
public void testBindable() {
    Intent startIntent = new Intent();
    startIntent.setClass(getContext(), LocalService.class);
    IBinder service = bindService(startIntent);
}
}
```

The constructor, as in other similar cases, invokes the parent constructor passing this service class as a parameter.

This is followed by a `testStartable()` test. It is annotated with the `SmallTest` annotation to categorize this test. Next we start the service using an Intent that we create here, setting its class to the class of the service under test. We also use the instrumented Context for this Intent. This class allows for some dependency injection, as every service depends on the Context in which it runs, and the application with which it is associated. This framework allows you to inject modified, mock, or isolated replacements for these dependencies, and thus performs a true unit test.

As we simply run our tests as-is, the `Service` will be injected with a fully-functional `Context`, and a generic `MockApplication` object.

Then we start the service using the `startService(startIntent)` method, in the same way as if it was started by `Context.startService()`, providing the arguments it supplied. If you use this method to start the service, it will automatically be stopped by `tearDown()`.

Another test, `testBindable()`, which is categorized as `MediumTest`, will be testing if the service can be bound. This test uses `bindService(startIntent)`, which starts the service under test, in the same way as if it was started by `Context.bindService()`, providing the arguments it supplied. It returns the communication channel to the service. It may return null if clients cannot bind to the service. Most probably this test should check for the null return value in the service with an assertion like `assertNotNull(service)` to verify that the service was bound correctly, but it doesn't. Be sure to include this test when you write code for similar cases.

The returned `IBinder` is usually for a complex interface that has been described using AIDL. In order to test with this interface, your service must implement a `getService()` method, as shown in `samples.ApiDemos.app.LocalService`, which has this implementation of that method:

```
/**
 * Class for clients to access.  Because we know this service
 * always runs in the same process as its clients,
 * we don't need to deal with IPC.
 */
public class LocalBinder extends Binder {
    LocalService getService() {
        return LocalService.this;
    }
}
```

*Testing Recipes*

# Extensive use of mock objects

In previous chapters we described and used the mock classes that are present in the Android SDK. While these classes could cover a great number of cases, that is not all and you may have the need for other mock objects to furnish your test cases.

Several libraries provide the infrastructure to satisfy our mocking needs, but we are now concentrating on EasyMock which is perhaps the most widely used in Android.

> This is not an EasyMock tutorial. We will just be analyzing its use in Android, so if you are not familiar with it I would recommend you take a look at the documentation available at its website: http://easymock.org/.

EasyMock, an Open Source software project available under the Apache 2.0 license, provides mock objects mainly for interfaces. It is a perfect match for Test Driven Development due to the way of recording expectations and its dynamically generated mock objects because they support refactoring, and test code will not break when renaming methods or changing its signature.

According to its documentation, the most relevant benefits of EasyMock are as follows:

- Hand-writing classes for Mock Objects are not needed.
- Supports refactoring-safe Mock Objects. Test code will not break at runtime when renaming methods or reordering method parameters.
- Supports return values and exceptions.
- Supports checking the order of method calls, for one or more Mock Objects.

To demonstrate its usage and to establish a style that can be later reproduced for other tests we are completing and expanding test cases produced before for our application.

In our previous `TemperatureConverter` example, we decided to extend `EditText` to create `EditNumber`, a text field that accepts only signed decimal numbers. `EditNumber` uses an `InputFilter` to provide this feature. In the following tests we will be exercising this filter to verify that the correct behavior is implemented.

To create the test we will be using a property that `EditNumber` inherits from `EditText`, that can add a listener, actually a `TextWatcher`, to provide methods that are called whenever the text of `EditText` changes. This `TextWatcher` is a collaborator for the test and we could have implemented it as a separate class, but this is tedious and may introduce more errors, so the approach taken is to use EasyMock to avoid the need of writing it.

And this is precisely how we are introducing a mock `TextWatcher` to check method invocations while text changes.

> The latest version of EasyMock supported by Android as of this writing is EasyMock 2.5.2. You may want to try out a different one but it is likely you will encounter problems.

The first thing we should do is add `easymock-2.5.2.jar` to the Test project properties.

The following screenshot shows how the easymock JAR file was added to the **Java Build Path** of the Test project:

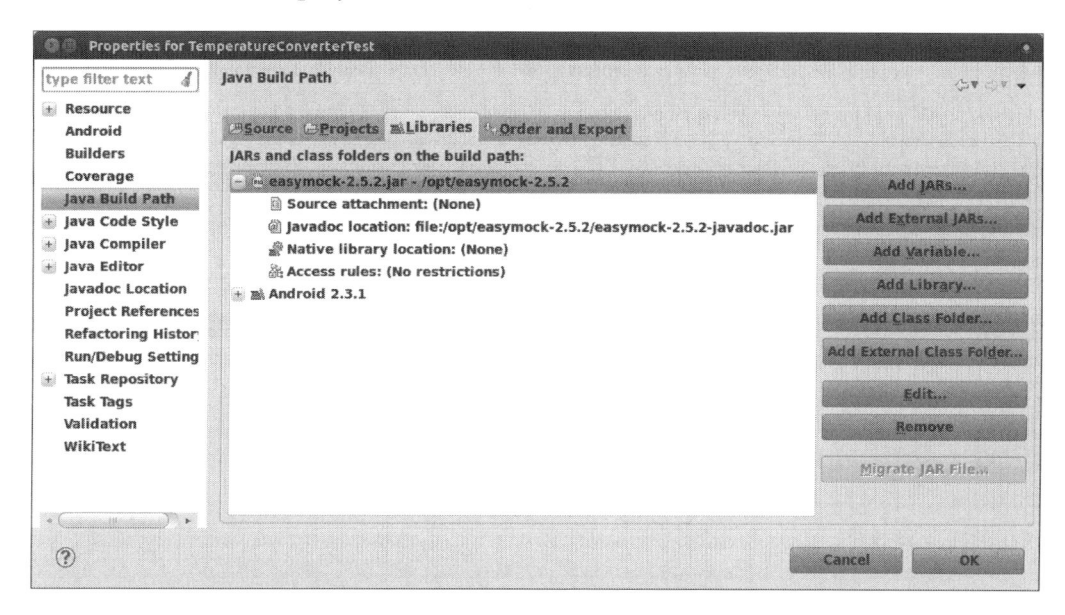

In order to use EasyMock in our tests we only need to statically import its methods from `org.easymockEasyMock`, which are the only non-internal, non-deprecated methods of EasyMock 2:

```
import static org.easymock.EasyMock.*;
```

It is preferable to use specific imports instead of using the wildcard, but it's not so easy to create the static import statement in Eclipse. However, if we organize imports (using **Source | Organize Imports** or the shortcut *Shift+Ctrl+O*), Eclipse will create the specific statements.

## Importing libraries

We have added an EasyMock library to the project's Java Build Path. This is usually not a problem, but sometimes rebuilding the project leads us to the following error that avoids the final APK. The problem is found when this final APK cannot be created because there is a problem while it is archived:

**[2010-10-28 01:12:29 - TemperatureConverterTest] Error generating final archive: duplicate entry: LICENSE**

This depends on how many libraries are included by the project and what they are.

Most of the available Open Source libraries have a similar content as proposed by GNU and include files like LICENSE, NOTICE, CHANGES, COPYRIGHT, INSTALL, among others. We will find this problem as soon as we try to include more than one in the same project to ultimately build a single APK.

The solution to this problem is to repackage the library content renaming these files; for example, `LICENSE` could be renamed to `LICENSE.<library>`. It is recommended to add the suffix **android** to the repackaged library to keep track of these changes.

This is an example of the steps you may need to rename those files:

```
$ mkdir mylib-1.0

$ (cd mylib-1.0; jar xf /path/to/mylib-1.0.jar)

$ mv mylib-1.0/META-INF/LICENSE  mylib-1.0/META-INF/LICENSE.mylib

$ mv mylib-1.0/META-INF/NOTICE   mylib-1.0/META-INF/NOTICE.mylib

$ (cd mylib-1.0; jar cf /path/to/mylib-1.0-android.jar .)
```

The idea is to move the common file names to a name suffixed by the library name to provide some uniqueness.

## The testTextChanged test

This test will exercise `EditNumber` behavior, checking the method calls on the `TextWatcher` mock and verifying the results.

We are using an `AndroidTestCase` because we are interested in testing `EditNumber` in isolation of other components or `Activities`.

This test defines two String arrays: sai and sar. sai stands for String array input and sar for String array result. As you may have guessed already, sai contains the input and sar the expected result for the corresponding element in the input after filters have been applied.

In real life you should select more descriptive names for the variables used in the tests as you should do for your code, but here we are constrained by the space and thus we have selected very short names. The names saInput and saResult would be good choices:

```java
/**
 * Test method for {@link com.example.aatg.tc.EditNumber}.
 * Several input strings are set and compared against the
 * expected results after filters are applied.
 * This test use {@link EasyMock}
 */
public final void testTextChanged() {
  final String[] sai = new String[] {
    null, "", "1", "123", "-123", "0", "1.2", "-1.2",
      "1-2-3", "+1", "1.2.3" };
  final String[] sar = new String[] {
    "",     "", "1", "123", "-123", "0", "1.2", "-1.2",
      "123", "1", "12.3" };
  // mock
  final TextWatcher watcher = createMock(TextWatcher.class);
  mEditNumber.addTextChangedListener(watcher);

  for (int i=1; i < sai.length; i++) {
    // record
    watcher.beforeTextChanged(stringCmp(sar[i-1]), eq(0),
      eq(sar[i-1].length()), eq(sar[i].length()));
    watcher.onTextChanged(stringCmp(sar[i]), eq(0),
      eq(sar[i-1].length()), eq(sar[i].length()));
    watcher.afterTextChanged(stringCmp(
      Editable.Factory.getInstance().newEditable(sar[i])));
    // replay
    replay(watcher);
    // exercise
    mEditNumber.setText(sai[i]);
    // test
    final String actual = mEditNumber.getText().toString();
    assertEquals(sai[i] + " => " + sar[i] + " => " + actual,
      sar[i], actual);
    // verify
    verify(watcher);
```

```
            // reset
            reset(watcher);
        }
    }
```

We begin creating `sai` and `sar`. As we explained before they are two `String` arrays containing the inputs and results expected.

Then we create a mock `TextWatcher` using `createMock(TextWatcher.class)` and assign it to `mEditNumber`, the `EditNumber` created in the test fixture.

We create a loop to iterate over every element of the `sai` array.

Next, we take the seven common steps usually needed to use the mock object:

1. Create the mock using `createMock()`, `createNiceMock()`, or `createStrictMock()`.
2. Record the expected behavior; all methods invoked will be recorded.
3. Replay, to change the state of the object from record to play when it really behaves like a mock object.
4. Exercise the methods, usually by invoking methods of the class under test.
5. Test the results of the exercised methods using asserts. This step is optional for simpler cases.
6. Verify that the behavior specified was actually followed. If this was not the case we will receive an exception.
7. Reset can be used to reuse a mock object, clearing its state.

In the record step we declare all the methods we are expecting to be invoked on the mock object together with its arguments. We use comparators for the arguments.

We will be using a special `Comparator`, `stringCmp()`, because we are interested in comparing the `String` content for different classes used by Android, such as `Editable`, `CharSequence`, `String`, and so on.

The other comparator, `eq()`, expects an `int` that is equal to the given value. The latter is provided by EasyMock for all primitive types and `Object`, but we need to implement `stringCmp()` as it supports some Android-specific usage.

EasyMock has a predefined matcher that would help us in creating our comparator:

```
public static <T> T cmp(T value, Comparator<? super T>
    comparator, LogicalOperator operator)
```

The cmp comparator method expects an argument that will be compared using the provided comparator using the operator. The comparison that will take place is comparator.compare(actual, value) operator 0 where operator can be one of logical operator values in EasyMock's LogicalOperator enum, representing <,<=,>,>=, or ==.

As you may have already realized, its frequent use in a test could be really complex and may lead to errors, so to simplify this process we will be using a helper class that we call StringComparator:

```
public static final class StringComparator<T> implements
  Comparator<T> {

  /* (non-Javadoc)
   * @see java.util.Comparator#compare(
     java.lang.Object, java.lang.Object)
   *
   * Return the {@link String} comparison of the arguments.
   */
  @Override
  public int compare(T object1, T object2) {
    return object1.toString().compareTo(object2.toString());
  }
}
```

This class implements the Comparator<T> interface, which has an abstract method named compare. We implement this method by returning the result of the comparison of the objects passed as arguments after they are converted to String. Remember that compareTo(String string) applied to a String compares the string specified as a parameter to the string using the Unicode values of the characters. Its return value is:

- 0 (zero) if the strings contain the same characters in the same order
- A negative integer if the first non-equal character in this string has a Unicode value which is less than the Unicode value of the character at the same position in the specified string, or if this string is a prefix of the specified string
- A positive integer if the first non-equal character in this string has a Unicode value which is greater than the Unicode value of the character at the same position in the specified string, or if the specified string is a prefix of this string

We could invoke EasyMock.cmp() directly using this comparator but to simplify things even further we will create a generic static method stringCmp:

```
/**
 * Return {@link EasyMock.cmp} using a {@link StringComparator} and
 * {@link LogicalOperator.EQUAL}
```

```
     *
     * @param <T> The original class of the arguments
     * @param o The argument to the comparison
     * @return {@link EasyMock.cmp}
     */
    public static <T> T stringCmp(T o) {
      return cmp(o, new StringComparator<T>(), LogicalOperator.EQUAL);
    }
```

This method will invoke `EasyMock.cmp()` using the right comparator for the specific type and using `EQUAL` as the operator.

That is why in our test we can simply use:

```
watcher.beforeTextChanged(stringCmp(sar[i-1]), …
```

# Introducing Hamcrest

While the previous method is valid, a more generic approach would be to introduce **hamcrest**, a library of matcher objects (also known as constraints or predicates) allowing *match* rules to be defined declaratively, to be used in other frameworks. Hamcrest also provides adaptors for EasyMock 2.

We will be revisiting our previous example introducing hamcrest for our matchers.

To be able to use hamcrest we need to include it to the **Java Build Path**.

> In this example we use hamcrest-1.2, which is the latest release. Instead of using `hamcrest-1.2-all.jar` we use the individual components and the method described before to avoid several `LICENSE.txt` files from clashing.

Download hamcrest library from `http://code.google.com/p/hamcrest`.

You need to include the following JAR files:

- `hamcrest-core`
- `hamcrest-library`
- `hamcrest-integration`

The following screenshot shows the new project properties after adding hamcrest libraries:

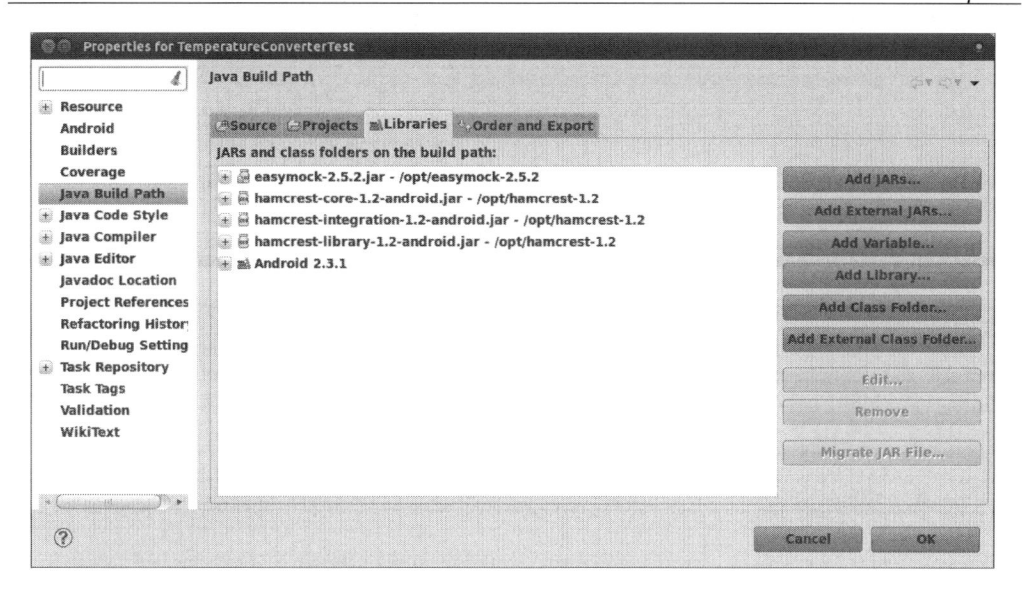

## Hamcrest matchers

Hamcrest comes with a library of useful matchers. Here are some of the most important ones:

- **Core**
    - **anything**: Always matches; useful if you don't care what the object under test is
    - **describedAs**: Decorator to adding custom failure description
    - **is**: Decorator to improve readability
- **Logical**
    - **allOf**: Matches if all matchers match, short circuits (like Java &&)
    - **anyOf**: Matches if any matchers match, short circuits (like Java ||)
    - **not**: Matches if the wrapped matcher doesn't match and vice versa
- **Object**
    - **equalTo**: Test object equality using `Object.equals`
    - **hasToString**: Test `Object.toString`
    - **instanceOf, isCompatibleType**: Test type
    - **notNullValue, nullValue**: Test for null
    - **sameInstance**: Test object identity

*Testing Recipes*

- **Beans**
    - **hasProperty**: Test JavaBeans properties
- **Collections**
    - **Array**: Test an array's elements against an array of matchers
    - **hasEntry, hasKey, hasValue**: Test a map containing an entry, key, or value
    - **hasItem, hasItems**: Test a collection containing elements
    - **hasItemInArray**: Test an array containing an element
- **Number**
    - **closeTo**: Test floating point values are close to a given value
    - **greaterThan, greaterThanOrEqualTo, lessThan, lessThanOrEqualTo**: Test ordering
- **Text**
    - **equalToIgnoringCase**: Test string equality ignoring case
    - **equalToIgnoringWhiteSpace**: Test string equality ignoring differences in runs of whitespace
    - **containsString, endsWith, startsWith**: Test string matching

## The hasToString matcher

Our next step is to create the matcher to replace the previous use of the `stringCmp()` Comparator. `EasyMock2Adapter` is an adapter class provided by hamcrest:

```
import org.hamcrest.integration.EasyMock2Adapter;
import org.hamcrest.object.HasToString;

    /**
     * Create an {@link EasyMock2Adapter} using a
     * {@link HasToString.hasToString}
     *
     * @param <T> The original class of the arguments
     * @param o The argument to the comparison
     * @return o
     */
    public static <T> T hasToString(T o) {
        EasyMock2Adapter.adapt(
            HasToString.hasToString(o.toString()));
        return o;
    }
}
```

Having this matcher implemented, the following step is still required. We need to adapt the `testTextChanged()` method to include this newly created matcher instead of `stringCmp()`:

```
// record
watcher.beforeTextChanged(hasToString(sar[i-1]), eq(0),
    eq(sar[i-1].length()), eq(sar[i].length()));
watcher.onTextChanged(hasToString(sar[i]), eq(0),
    eq(sar[i-1].length()), eq(sar[i].length()));
watcher.afterTextChanged(hasToString(
    Editable.Factory.getInstance().newEditable(sar[i])));
```

## Testing Views in isolation

The test we are analyzing here also belongs to the ApiDemos project. It demonstrates how some properties of the `Views` conforming a `Layout` can be tested when the behavior itself cannot be isolated. Testing focus is one of these situations.

To avoid creating the full `Activity`, this test is extending `AndroidTestCase`:

```
/*
 * Copyright (C) 2008 The Android Open Source Project
 *
 * Licensed under the Apache License, Version 2.0 (the "License");
 * you may not use this file except in compliance with the License.
 * You may obtain a copy of the License at
 *
 *      http://www.apache.org/licenses/LICENSE-2.0
 *
 * Unless required by applicable law or agreed to in writing,
 * software distributed under the License is distributed on an
 * "AS IS" BASIS, WITHOUT WARRANTIES OR CONDITIONS OF ANY KIND,
 * either express or implied.
 * See the License for the specific language governing permissions
 * and limitations under the License.
 */
package com.example.android.apis.view;

import com.example.android.apis.R;

import android.content.Context;
import android.test.AndroidTestCase;
import android.test.suitebuilder.annotation.SmallTest;
import android.view.FocusFinder;
import android.view.LayoutInflater;
```

## Testing Recipes

```
import android.view.View;
import android.view.ViewGroup;
import android.widget.Button;
```

As in previous cases we start with the required copyright and imports:

```
/**
 * This exercises the same logic as {@link Focus2ActivityTest} but in
 * a lighter weight manner; it doesn't need to launch the activity,
 * and it can test the focus behavior by calling {@link FocusFinder}
 * methods directly.
 *
 * {@link Focus2ActivityTest} is still useful to verify that, at an
 * end to end level, key events actually translate to focus
 * transitioning in the way we expect.
 * A good complementary way to use both types of tests might be to
 * have more exhaustive coverage in the lighter weight test case,
 * and a few end to end scenarios in the functional {@link
 * android.test.ActivityInstrumentationTestCase}.
 * This would provide reasonable assurance that the end to end
 * system is working, while avoiding the overhead of
 * having every corner case exercised in the slower,
 * heavier weight way.
 *
 * Even as a lighter weight test, this test still needs access to a
 * {@link Context} to inflate the file, which is why it extends
 * {@link AndroidTestCase}.
 *
 * If you ever need a context to do your work in tests, you can
 * extend {@link AndroidTestCase}, and when run via an {@link
 * android.test.InstrumentationTestRunner},
 * the context will be injected for you.
 *
 * See {@link com.example.android.apis.app.ForwardingTest} for
 * an example of an Activity unit test.
 *
 * See {@link com.example.android.apis.AllTests} for
 * documentation on running
 * all tests and individual tests in this application.
 */
public class Focus2AndroidTest extends AndroidTestCase {
```

As we mentioned before, this test extends `AndroidTestCase` to provide a lightweight alternative to `ActivityInstrumentationTestCase<Activity>` when possible.

You may have thought about using just `TestCase`, but unfortunately this is not possible as we need a `Context` to inflate the XML layout via `LayoutInflater`, and `AndroidTestCase` will provide us with this component:

```
private FocusFinder mFocusFinder;
private ViewGroup mRoot;
private Button mLeftButton;
private Button mCenterButton;
private Button mRightButton;

@Override
protected void setUp() throws Exception {
    super.setUp();

    mFocusFinder = FocusFinder.getInstance();

    // inflate the layout
    final Context context = getContext();
    final LayoutInflater inflater = LayoutInflater.from(context);
    mRoot = (ViewGroup) inflater.inflate(R.layout.focus_2, null);

    // manually measure it, and lay it out
    mRoot.measure(500, 500);
    mRoot.layout(0, 0, 500, 500);

    mLeftButton = (Button) mRoot.findViewById(R.id.leftButton);
    mCenterButton = (Button)
        mRoot.findViewById(R.id.centerButton);
    mRightButton = (Button) mRoot.findViewById(
        R.id.rightButton);
}
```

The fixture set up is as follows:

1. `FocusFinder` is a class that provides the algorithm used to find the next focusable `View`. It implements the singleton pattern and that's why we use `FocusFinder.getInstance()` to obtain a reference to it. This class has several methods to help us find focusable and touchable items as we mentioned, given various conditions as the nearest in a given direction or searching from a particular rectangle.

2. Then we get the `LayoutInflater` and inflate the layout under test.

3. One thing we need to take into account, as our test is isolated from other parts of the system, is that we have to manually measure and layout the components.

*Testing Recipes*

4. Then, we use the *find views* pattern and we assign the found views to the fields:

```
/**
 * The name 'test preconditions' is a convention to signal
 * that if this test doesn't pass, the test case was not
 * set up properly and it might explain any and all failures
 * in other tests.  This is not guaranteed to run before
 * other tests, as junit uses reflection to find the tests.
 */
@SmallTest
public void testPreconditions() {
    assertNotNull(mLeftButton);
    assertTrue("center button should be right of left button",
            mLeftButton.getRight() < mCenterButton.getLeft());
    assertTrue("right button should be right of center button",
            mCenterButton.getRight() < mRightButton.getLeft());
}
```

Once the fixture has been configured we describe the precondition in a test which, as we mentioned earlier is named `testPreconditions()`. However, because tests are found using reflection, there is no guarantee that it will run in a particular order, as all of the test methods are looked for by evaluating if their name begins with test.

These preconditions include the verification of the relative position on the screen for the components. In this case their edges relative to the parent are used.

In a previous chapter we enumerated all the available asserts in our arsenal and you may remember that to test `Views` position, we had a complete set of assertions in the `ViewAsserts` class. However, this depends on how the layout is defined:

```
    @SmallTest
    public void
      testGoingRightFromLeftButtonJumpsOverCenterToRight() {
        assertEquals("right should be next focus from left",
          mRightButton, mFocusFinder.findNextFocus(
          mRoot, mLeftButton, View.FOCUS_RIGHT));
    }
    @SmallTest
    public void testGoingLeftFromRightButtonGoesToCenter() {
        assertEquals("center should be next focus from right",
          mCenterButton, mFocusFinder.findNextFocus(
          mRoot, mRightButton, View.FOCUS_LEFT));
    }
}
```

The method `testGoingRightFromLeftButtonJumpsOverCenterToRight()`, as its name suggests, tests the focus gained by the right button when the focus moves from the right to the left button. To achieve this search, the instance of `FocusFinder` obtained during the `setUp()` method is employed. This class has a `findNextFocus()` method to obtain the View receiving focus in a given direction. The value obtained is checked against our expectations.

In a similar way, the test `testGoingLeftFromRightButtonGoesToCenter()`, tests the focus going in the other direction.

## Testing parsers

There are many occasions where your Android application relies on external XML, JSON messages, or documents obtained from web services. These documents are used for data interchange between the local application and the server. There are many use cases where XML or JSON documents are obtained from the server or generated by the local application to be sent to the server. Ideally, methods invoked by these activities have to be tested in isolation to have real unit tests and to achieve this, we need to include some mock files somewhere in our APK to run the tests.

But the question is where can we include these files?

Let's find out.

## Android assets

To begin, a brief review of the assets definition can be found in the Android SDK documentation:

> *The difference between "resources" and "assets" isn't much on the surface, but in general, you'll use resources to store your external content much more often than you'll use assets. The real difference is that anything placed in the resources directory will be easily accessible from your application from the R class, which is compiled by Android. Whereas, anything placed in the assets directory will maintain its raw file format and, in order to read it, you must use the AssetManager to read the file as a stream of bytes. So keeping files and data in resources (res/) makes them easily accessible.*

Clearly, assets are what we need to store the files that will be parsed to test the parser.

So our XML or JSON files should be placed on the assets folder to prevent manipulation at compile time and to be able to access their raw content while the application or test run.

But be careful; we need to place them in the assets folder of our **test project** because they are not part of the application and we don't want them packed with it.

## The parser activity

This is an extremely simple activity to demonstrate the case. Our activity obtains an XML or JSON document from a server and then parses it. Let's assume we have a `parseXml` method:

```
package com.example.aatg.parserexample;

import org.xmlpull.v1.XmlPullParser;
import org.xmlpull.v1.XmlPullParserFactory;

import android.app.Activity;
import android.os.Bundle;

import java.io.InputStream;
import java.io.InputStreamReader;

public class ParserExampleActivity extends Activity {
  /** Called when the activity is first created. */
  @Override
  public void onCreate(Bundle savedInstanceState) {
    super.onCreate(savedInstanceState);
    setContentView(R.layout.main);
  }

  public String parseXml(InputStream xml) {
    try {
      XmlPullParserFactory factory =
        XmlPullParserFactory.newInstance();
      factory.setNamespaceAware(true);
      XmlPullParser parser = factory.newPullParser();
      parser.setInput(new InputStreamReader(xml));

      int eventType = parser.getEventType();
      StringBuilder sb = new StringBuilder();
      while (eventType != XmlPullParser.END_DOCUMENT) {
        if(eventType == XmlPullParser.TEXT) {
          sb.append(parser.getText());
        }
        eventType = parser.next();
      }
      return sb.toString();
    }
    catch (Exception e) {
      // TODO Auto-generated catch block
```

```
            e.printStackTrace();
        }
        return null;
    }
}
```

This is an oversimplified example of an activity that includes a parser method to illustrate the use of assets. Your real application may look very different and your parser could be implemented as an external class that could be tested in isolation and integrated at a later stage.

## The parser test

This test implements an `ActivityInstrumentationTestCase2` for the `ParserExampleActivity` class:

```
package com.example.aatg.parserexample.test;

import com.example.aatg.parserexample.ParserExampleActivity;

import android.test.ActivityInstrumentationTestCase2;

import java.io.IOException;
import java.io.InputStream;

public class ParserExampleActivityTest extends
    ActivityInstrumentationTestCase2<ParserExampleActivity> {
  public ParserExampleActivityTest() {
    super(ParserExampleActivity.class);
  }

  protected void setUp() throws Exception {
    super.setUp();
  }

  protected void tearDown() throws Exception {
    super.tearDown();
  }

  public final void testParseXml() {
    ParserExampleActivity activity = getActivity();
    String result = null;
    try {
      InputStream myxml = getInstrumentation().getContext().
        getAssets().open("my_document.xml");
      result = activity.parseXml(myxml);
    } catch (IOException e) {
      fail(e.getLocalizedMessage());
    }
```

```
        assertNotNull(result);
    }
}
```

Almost all the methods are simple implementations of the default ones and the only interesting method for us is `testParseXml()`. Firstly, the activity is obtained by invoking `getActivity()`. Then an `InputStream` is obtained, opening the file `my_document.xml` from the assets by `getInstrumentation().getContext().getAssets()`. Note that the `Context` and thus the assets obtained here are from the tests package not from the `Activity` under test.

Next, the activity `parseXml()` method is invoked using the recently obtained `InputStream`. If there is an `Exception`, `fail()` is invoked and if everything goes well we test that the result is not null.

We should then provide the XML we want to use for the test in an asset named `my_document.xml`.

The content could be:

```
<?xml version="1.0" encoding="UTF-8"?>
<!-- place this file in assets/my_document.xml -->
<my>This is my document</my>
```

# Testing for memory leaks

Sometimes memory consumption is an important factor to measure the good behavior of the test target, be it an Activity, Service, ContentProvider, or other Component.

To test for this condition, we can use a utility test that you can invoke from other tests mainly after having run a test loop:

```
public final void assertNotInLowMemoryCondition() {
  //Verification: check if it is in low memory
  ActivityManager.MemoryInfo mi = new
    ActivityManager.MemoryInfo();
  ((ActivityManager)getActivity().getSystemService(
    Context.ACTIVITY_SERVICE)).getMemoryInfo(mi);
  assertFalse("Low memory condition", mi.lowMemory);
}
```

This assertion can be called from other tests. At the beginning it obtains the `MemoryInfo` from `ActivityManager` using `getMemoryInfo()`, after getting the instance using `getSystemService()`. The field `lowMemory` is set to true if the system considers itself to currently be in a low memory situation.

*Chapter 7*

In some cases we want to dive even deeper in the resource usage and we can obtain more detailed information from the process table.

We can create another helper method to obtain process information and use it in our tests:

```java
public final String captureProcessInfo() {
    String cmd = "ps";
    String memoryUsage = null;
    int ch; // the character read
    try {
        Process p = Runtime.getRuntime().exec(cmd);
        InputStream in = p.getInputStream();
        StringBuffer sb = new StringBuffer(512);
        while ((ch = in.read()) != -1) {
            sb.append((char) ch);
        }
        memoryUsage = sb.toString();
    } catch (IOException e) {
        fail(e.getLocalizedMessage());
    }
    return memoryUsage;
}
```

To obtain this information, a command (in this case, `ps` is used but you can adapt it to your needs) is executed using `Runtime.exec()`. The output of this command is concatenated in a `String` that is later returned. We can use the return value to print it to the logs in our test or we can further process the content to obtain summary information.

This is an example if logging the output:

```java
Log.d(TAG, captureProcessInfo());
```

When this test is run we obtain information about the running processes:

11-12 21:10:29.182: DEBUG/ActivityTest(1811): USER    PID  PPID  VSIZE  RSS  WCHAN    PC         NAME

11-12 21:10:29.182: DEBUG/ActivityTest(1811): root     1    0    312    220  c009b74c 0000ca4c S /init

11-12 21:10:29.182: DEBUG/ActivityTest(1811): root     2    0    0      0    c004e72c 00000000 S kthreadd

11-12 21:10:29.182: DEBUG/ActivityTest(1811): root     3    2    0      0    c003fdc8 00000000 S ksoftirqd/0

11-12 21:10:29.182: DEBUG/ActivityTest(1811): root    4  2  0  0  c004b2c4 00000000 S events/0

11-12 21:10:29.182: DEBUG/ActivityTest(1811): root    5  2  0  0  c004b2c4 00000000 S khelper

11-12 21:10:29.182: DEBUG/ActivityTest(1811): root    6  2  0  0  c004b2c4 00000000 S suspend

11-12 21:10:29.182: DEBUG/ActivityTest(1811): root    7  2  0  0  c004b2c4 00000000 S kblockd/0

11-12 21:10:29.182: DEBUG/ActivityTest(1811): root    8  2  0  0  c004b2c4 00000000 S cqueue

11-12 21:10:29.182: DEBUG/ActivityTest(1811): root    9  2  0  0  c018179c 00000000 S kseriod

[...]

The output was cut for brevity but you will get the complete list of processes running on the system.

A brief explanation of the information obtained is as follows:

| Column | Description |
| --- | --- |
| USER | This is the textual user ID. |
| PID | Process ID number of the process. |
| PPID | Parent process ID. |
| VSIZE | Virtual memory size of the process in KiB. This is the virtual memory the process reserves. |
| RSS | Resident set size, the non-swapped physical memory that a task has used (in pages). This is the actual amount of real memory the process takes in pages. |
| | This does not include pages which have not been demand-loaded in. |
| WCHAN | This is the "channel" in which the process is waiting. It is the address of a system call, and can be looked up in a namelist if you need a textual name. |
| PC | The current EIP (instruction pointer). |
| State (no header) | The process state.<br>• S for sleeping in an interruptible state<br>• R for running<br>• T for a stopped process<br>• Z for a zombie |

| Column | Description |
|---|---|
| NAME | Command name. Application processes in Android are renamed after its package name. |

# Summary

In this chapter, several real world examples of tests that cover a wide range of cases were presented. You can use them as a starting point while creating your own tests.

We covered a variety of testing recipes that you can extend for your own tests. We used mock contexts and showed how a `RenamingDelegatingContext` can be used in various situations to change the data obtained by the tests. We also analyzed the injection of these mock context into test dependencies.

Then, we used `ActivityUnitTestCase` to test Activities in complete isolation. We tested Views in isolation using `AndroidTestCase`. We demonstrated the use of EasyMock 2 to mock objects combined with Hamcrest to provide comparators. Finally we treated the analysis of potential memory leaks.

The next chapter focuses on automating the testing process using Continuous Integration.

# 8
# Continuous Integration

**Continuous Integration** is one agile technique for software engineering that aims to improve the software quality and to reduce the time taken to integrate changes by continuously applying integration and testing frequently, opposed to the more traditional approach of integrating and testing by the end of the development cycle. The original article was written by Martin Fowler back in 2000 (http://www.martinfowler.com/articles/continuousIntegration.html), and describes the experience of putting together Continuous Integration on a large software project.

Continuous Integration has received a broad adoption in recent years, and a proliferation of commercial tools and Open Source projects is a clear demonstration of its success. That is not very difficult to understand, as anybody who during their professional career has participated in a software development project using a traditional approach, is very likely to have experienced the so called *integration hell*, where the time it takes to integrate the changes exceeds the time it took to make the changes. Does this remind you of anything?

On the contrary, Continous Integration is the practice to integrate changes frequently and in small steps. These steps are negligible and usually no errors as a product of the integration can arise without beign noticed immediately. The most common practice is to trigger the build process after every commit to the source code repository.

This practice also implies other requirements, beside the source code being maintained by a Version Control System (VCS):

- Builds should be automated by running a single command. This feature has been supported for a very long time by tools like `make` and more recently by `ant` and `maven`.
- The build should be self tested to confirm that the newly built software meets the expectations of the developers, and this has been the subject of this book so far.
- The artifacts and results of the tests should be easy to find and view.

In previous chapters, we have written some tests for our Android projects and now we would like to take Continuous Integration into account. To achieve this we want to create a model that coexists with the traditional Eclipse and Android ADT environments, so both alternatives are supported from the source tree.

In this chapter we are going to discuss:

- Automating the build process
- Introducing Version Control Systems to the process
- Continuous Integration with Hudson
- Automating tests

After this chapter you will be able to apply Continuous Integration to your own project no matter its size, whether it is a medium or large software project employing dozens of developers or it is just you programming solo.

# Building Android applications manually using Ant

If we aim to incorporate **Continuous Integration** in our development process, the first step will be building Android applications manually, as we can combine it with this technique to automate the procedure.

In doing this we intend to keep our project compatible with the Eclipse and ADT plugin building process, and this is what we are going to do. As I understand, this is a great advantage and speeds up the development process by automatically building and eventually showing the errors that may exist in your project immediately. This is an invaluable tool too when editing resources or other files that generate intermediate classes, otherwise some simple errors would be discovered too late in the building process.

Fortunately, Android supports this alternative with the existing tooling and not much effort is needed to merge both approaches in the same project. In such cases, building manually with **ant** is supported. However, other options exist too, though not supported *out-of-the-box*, like using **maven** or even **make**.

> Ant is a software command-line tool and a Java library to automate software build process by describing it in XML files containing targets and dependencies.
>
> More information can be found at its home page, `http://ant.apache.org/`.
>
> The Android Ant based build system requires at least Ant 1.8 or newer versions.

Here it is worth noting that the entire Android platform is built by an incredibly complex structure of makefiles and this method is used even for building the applications that are included by the platform like Calculator, Contacts, Browser, and so on.

If you are already building a project with Eclipse, you can convert it using the `android` tool. `android` is available in the tools directory of the Android SDK. If you are using Microsoft Windows you should adapt the following examples to use valid Windows paths and replace the variables that are not available, like PWD in the following example, by their values.

Firstly, we change our current directory to the project; though not strictly necessary, this simplifies things a bit.

Then using the `android` command we convert the project to be built with `ant` and the `build.xml` buildfile is created:

```
$ cd <path/to>/TemperatureConverter
$ android update project --path $PWD --name TemperatureConverter
```

This is the output obtained:

**Updated local.properties**

**Added file <path/to>/TemperatureConverter/build.xml**

**Updated file <path/to>/TemperatureConverter/proguard.cfg**

Immediately after finishing this step we are ready to build the project manually from the command line. This buildfile features the following targets:

| Target | Description |
| --- | --- |
| help | Displays a short help. |
| clean | Removes output files created by other targets. |
| compile | Compiles project's `.java` files into `.class` files. |
| debug | Builds the application and signs it with a debug key. |
| release | Builds the application. The generated `.apk` file must be signed before it is published. |
| install | Installs/reinstalls the debug package onto a running emulator or device. |
|  | If the application was previously installed, the signatures must match. |
| uninstall | Uninstalls the application from a running emulator or device. |

Some of these targets operate on a device or emulator. If there are several devices or emulators connected to the build machine we need to specify the specific target on the command line. For this reason the targets uses a variable named `adb.device.arg` for us to specify the target:

```
$ ant -Dadb.device.arg='-s emulator-5554' install
```

This is the output generated:

**Buildfile: build.xml**

   [setup] Android SDK Tools Revision 9

   [setup] Project Target: Android 2.3.1

   [setup] API level: 9

   [setup] Importing rules file: platforms/android-8/ant/ant_rules_r2.xml

-compile-tested-if-test:

-dirs:

   [echo] Creating output directories if needed...

   [mkdir] Created dir: TemperatureConverter/bin/classes

-resource-src:

   [echo] Generating R.java / Manifest.java from the resources...

-aidl:

   [echo] Compiling aidl files into Java classes...

compile:

   [javac] Compiling 6 source files to TemperatureConverter/bin/classes

-dex:

   [echo] Converting compiled files and external libraries into TemperatureConverter/bin/classes.dex...

-package-resources:

   [echo] Packaging resources

 [aaptexec] Creating full resource package...

-package-debug-sign:

[apkbuilder] Creating TemperatureConverter-debug-unaligned.apk and signing it with a debug key...

[apkbuilder] Using keystore: .android/debug.keystore

debug:

   [echo] Running zip align on final apk...

   [echo] Debug Package: TemperatureConverter/bin/TemperatureConverter-debug.apk

install:

   [echo] Installing TemperatureConverter/bin/TemperatureConverter-debug.apk onto default emulator or device...

   [exec] 371 KB/s (18635 bytes in 0.049s)

   [exec] pkg: /data/local/tmp/TemperatureConverter-debug.apk

   [exec] Success

**BUILD SUCCESSFUL**

**Total time: 6 seconds**

That is, running the command line mentioned, the following steps are executed:

- Environment setup, including the specific rules for the version used
- Create the output directories if needed
- Compile the sources, including resources, aidl, and Java files
- Convert the compiled files into `dex`
- Package creation and signing
- Installation onto the given device or emulator

Once we have the APK installed, and because we are now doing everything from the command line, we can even start the `TemperatureConverterActivity`. Using the `am start` command and an `Intent` using the action `MAIN` and the `Activity` we are interested to launch as the component, we can create a command line as follows:

```
$ adb -s emulator-5554 shell am start -a android.intent.action.MAIN -n com.example.aatg.tc/.TemperatureConverterActivity
```

The Activity is started as you can verify in the emulator. Then, we can proceed in a similar way for the test project:

```
$ cd </path/to>/TemperatureConverterTest
$ android update test-project --path $PWD --main <path/to>/TemperatureConverter
```

Running this command, we will obtain output similar to the following if everything goes well:

**Updated default.properties**

**Updated local.properties**

**Added file <path/to>/TemperatureConverterTest/build.xml**

**Updated file <path/to>/TemperatureConverterTest/proguard.cfg**

**Updated build.properties**

Also as we did before with the main project, we can build and install the tests. To do it, once we have our test project converted we can build it using ant as we did for the main project. To build and install it on a running emulator, use:

```
$ ant -Dadb.device.arg='-s emulator-5554' install
```

It is worth noting that to be able to build the project successfully we need the libraries used to reside in the libs directory inside the project. You can create symbolic links to their original location to avoid copying them if you prefer.

Also, it is a good practice to keep the Eclipse and Ant build processes synchronized, so if you add the required libraries to the libs directory you can also replace the locations of the libraries in the Eclipse project using **Properties | Java Build Path | Libraries**.

Now we can run the tests from the command line as we already discussed in previous chapters:

```
$ adb -e shell am instrument -w com.example.aatg.tc.test/android.test.InstrumentationTestRunner
```

Running the command we will obtain the tests results:

**com.example.aatg.tc.test.EditNumberTests:........**

**com.example.aatg.tc.test.TemperatureConverterActivityTests:..........**

**com.example.aatg.tc.test.TemperatureConverterApplicationTests:.....**

**com.example.aatg.tc.test.TemperatureConverterTests:....**

**Test results for InstrumentationTestRunner=..........................**

**Time: 12.125**


**OK (28 tests)**

We have done everything from the command line by just invoking some simple commands, which is what we were looking for in order to feed this into a **Continuous Integration** process.

# Git—the fast version control system

**Git** is a free and Open Source, distributed version control system designed to handle everything from small to very large projects with speed and efficiency. It is very simple to setup so I strongly recommend its use even for personal projects. There is no project simpler enough that could not benefit from the application of this tool. You can find information and downloads at http://git-scm.com/.

On the other hand, a version control system or VCS (also known as **Source Code Management** or **SCM**) is an unavoidable element for development projects where more than one developer is involved. Furthermore, even if it is possible to apply continuous integration with no VCS in place, as it is not a requisite clearly, is not a reasonable practice.

Other, and probably more traditional, options exist in the VCS arena such as Subversion or CVS that you are free to use if you feel more comfortable. Anyway, Git is used extensively by the Android project so it is worth investing some time to at least understand the basics.

Having said that and remembering that this is a very broad subject to justify a book in itself (and certainly there are some good books about it) we are discussing here the most basic topics and supplying examples to get you started if you haven't embraced this practice yet.

## Creating a local git repository

These are the simplest possible commands to create a local repository and populate it with the initial source code for our projects. In this case again we are using `TemperatureConverter` and `TemperatureConverterTest` projects created and used in previous chapters. We are selecting a directory named `git-repos` as the parent for both projects and copying the code we used in the previous section, where we built manually:

```
$ cd <path/to>/git-repos
$ mkdir TemperatureConverter
$ cd TemperatureConverter
$ git init
$ cp -a <path/to>/TemperatureConverter/. .
$ ant clean
$ rm local.properties
$ git add .
$ git commit -m "Initial commit"
```

*Chapter 8*

That is, we create the parent for the repositories, create the project directory, initialize the git repository, copy the initial content, clean our previous built, remove the `local.properties` file, add everything to the repository, and commit.

> The `local.properties` file must never be checked in a Version Control System as it contains information specific to your local configuration.

Then, the same should be done for the `TemperatureConverterTest` project:

```
$ cd <path/to>/git-repos
$ mkdir TemperatureConverterTest
$ cd TemperatureConverterTest
$ git init
$ cp -a <path/to>/TemperatureConverterTest/. .
$ ant clean
$ rm local.properties
$ git add .
$ git commit -m "Initial commit"
```

At this point we have two project repositories containing the initial source code for the `TemperatureConverter` and `TemperatureConverterTest` projects. We haven't altered their structure so they are also compatible with **Eclipse** and the **Android ADT** plugin to build while we develop in an IDE.

The next step is to have both projects built and tested automatically every time we commit a change to the source code.

# Continuous Integration with Hudson

**Hudson** is an Open Source, extensible **Continuous Integration** server which has the ability to build and test software projects or to monitor the execution of external jobs. Hudson has an easy installation and configuration and does a very decent job and this is the reason why we are basing our example on it.

> Recently (January 2011) a proposal was made to change the name from Hudson to Jenkins to avoid future legal problems as Oracle has submitted a trademark registration. Consequently now two different forked projects exist. Though these examples are based on Hudson you should monitor the evolution of the individual projects to find the one that better suites your needs.

## Installing and configuring Hudson

We mentioned easy installation as one of Hudson's advantages and installation could not be any easier.

Download the native package for the operating system of your choice from `http://hudson-ci.org/`. There are native packages for Debian/Ubuntu, RedHat/Fedora/Centos, openSUSE, OpenSolaris/Nevada, and FreeBSD or download the latest generic `hudson.war` (which will work on Mac and Windows as well). In the following examples we will be using version 2.0. We will show the latter as it is the one that does not require administrative privileges to install, configure, and run.

Once finished, copy it into a selected directory, let's say `~/hudson`, and then run the following:

```
$ java -jar hudson-2.0.0.war
```

This expands and starts Hudson.

The default configuration uses port 8080 as the HTTP listener port, so pointing your browser of choice to `http://localhost:8080` should present you with the Hudson home page.

You can verify and change Hudson's operating parameter if required, by accessing the **Manage Hudson** screen. We should add to this configuration the plugins needed for Git integration and support for Android emulator during builds. These plugins are named **Hudson GIT plugin** and **Android Emulator Plugin** respectively.

This screenshot displays the information you can obtain about the plugins following the hyperlinks available on the Hudson administration page:

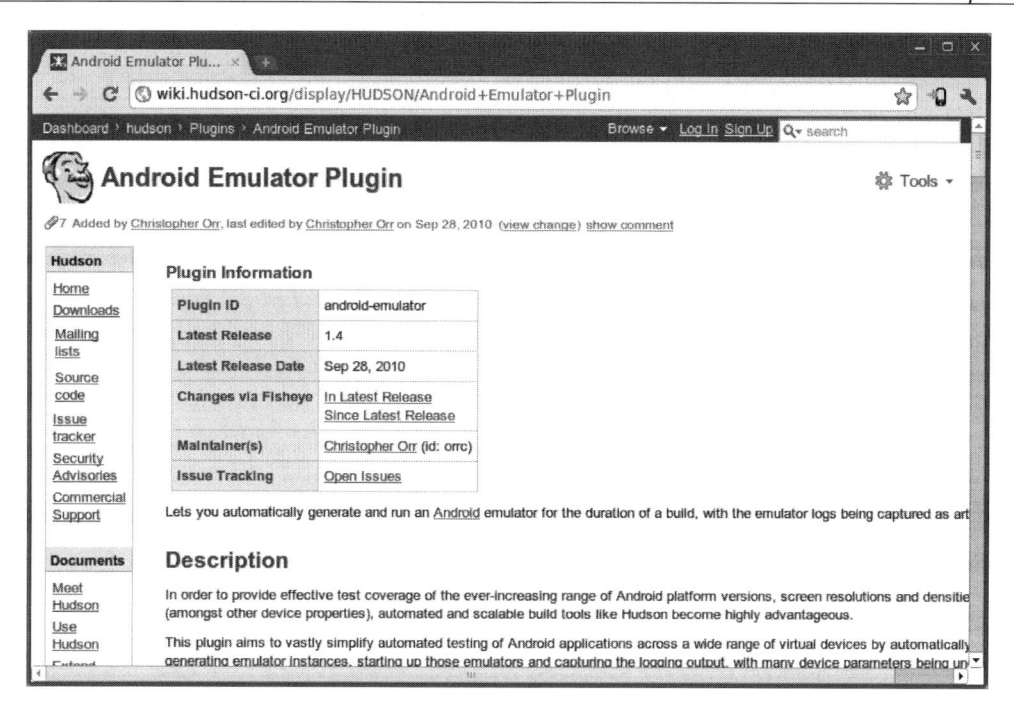

After installing and restarting Hudson these plugins will be available for use. Our next step is to create the jobs necessary to build the projects.

## Creating the jobs

Let's start by creating the `TemperatureConverter` job using **New Job in the Hudson home page**. Different kind of jobs can be created; in this case we are selecting **Build a free-style software project**, allowing you to connect any SCM with any build system.

## Continuous Integration

After clicking on the OK button you will be presented with the specific job options, which that are described in the following table. This is the job properties page:

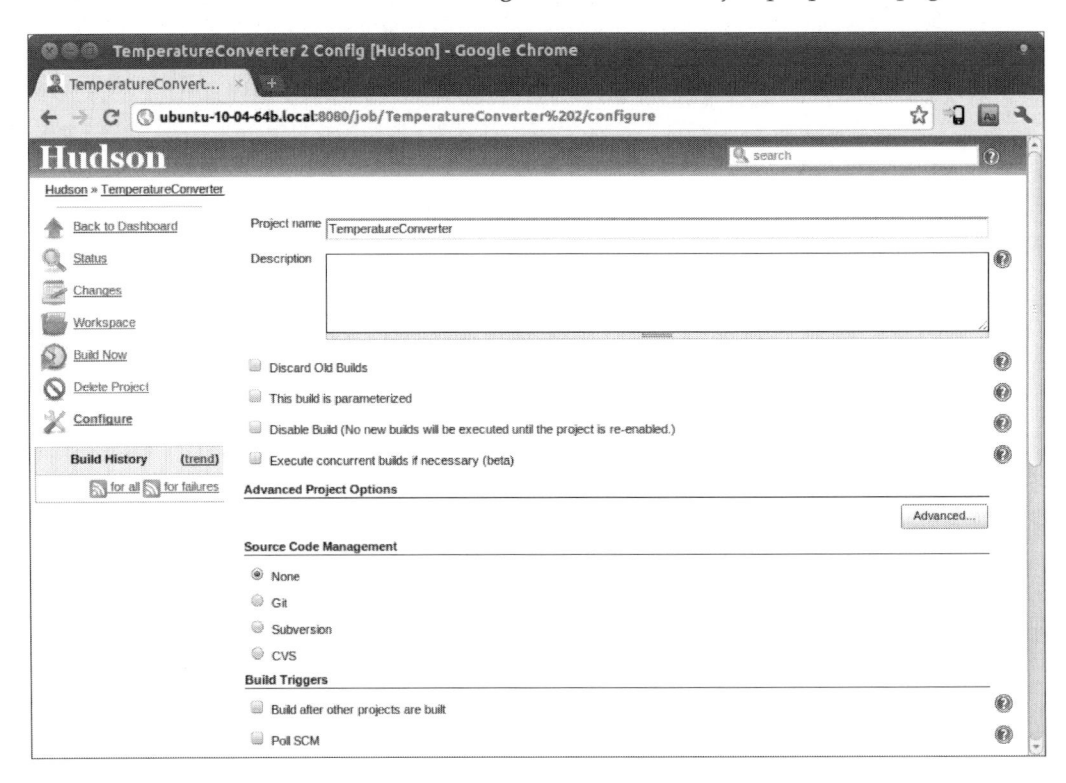

All of the options in the **New Job** screen have a help text associated, so here we are only explaining the ones we are entering:

| Option | Description |
| --- | --- |
| Project name | The name given to the project. |
| Description | Optional description. |
| Discard Old Builds | This helps you save on disk consumption by managing how long to keep records of the builds (such as console output, build artifacts, and so on.) |
| This build is parameterized | This allows you to configure parameters that are passed to the build process to create parameterized builds. |
| Disable Build (No new builds will be executed until the project is re-enabled.) | Temporarily disable the project. |
| Execute concurrent builds if necessary (beta) | This permits the execution of several builds concurrently. |

| Option | Description |
| --- | --- |
| Source Code Management | Also know as VCS. |
| | Where is the source code for the project? In this case we are using git and a repository where the URL is the absolute path of the repository we created earlier. For example, /home/diego/aatg/git-repos/TemperatureConverter. |
| Build Triggers | How this project is automatically built. In this case we want that every change in the source code triggers the automatic build so we are selecting **Poll SCM**.<br>The other option is to use **Build periodically**. This feature is primarily for using Hudson as a cron replacement, and it is not ideal for continuously building software projects. When people first start continuous integration, they are often so used to the idea of regularly scheduled builds like nightly/weekly that they use this feature. However, the point of continuous integration is to start a build as soon as a change is made, to provide a quick feedback to the change. |
| Schedule | This field follows the syntax of cron (with minor differences). Specifically, each line consists of five fields separated by TAB or whitespace:<br>MINUTE HOUR DOM MONTH DOW.<br><br>For example if we want to poll continuously at thirty minutes past the hour specify:<br>30 * * * *<br><br>Check the documentation for a complete explanation of all the options. |
| Build environment | Lets you specify different options for the build environment and for the Android emulator that may run during the build. |
| Build | This describes the build steps. We are selecting **Invoke Ant** as we are reproducing the steps we did before to manually build the project.<br><br>The target we use here is debug as we only want to compile the project and generate the APK, and not install or run it. Additionally, using the **Advanced...** options we need to specify the Android SDK directory and the Android target version **Properties**.<br><br>sdk.dir=/opt/android-sdk<br>target=android-9 |
| Post build actions | These are a series of actions we can do after the build is done. We are interested in saving the APKs so we are enabling **Archive the artifacts** and then defining the path for them as **Files to archive**; in this precise case it is **/*-debug.apk. |

*Continuous Integration*

Now there are two options: you can force a build using **Build now**, or introduce some changes to the source code through Git and wait for them to be detected by our polling strategy. Either way, we would get our project built and our artifacts ready to be used for other purposes, such as dependency projects or QA.

So far we haven't run any tests and this is just what we are presenting now. Hudson has the ability to handle dependencies between projects, so we are now creating a Hudson job, `TemperatureConverterTest` depending on `TemperatureConverter`.

Proceed in the same way as before. We are only pinpointing the differences in setting up this project against the previous setup.

| Option | Description |
| --- | --- |
| Build Triggers | This is how we trigger the build of this project. **Built after other projects are built** is selected so that when some other projects finish building, a new build is scheduled for this project. We need this to be built after `TemperatureConverter`. |
| | This is convenient for running an extensive test after a build is complete as in this example. |
| Build environment | Our intention is to install and run the tests on an emulator so for our build environment we use the facilities provided by the **Android Emulator Plugin**. This comes in handy if you wish to automatically start an Android emulator of your choice before the build steps execute, with the emulator being stopped after building is complete. |
| | You can choose to start a pre-defined, existing Android emulator instance (AVD). |
| | Alternatively, the plugin can automatically create a new emulator on the build slave with properties you specify here. |
| | In any case, the `logcat` output will automatically be captured and archived. |
| | Then select 2.3 for the **Android OS version**, 240 DPI for the **Screen density** and WVGA for **Screen resolution**. |
| | Feel free to experiment and select the options that better suit your needs. |
| Common emulator options | We would like to **Reset emulator state at start-up** to wipe user data and disable **Show emulator window**, so the emulator window is not displayed. |

| Option | Description |
| --- | --- |
| Build | Select **Invoke ant** as the build step and `install` as the **Target**. Here again, as we did in `TemperatureConverter`, we have to set some variables to build and install the current job. Using the **Advanced...** options set:<br><br>`sdk.dir=/opt/android-sdk`<br><br>`target=android-9`<br><br>`tested.project.dir=../../TemperatureConverter/workspace/`<br><br>`adb.device.arg=-s $ANDROID_AVD_DEVICE`<br><br>As before, we specified the Android SDK directory and the target version. Additionally, here we should specify the target project directory, that is the SUT, and the device where we want to install the APK. We are using a special variable set by the **Android Emulator Plugin** to identify the ADV that was chosen as the target. |

After configuring and building this project, we have the APK installed on the target emulator. Some steps are still needed as we still miss running the tests and obtaining the results to be displayed in Hudson.

## Obtaining Android test results

To be able to display test results we should store raw XML results in the test runner. The default `android.test.InstrumentationTestRunner` does not support storing raw XML so the solution here is to extend it to provide the missing functionality.

I found the `nbandroid-utils` (http://code.google.com/p/nbandroid-utils/) project hosted in Google code that provides almost the same functionality that we need.

The `com.neenbedankt.android.test.InstrumentationTestRunner` class extends the Android one so that an XML of the test results is written to the device when running the tests.

We also want the ability to specify the filename from the test arguments and be able to store files in external storage just in case test results become very large, so we are slightly modifying the class to support these features. Also, to make these changes evident we are naming the new class `XMLInstrumentationTestRunner`:

```java
package com.neenbedankt.android.test;

import java.io.File;
import java.io.FileWriter;
import java.io.IOException;
import java.io.Writer;

import org.xmlpull.v1.XmlPullParserFactory;
import org.xmlpull.v1.XmlSerializer;

import android.os.Bundle;
import android.util.Log;
/*
 * Copyright (C) 2010 Diego Torres Milano
 *
 * Base on previous work by
 * Copyright (C) 2007 Hugo Visser
 *
 * Licensed under the Apache License, Version 2.0 (the "License");
 * you may not use this file except in compliance with the License.
 * You may obtain a copy of the License at
 *
 *      http://www.apache.org/licenses/LICENSE-2.0
 *
 * Unless required by applicable law or agreed to in writing,
 * software distributed under the License is distributed on an
 * "AS IS" BASIS,WITHOUT WARRANTIES OR CONDITIONS OF ANY KIND,
 * either express or implied.
 * See the License for the specific language governing permissions
 * and limitations under the License.
 */
/**
 * This test runner creates an xml in the files directory of
 * the application under test. The output is compatible with
 * that of the junitreport ant task, the format that is
 * understood by Hudson. Currently this implementation does not
 * implement the all aspects of the junitreport format, but
 * enough for Hudson to parse the test results.
 */
public class XMLInstrumentationTestRunner extends android.test.InstrumentationTestRunner {
    private Writer mWriter;
    private XmlSerializer mTestSuiteSerializer;
    private long mTestStarted;
```

Here we are providing the field to keep the name of the output file as well as its default value.

We are also defining the name of the argument our test runner will use to receive this value:

```
/**
 * Output file name.
 */
private String mOutFileName;
/**
 * Outfile argument name.
 * This argument can be passed to the instrumentation using
     <code>-e</code>.
 */
private static final String OUT_FILE_ARG = "outfile";
/**
 * Default output file name.
 */
private static final String OUT_FILE_DEFAULT = "test-results.xml";
```

In our `onCreate()` method we verify if the argument has been provided and if so we store it in the previously defined field:

```
@Override
public void onCreate(Bundle arguments) {
  if ( arguments != null ) {
    mOutFileName = arguments.getString(OUT_FILE_ARG);
  }
  if ( mOutFileName == null ) {
    mOutFileName = OUT_FILE_DEFAULT;
  }
  super.onCreate(arguments);
}
```

In the `onStart()` method we create the file and we use it as the JUnit output:

```
@Override
public void onStart() {
  try {
    File dir = getTargetContext().getExternalFilesDir(null);
    if ( dir == null ) {
      dir = getTargetContext().getFilesDir();
    }
```

## Continuous Integration

```java
      final File outFile = new File(dir, mOutFileName);
      startJUnitOutput(new FileWriter(outFile));
    } catch (IOException e) {
      throw new RuntimeException(e);
    }
    super.onStart();
  }
```

The following code is the original code for this test runner:

```java
    void startJUnitOutput(Writer writer) {
      try {
        mWriter = writer;
        mTestSuiteSerializer = newSerializer(mWriter);
        mTestSuiteSerializer.startDocument(null, null);
        mTestSuiteSerializer.startTag(null, "testsuites");
        mTestSuiteSerializer.startTag(null, "testsuite");
      } catch (Exception e) {
        throw new RuntimeException(e);
      }
    }

    private XmlSerializer newSerializer(Writer writer) {
      try {
        XmlPullParserFactory pf =
          XmlPullParserFactory.newInstance();
        XmlSerializer serializer = pf.newSerializer();
        serializer.setOutput(writer);
        return serializer;
      } catch (Exception e) {
        throw new RuntimeException(e);
      }
    }

    @Override
    public void sendStatus(int resultCode, Bundle results) {
      super.sendStatus(resultCode, results);
      switch (resultCode) {
        case REPORT_VALUE_RESULT_ERROR:
        case REPORT_VALUE_RESULT_FAILURE:
        case REPORT_VALUE_RESULT_OK:
        try {
          recordTestResult(resultCode, results);
        } catch (IOException e) {
          throw new RuntimeException(e);
        }
```

```
      break;
    case REPORT_VALUE_RESULT_START:
        recordTestStart(results);
    default:
    break;
  }
}
void recordTestStart(Bundle results) {
  mTestStarted = System.currentTimeMillis();
}
void recordTestResult(int resultCode, Bundle results)
throws IOException {
  float time = (System.currentTimeMillis() -
    mTestStarted) / 1000.0f;
  String className = results.getString(REPORT_KEY_NAME_CLASS);
  String testMethod = results.getString(REPORT_KEY_NAME_TEST);
  String stack = results.getString(REPORT_KEY_STACK);
  int current = results.getInt(REPORT_KEY_NUM_CURRENT);
  int total = results.getInt(REPORT_KEY_NUM_TOTAL);

  mTestSuiteSerializer.startTag(null, "testcase");
  mTestSuiteSerializer.attribute(null, "classname", className);
  mTestSuiteSerializer.attribute(null, "name", testMethod);

  if (resultCode != REPORT_VALUE_RESULT_OK) {
    mTestSuiteSerializer.startTag(null, "failure");
    if (stack != null) {
      String reason = stack.substring(0,
        stack.indexOf('\n'));
      String message = "";
      int index = reason.indexOf(':');
      if (index > -1) {
        message = reason.substring(index+1);
        reason = reason.substring(0, index);
      }
      mTestSuiteSerializer.attribute(null,
        "message", message);
      mTestSuiteSerializer.attribute(null, "type", reason);
      mTestSuiteSerializer.text(stack);
    }
    mTestSuiteSerializer.endTag(null, "failure");
  } else {
    mTestSuiteSerializer.attribute(null,
      "time", String.format("%.3f", time));
  }
```

```
            mTestSuiteSerializer.endTag(null, "testcase");
            if (current == total) {
              mTestSuiteSerializer.startTag(null, "system-out");
              mTestSuiteSerializer.endTag(null, "system-out");
              mTestSuiteSerializer.startTag(null, "system-err");
              mTestSuiteSerializer.endTag(null, "system-err");
              mTestSuiteSerializer.endTag(null, "testsuite");
              mTestSuiteSerializer.flush();
            }
        }
        @Override
        public void finish(int resultCode, Bundle results) {
           endTestSuites();
           super.finish(resultCode, results);
        }
        void endTestSuites() {
          try {
            if ( mTestSuiteSerializer != null ) {
              mTestSuiteSerializer.endTag(null, "testsuites");
              mTestSuiteSerializer.endDocument();
              mTestSuiteSerializer.flush();
            }
            if ( mWriter != null) {
              mWriter.flush();
              mWriter.close();
            }
          } catch (IOException e) {
            throw new RuntimeException(e);
          }
        }
    }
```

There are still a few steps required to achieve our objective. The first is to add this test runner to our project using the combination `git add`/`git commit`.

You can simply use these commands:

```
$ git add src/com/neenbedankt/
$ git commit -a -m "Added XMLInstrumentationTestRunner"
```

Then we need to declare the instrumentation using the test runner in `AndroidManifest.xml`. That is use the recently created test runner `com.neenbedankt.android.test.XMLInstrumentationTestRunner` as the instrumentation for the `com.example.aatg.tc` package:

```
<instrumentation
    android:targetPackage="com.example.aatg.tc"
    android:label="TemperatureConverter tests"
    android:name="com.neenbedankt.android.test.
        XMLInstrumentationTestRunner"
/>
```

Also, add it to the repository as we did before with other files.

And finally, as we have the ability to add a step in the build process by using **Add build step** that executes arbitrary commands in a shell script, we add this as an **Execute shell** step in the job configuration page. We are using some shell variables to be able to re-utilize this step for other projects:

```
PKG=com.example.aatg.tc
OUTDIR=/data/data/${PKG}/files/
OUTFILE=test-results.xml
ADB=/opt/android-sdk/platform-tools/adb
$ADB -s $ANDROID_AVD_DEVICE install -r "$WORKSPACE/../../
  TemperatureConverter/lastSuccessful/
  archive/bin/TemperatureConverter-debug.apk"
$ADB -s $ANDROID_AVD_DEVICE shell am instrument -w -e
outfile "$OUTFILE" $PKG.test/com.neenbedankt.android.test.
XMLInstrumentationTestRunner
$ADB -s $ANDROID_AVD_DEVICE pull "$OUTDIR/$OUTFILE"
"$WORKSPACE/$OUTFILE"
```

Let us explain these steps in greater detail:

- We assign a specific project package name to PKG variable.
- OUTDIR is the name of the directory where the test runner will leave the file OUTFILE. Note that this is a directory on the emulator or device, not a local directory.
- Install the package under test onto the emulator or device.
- Run the instrumentation from the command line, as we have seen previously, but in this case adding an extra argument -e outfile with the name of the file we are expecting to receive.
- Get the test results from that file, pulling from the device to the local workspace.

*Continuous Integration*

Almost everything is in place. The only thing left is to tell Hudson where to expect these test results. In this scenario we use the **Post Build Actions also in the job configuration page**.

| Option | Description |
|---|---|
| Publish Junit test results report | When this option is configured, Hudson can provide useful information about test results, such as historical test result trends, a web UI for viewing test reports, tracking failures, and so on. |
| | To use this feature, first set up your build to run tests, then use `com.neenbedankt.android.test.XMLInstrumentationTestRunner` as the test runner, specify the output using `-e outfile` in the instrumentation, and use this same name to tell Hudson where to find the results. Ant glob syntax, such as `**/build/test-reports/*.xml`, can also be used. |
| | Be sure not to include any non-report files into this pattern. |
| | In simple terms, this is simply `test-results.xml` as we specified in the `OUTFILE` variable before. |
| | Once there are a few builds running with test results, you should start seeing some trend charts displaying the evolution of tests. |

Having done all of the steps described before, only forcing a build is left to see the results. Press **Build now** as usual and after a few moments you will see your test results and statistics displayed in a similar way as the following screenshot depicts:

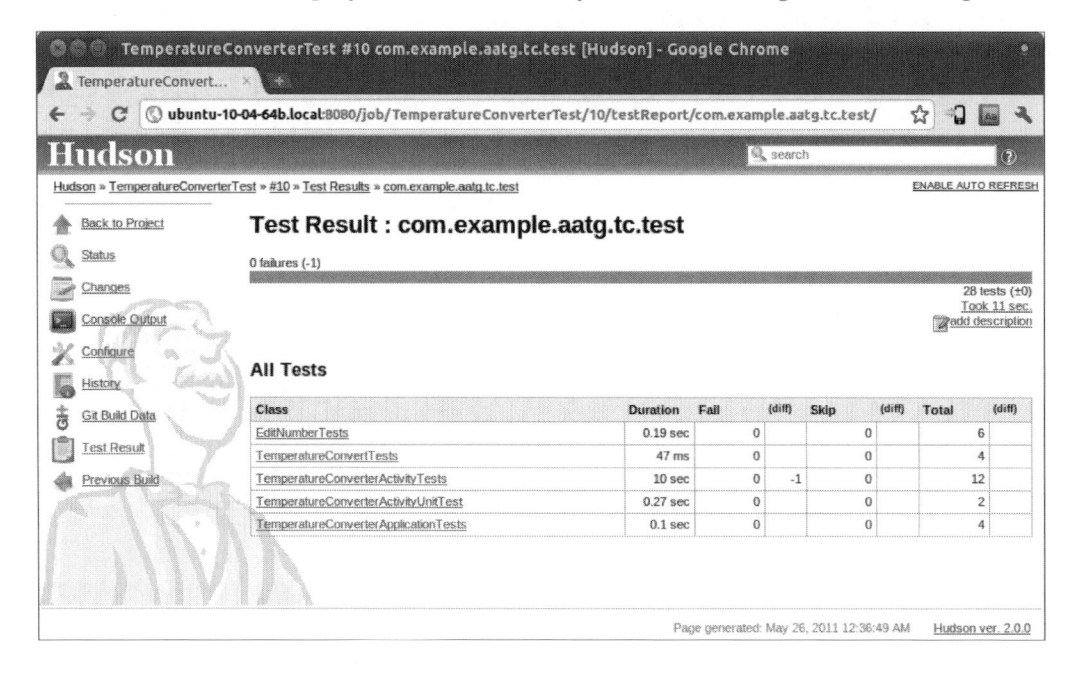

**Test Result : com.example.aatg.tc.test**

0 failures (-1)

28 tests (±0)
Took 11 sec.

**All Tests**

| Class | Duration | Fail | (diff) | Skip | (diff) | Total | (diff) |
|---|---|---|---|---|---|---|---|
| EditNumberTests | 0.19 sec | 0 | | 0 | | 6 | |
| TemperatureConvertTests | 47 ms | 0 | | 0 | | 4 | |
| TemperatureConverterActivityTests | 10 sec | 0 | -1 | 0 | | 12 | |
| TemperatureConverterActivityUnitTest | 0.27 sec | 0 | | 0 | | 2 | |
| TemperatureConverterApplicationTests | 0.1 sec | 0 | | 0 | | 4 | |

**[ 238 ]**

From here we can easily understand our project status, knowing how many tests failed and why. Digging through the failed tests we can also find the extensive **Error message** and **Stack trace**.

It is also really helpful to understand the evolution of a project through the evaluation of different trends and Hudson is able to provide such information. Every project presents the current trends using weather-like icons from sunny, when the health of the project increases 80%, and to thunderstorm when the health lies bellow 20%. In addition, for every project the evolution of the trend of the tests success versus failure ratio is displayed in a chart that is reproduced here:

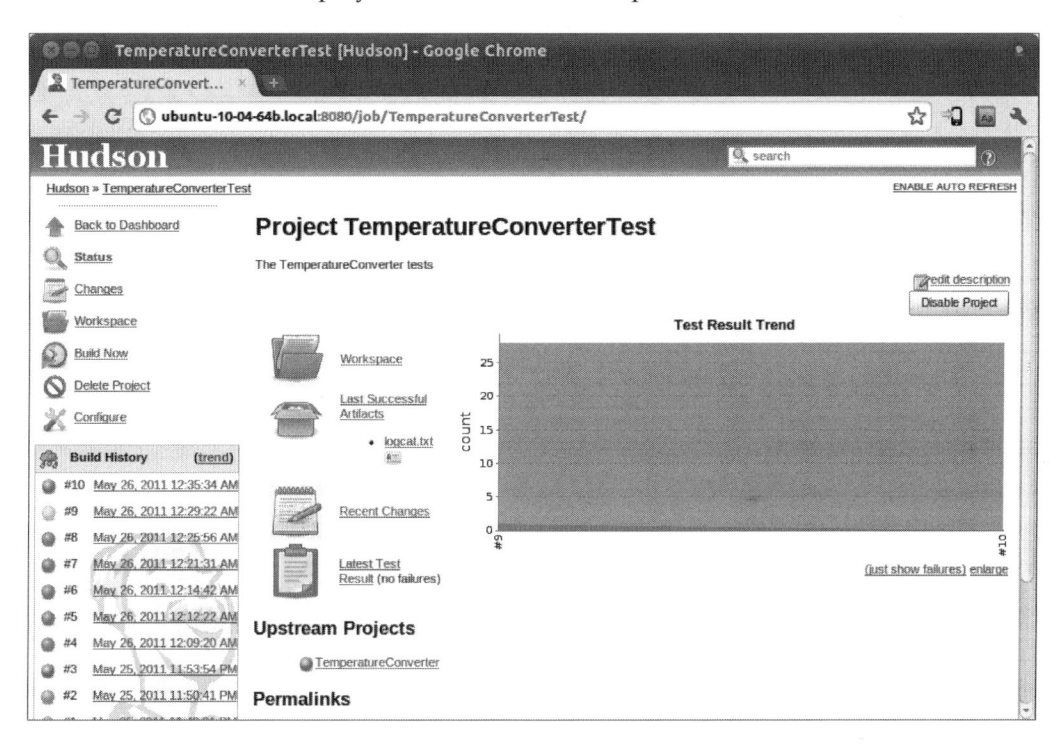

In this case we can see how since the last build, one test started to fail.

To see how a project status changes by forcing a failure let's add a failing test like the following:

```
public final void testForceFailure1() {
  fail("Forced fail");
}
```

*Continuous Integration*

Yet another very interesting feature that is worth mentioning is the ability of Hudson to keep and display the Timeline and Build Time Trend, as shown in the following screenshot:

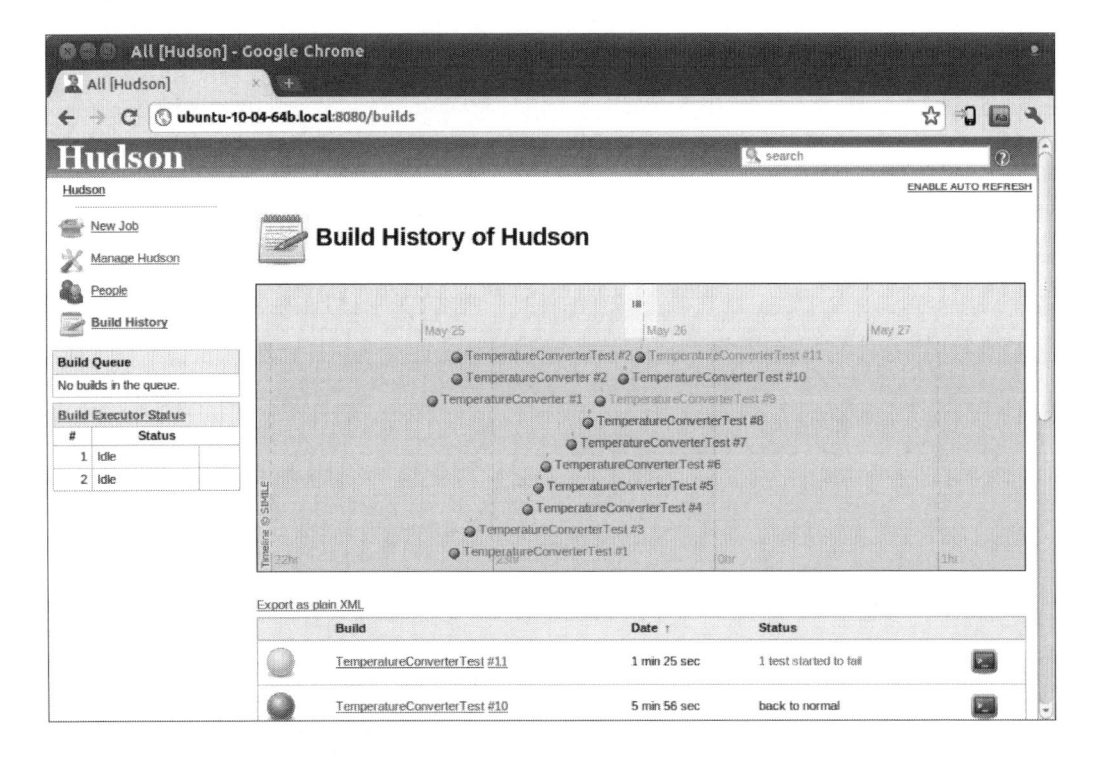

This page presents the build history with hyperlinks to every particular build that you can follow to see the details.

Now we have less concern to be worried about and every time somebody in the developer team commits changes to the repository we know that these changes will be immediately integrated and the whole project will be built and tested and if we further configure Hudson we can even receive the status by e-mail. To achieve this, in the job configuration page enable **E-mail Notification** and enter the desired **Recipients**.

## Summary

This chapter has introduced **Continuous Integration** in practice providing valuable information to start applying it soon to your projects no matter what their size is, whether you are developing solo or on a big company team.

The techniques presented focus on the particularities of Android projects maintaining and supporting widely used development tools like Eclipse and Android ADT.

We introduced real-world examples with real-world tools available from the vast Open Source arsenal. We employed Ant to automate the building process, git to create a simple version control system repository to store our source code and manage the changes, and finally installed and configured Hudson as the Continuous Integration of choice.

In this course we detailed the creation of jobs for automating the creation of `TemperatureConverter` and its tests and we emphasized on the relationship between the projects.

Finally, we analyzed a way of getting XML results from Android tests and implemented this to obtain an attractive interface to monitor the running of tests, their results, and the existing trends.

The next chapter deals with a different aspect of testing concentrating on performance and profiling which is probably the natural step to follow after we have our application behaving correctly and according to our specifications.

# 9
# Performance Testing and Profiling

In the previous chapters, we studied and developed tests for our Android application. Those tests let us evaluate the compliance to a certain number of specifications and allow us to determine if the software is behaving correctly or according to these rules by taking a binary verdict, whether it complies or not. If it does the software is correct; if it does not we have to fix it until it does.

In many other cases, mainly after we have verified that the software conforms to all these specifications, we want to move forward and know how or in what manner they are satisfied, and at the same time how the system performs under different situations to analyze other attributes such as usability, speed, response time, and reliability.

According to Android Developer's Guide (`http://developer.android.com/guide/index.html`), these are the best practices when it comes to designing our application:

- Designing for performance
- Designing for responsiveness
- Designing for seamlessness

It's extremely important to follow these best practices and start thinking mainly in terms of performance and responsiveness from the very beginning of the design. Since our application will run on mobile devices with limited computer power, the bigger gains are obtained by identifying the targets for the optimization once our application is built, at least partially, and applying the performance testing that we will be discussing soon.

As Donald Knuth popularized years ago:

> "*Premature optimization is the root of all evil*".

These optimizations, which are based on guesses, intuition, and even superstition often interfere with the design over short term periods, and with readability and maintainability over long term periods. On the contrary, *micro-optimizations* are based on identifying the bottlenecks or hot-spots that require optimization, apply the changes, and then benchmark again to evaluate the improvements of the optimization. So the point we are concentrating on here is on measuring the existing performance and the optimization alternatives.

This chapter will introduce a series of concepts related to benchmarking and profiles as follows:

- Traditional logging statement methods
- Creating Android performance tests
- Using profiling tools
- Microbenchmarks using Caliper

## Ye Olde Logge method

Sometimes this is too simplistic for real scenarios but I'm not going to say that it could not help in some cases mainly because its implementation takes minutes and you only need the `logcat` text output to analyze the case, which comes in handy during situations as described in previous chapters where you want to automate procedures or apply Continuous Integration.

This method consists in timing a method, and or a part of it, surrounding it by two time measures and logging the difference at the end:

```
/* (non-Javadoc)
 * @see android.text.TextWatcher#onTextChanged(
 * java.lang.CharSequence, int, int, int)
 */
public void onTextChanged(CharSequence s, int start,
   int before, int count) {
   if (!mDest.hasWindowFocus() || mDest.hasFocus() ||
      s == null ) {
      return;
   }
   final String str = s.toString();
   if ( "".equals(str) ) {
```

```
        mDest.setText("");
        return;
      }
      final long t0;
      if ( BENCHMARK_TEMPERATURE_CONVERSION ) {
        t0 = System.currentTimeMillis();
      }

      try {
        final double temp = Double.parseDouble(str);
        final double result = (mOp == OP.C2F) ?
          TemperatureConverter.celsiusToFahrenheit(temp) :
          TemperatureConverter.fahrenheitToCelsius(temp);
        final String resultString = String.format("%.2f", result);
        mDest.setNumber(result);
        mDest.setSelection(resultString.length());
      } catch (NumberFormatException e) {
        // WARNING
        // this is generated while a number is entered,
        // for example just a '-'
        // so we don't want to show the error
      } catch (Exception e) {
        mSource.setError("ERROR: " + e.getLocalizedMessage());
      }
      if ( BENCHMARK_TEMPERATURE_CONVERSION ) {
        long t = System.currentTimeMillis() - t0;
        Log.i(TAG, "TemperatureConversion took " + t +
          " ms to complete.");
      }
    }
```

This is very straightforward. We take the times and log the difference. For this we are using the Log.i() method and we can see the output in logcat while we run the application. You can control the execution of this benchmark by setting true or false to the BENCHMARK_TEMPERATURE_CONVERSION constant that you should have defined elsewhere.

When we launch the activity with the BENCHMARK_TEMPERATURE_CONVERSION constant set to true in the logcat, we will receive messages like these every time the conversion takes place:

**INFO/TemperatureConverterActivity(392): TemperatureConversion took 55 ms to complete.**

INFO/TemperatureConverterActivity(392): TemperatureConversion took 11 ms to complete.

INFO/TemperatureConverterActivity(392): TemperatureConversion took 5 ms to complete.

Something you should take into account is that these benchmark-enabling constants should not be enabled in the production build, as other common constants are used like DEBUG or LOGD. To avoid this mistake you should integrate the verification of these constants values in the build process you are using for automated builds such as Ant or Make.

Pretty simple, but this would not apply for more complex cases.

# Performance tests in Android SDK

If the previous method of adding log statements does not suit you, there is a different method of getting performance test results from our application.

Unfortunately, performance tests in Android SDK are half baked (at least up to Android 2.3 Gingerbread, the latest version available at the time this book was written). There is no reasonable way of getting performance test results from an Android SDK application as the classes used by Android tests are hidden in the Android SDK and only available to system applications, that is to applications that are built as part of the main build or system image. This strategy is not available for SDK applications so we are not digging deeper in that direction and we will focus on other available choices.

## Launching the performance test

These tests are based on a similar approach like the one used by Android to test system applications. The idea is to extend `android.app.Instrumentation` to provide performance snapshots, automatically creating a framework that we can even extend to satisfy other needs. We are presenting a simple case here due to the limitations imposed by this medium.

## Creating the LaunchPerformanceBase instrumentation

Our first step is to extend `Instrumentation` to provide the functionality we need. We are using a new package named `com.example.aatg.tc.test.launchperf` to keep our tests organized:

```
package com.example.aatg.tc.test.launchperf;
import android.app.Instrumentation;
import android.content.Intent;
import android.os.Bundle;
import android.util.Log;
/**
 * Base class for all launch performance Instrumentation classes.
 */
public class LaunchPerformanceBase extends Instrumentation {
  public static final String TAG = "LaunchPerformanceBase";
  protected Bundle mResults;
  protected Intent mIntent;
  /**
   * Constructor.
   */
  public LaunchPerformanceBase() {
    mResults = new Bundle();
    mIntent = new Intent(Intent.ACTION_MAIN);
    mIntent.setFlags(Intent.FLAG_ACTIVITY_NEW_TASK);
    setAutomaticPerformanceSnapshots();
  }
  /**
   * Launches intent {@link #mIntent}, and waits for idle before
   * returning.
   */
  protected void LaunchApp() {
    startActivitySync(mIntent);
    waitForIdleSync();
  }
  @Override
  public void finish(int resultCode, Bundle results) {
    Log.v(TAG, "Test reults = " + results);
    super.finish(resultCode, results);
  }
}
```

We are extending `Instrumentation` here. The constructor initialized the two fields in this class: `mResults` and `mIntent`. At the end we invoke the method `setAutomaticPerformanceSnapshots()` which is the key here to create this performance test.

*Performance Testing and Profiling*

The method `LaunchApp()` is in charge of starting the desired `Activity` and waiting before returning.

The `finish()` method logs the results received and then invokes `Instrumentation`'s `finish()`.

# Creating the TemperatureConverterActivityLaunchPerformance class

This class sets up the `Intent` to invoke the `TemperatureConverterActivity` and furnish the infrastructure provided by the `LaunchPerformanceBase` class to test the performance of launching our `Activity`:

```
package com.example.aatg.tc.test.launchperf;

import com.example.aatg.tc.TemperatureConverterActivity;
import android.app.Activity;
import android.os.Bundle;
/**
 * Instrumentation class for {@link TemperatureConverterActivity}
 launch performance testing.
 */
public class TemperatureConverterActivityLaunchPerformance extends
LaunchPerformanceBase {
  /**
   * Constructor.
   */
  public TemperatureConverterActivityLaunchPerformance() {
    super();
  }

  @Override
  public void onCreate(Bundle arguments) {
    super.onCreate(arguments);

    mIntent.setClassName("com.example.aatg.tc",
      "com.example.aatg.tc.TemperatureConverterActivity");
    start();
  }
  /**
   * Calls LaunchApp and finish.
   */
  @Override
  public void onStart() {
```

```
        super.onStart();
        LaunchApp();
        finish(Activity.RESULT_OK, mResults);
    }
}
```

Here, `onCreate()` calls `super.onCreate()` as the Android lifecycle dictates. Then the `Intent` is set, specifying the class name and the package. Then one of the `Instrumentation`'s methods is called, `start()`, which creates and starts a new thread in which to run instrumentation. This new thread will make a call to `onStart()`, where you can implement the instrumentation.

Then `onStart()` implementation follows, invoking `LaunchApp()` and `finish()`.

## Running the tests

To be able to run this test we need to define the specific `Instrumentation` in the `AndroidManifest.xml` of the `TemperatureConverterTest` project.

This is the snippet of code we have to add to the manifest:

```
<?xml version="1.0" encoding="utf-8"?>
<manifest xmlns:android="http://schemas.android.com/apk/res/android"
   package="com.example.aatg.tc.test" android:versionCode="1"
   android:versionName="1.0">

   <application android:icon="@drawable/icon"
      android:label="@string/app_name">
      <uses-library android:name="android.test.runner" />
   </application>

   <uses-sdk android:minSdkVersion="9" />
   <instrumentation android:targetPackage="com.example.aatg.tc"
      android:name="android.test.InstrumentationTestRunner"
      android:label="Temperature Converter Activity Tests"
      android:icon="@drawable/icon" />

   <instrumentation android:targetPackage="com.example.aatg.tc"
      android:label="Temperature Converter Activity Launch Performance"
      android:name=".launchperf.TermeratureConverterActivity
      LaunchPerformance" />

</manifest>
```

Once everything is in place we are ready to start running the test.

## Performance Testing and Profiling

First, install the APK that includes these changes. Then, we have several options to run the tests as we have reviewed in previous chapters. In this case we are using the command line as it is the easiest way of getting all the details. Replace the serial number for what is applicable in your case:

```
$ adb -s emulator-5554 shell am instrument -w com.example.aatg.tc.test/.
launchperf.TermeratureConverterActivityLaunchPerformance
```

We receive the set of results for this test in the standard output:

```
INSTRUMENTATION_RESULT: other_pss=13430
INSTRUMENTATION_RESULT: java_allocated=2565
INSTRUMENTATION_RESULT: global_freed_size=16424
INSTRUMENTATION_RESULT: native_private_dirty=504
INSTRUMENTATION_RESULT: native_free=6
INSTRUMENTATION_RESULT: global_alloc_count=810
INSTRUMENTATION_RESULT: other_private_dirty=12436
INSTRUMENTATION_RESULT: global_freed_count=328
INSTRUMENTATION_RESULT: sent_transactions=-1
INSTRUMENTATION_RESULT: java_free=2814
INSTRUMENTATION_RESULT: received_transactions=-1
INSTRUMENTATION_RESULT: pre_sent_transactions=-1
INSTRUMENTATION_RESULT: other_shared_dirty=5268
INSTRUMENTATION_RESULT: pre_received_transactions=-1
INSTRUMENTATION_RESULT: execution_time=4563
INSTRUMENTATION_RESULT: native_size=11020
INSTRUMENTATION_RESULT: native_shared_dirty=1296
INSTRUMENTATION_RESULT: cpu_time=1761
INSTRUMENTATION_RESULT: java_private_dirty=52
INSTRUMENTATION_RESULT: native_allocated=11013
INSTRUMENTATION_RESULT: gc_invocation_count=0
INSTRUMENTATION_RESULT: java_shared_dirty=1860
INSTRUMENTATION_RESULT: global_alloc_size=44862
INSTRUMENTATION_RESULT: java_pss=1203
INSTRUMENTATION_RESULT: java_size=5379
INSTRUMENTATION_RESULT: native_pss=660
INSTRUMENTATION_CODE: -1
```

We have highlighted two of the values we are interested in: **execution_time** and **cpu_time**. They account for the total execution time and the CPU time used respectively.

Running this test on an emulator increases the potential for mis-measurement, because the host computer is running other processes that also take on the CPU, and the emulator does not necessarily represent the performance of a real piece of hardware.

Because of this we are taking these two measures into account. The `execution_time` gives us the real time and `cpu_time` the total time used by the CPU to compute our code.

Needless to say, that in this and any other case where you measure something that is variable over time, you should use a measurement strategy and run the test several times to obtain different statistical values, such as average or standard deviation.

Unfortunately, the current implementation of Android ADT does not allow using an instrumentation that does not extend `android.test.InstrumentationTestRunner`, though `.launchperf.TemperatureConverterActivityLaunchPerformance` extends `LaunchPerformaceBase` that extends `Instrumentation`.

This screenshot shows the error trying to define this Instrumentation in Eclipse Run Configurations:

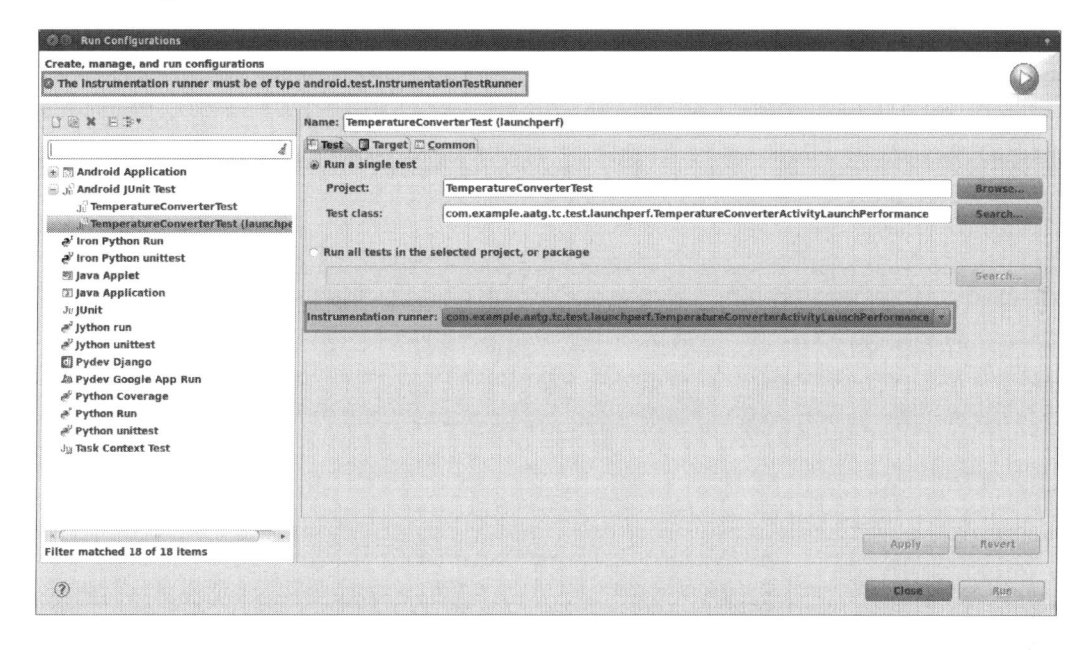

# Using the Traceview and dmtracedump platform tools

The Android SDK includes among its various tools two that are specially intended to analyze performance problems and potentially determine the target to apply optimizations.

## Performance Testing and Profiling

These tools have an advantage over other alternatives: usually no modification to the source code is needed for simpler tasks. However, for more complex cases some additions are needed, but they are very simple as we will see shortly.

If you don't need precision about starting and stopping tracing, you can drive it from the command line or Eclipse. For example, to start tracing from the command line you can use the following command. Remember to replace the serial number for what is applicable in your case:

```
$ adb -s emulator-5554 am start -n com.example.aatg.tc/.TemperatureConverterActivity
$ adb -s emulator-5554 shell am profile com.example.aatg.tc start /mnt/sdcard/tc.trace
```

Do something, for example enter a temperature in the Celsius field to force a conversion.

```
$ adb -s emulator-5554 shell am profile com.example.aatg.tc stop
$ adb -s emulator-5554 pull /mnt/sdcard/tc.trace /tmp/tc.trace
1132 KB/s (2851698 bytes in 2.459s)
$ traceview /tmp/tc.trace
```

Otherwise, if you need more precision about when profiling starts, you can add this piece of code instead of the previous one:

```
        @Override
        public void onTextChanged(CharSequence s, int start,
          int before, int count) {
          if (!dest.hasWindowFocus() || dest.hasFocus() || s == null ) {
            return;
          }
          final String ss = s.toString();
          if ( "".equals(ss) ) {
            dest.setText("");
            return;
          }
          if ( BENCHMARK_TEMPERATURE_CONVERSION ) {
            Debug.startMethodTracing();
          }
          try {
            final double result = (Double) convert.invoke(
              TemperatureConverter.class, Double.parseDouble(ss));
            dest.setNumber(result);
```

## Chapter 9

```
        dest.setSelection(dest.getText().toString().length());
    } catch (NumberFormatException e) {
        // WARNING
        // this is generated while a number is entered,
        //for example just a '-'
        // so we don't want to show the error
    } catch (Exception e) {
        dest.setError(e.getCause().getLocalizedMessage());
    }
    if ( BENCHMARK_TEMPERATURE_CONVERSION ) {
      Debug.stopMethodTracing();
    }
}
```

This will create a trace file, using the default name `dmtrace.trace` in the Sdcard by invoking `Debug.startMethodTracing()`, which starts method tracing with the default log name and buffer size. When we are done, we call `Debug.stopMethodTracing()` to stop the profiling.

> To be able to write to the Sdcard the application requires a `android.permission.WRITE_EXTERNAL_STORAGE` permission added in the manifest.
>
> For VMs earlier than Android 2.2, the permission is required even for doing this from Eclipse as the file is also generated. Starting with Android 2.2, the stream is sent through the JDWP connection and the permission is not needed anymore.

You need to exercise the application in order to obtain the trace file. This file needs to be pulled to the development computer to be further analyzed using `traceview`:

```
$ adb -s emulator-5554 pull /mnt/sdcard/dmtrace.trace /tmp/dmtrace.trace
375 KB/s (50664 bytes in 0.131s)
$ traceview /tmp/dmtrace.trace
```

[ 253 ]

*Performance Testing and Profiling*

After running this command `traceview`'s window appears displaying all the information collected:

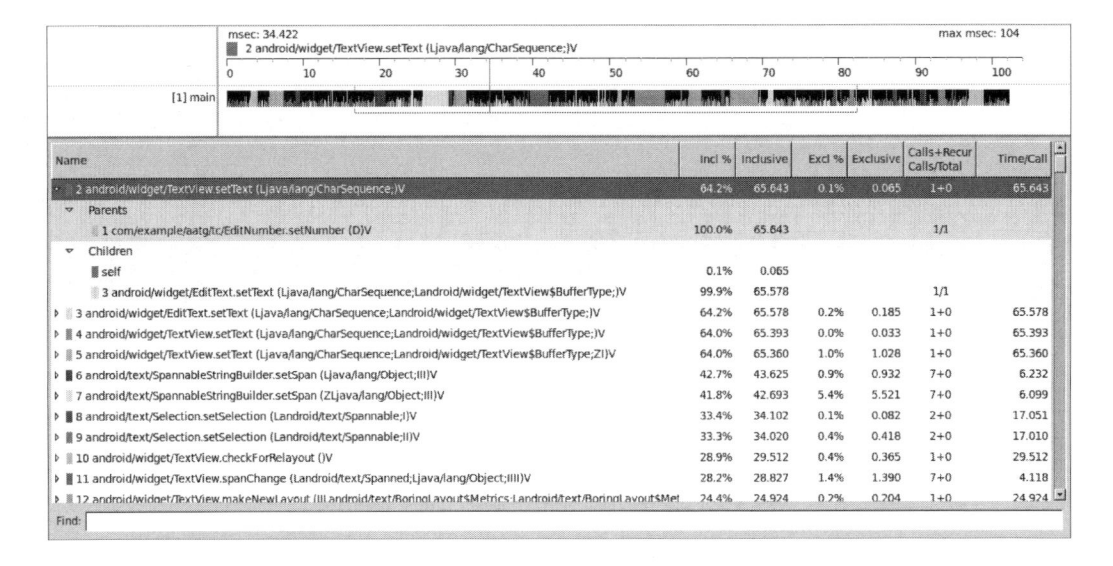

| Name | Incl % | Inclusive | Excl % | Exclusive | Calls+Recur Calls/Total | Time/Call |
|---|---|---|---|---|---|---|
| 2 android/widget/TextView.setText (Ljava/lang/CharSequence;)V | 64.2% | 65.643 | 0.1% | 0.065 | 1+0 | 65.643 |
| Parents | | | | | | |
| 1 com/example/aatg/tc/EditNumber.setNumber (D)V | 100.0% | 65.643 | | | 1/1 | |
| Children | | | | | | |
| self | 0.1% | 0.065 | | | | |
| 3 android/widget/EditText.setText (Ljava/lang/CharSequence;Landroid/widget/TextView$BufferType;)V | 99.9% | 65.578 | | | 1/1 | |
| 3 android/widget/EditText.setText (Ljava/lang/CharSequence;Landroid/widget/TextView$BufferType;)V | 64.2% | 65.578 | 0.2% | 0.185 | 1+0 | 65.578 |
| 4 android/widget/TextView.setText (Ljava/lang/CharSequence;Landroid/widget/TextView$BufferType;)V | 64.0% | 65.393 | 0.0% | 0.033 | 1+0 | 65.393 |
| 5 android/widget/TextView.setText (Ljava/lang/CharSequence;Landroid/widget/TextView$BufferType;ZI)V | 64.0% | 65.360 | 1.0% | 1.028 | 1+0 | 65.360 |
| 6 android/text/SpannableStringBuilder.setSpan (Ljava/lang/Object;III)V | 42.7% | 43.625 | 0.9% | 0.932 | 7+0 | 6.232 |
| 7 android/text/SpannableStringBuilder.setSpan (ZLjava/lang/Object;III)V | 41.8% | 42.693 | 5.4% | 5.521 | 7+0 | 6.099 |
| 8 android/text/Selection.setSelection (Landroid/text/Spannable;I)V | 33.4% | 34.102 | 0.1% | 0.082 | 2+0 | 17.051 |
| 9 android/text/Selection.setSelection (Landroid/text/Spannable;II)V | 33.3% | 34.020 | 0.4% | 0.418 | 2+0 | 17.010 |
| 10 android/widget/TextView.checkForRelayout ()V | 28.9% | 29.512 | 0.4% | 0.365 | 1+0 | 29.512 |
| 11 android/widget/TextView.spanChange (Landroid/text/Spanned;Ljava/lang/Object;III)V | 28.2% | 28.827 | 1.4% | 1.390 | 7+0 | 4.118 |
| 12 android/widget/TextView.makeNewLayout (IILandroid/text/BoringLayout$Metrics;Landroid/text/BoringLayout$Met... | 24.4% | 24.924 | 0.2% | 0.204 | 1+0 | 24.924 |

> Remember that enabling profiling really slows down the application execution so the measure should be interpreted by its relative weight not by their absolute values.

The top part of the window shows the **timeline panel** and a colored area for every method. Time increases to the right. There are also small lines under the colored row displaying the extent of all the calls to the selected method.

We profiled a small segment of our application so only the main thread was running. In other cases where other threads were running during the profiling, this information will also be displayed.

The bottom part shows the **profile panel** and every method executed and its parent-child relationship. We refer to calling methods as *parents* and called methods as *children*. When clicked, a method expands to show its parents and children. Parents are shown with a purple background and children with a yellow background.

Also the color selected for the method, done in a round-robin fashion, is displayed before the method name.

Finally, at the bottom there's a **Find:** field where we can enter a filter to reduce the amount of information displayed. For example if we are only interested in displaying methods in the `com.example.aatg.tc` package, we should enter **com/example/aatg/tc**.

Clicking on a column will set the order of the list according to this column in ascending or descending order.

This table describes the available columns and their descriptions:

| Column | Description |
| --- | --- |
| name | The name of the method including its package name in the form described above, which is using "/" (slash) as the delimiter. Also the parameters and the return type are displayed. |
| Incl% | The inclusive time, as a percentage of the total time, used by the method. That is including all of its children. |
| Inclusive | The inclusive time, in milliseconds, used by this method. That is including this method and all of its children. |
| Excl% | The exclusive time, as a percentage of the total time, used by the method. That is excluding all of its children. |
| Exclusive | The exclusive time, in milliseconds, this is the total time spent in this method. That is excluding all of its children. |
| Calls+Recur | This column shows the number of calls for this method and the number of recursive calls. |
| Calls/Total | The number of calls compared with the total number of calls made to this method. |
| Time/Call | The time in milliseconds of every call. That is Inclusive/Calls. |

# Microbenchmarks

Benchmarking is the act of running a computer program or operation in order to compare operations in a way that produces quantitative results, normally by running a set of tests and trials against them.

Benchmarks can be organized in two big categories:

- Macrobenchmarks
- Microbenchmarks

**Macrobenchmarks** exist as a means to compare different platforms in specific areas such as processor speed, number of floating point operations per unit of time, graphics and 3D performance, and so on. They are normally used against hardware components but can also be used to test software specific areas, such as compiler optimization or algorithms.

As opposed to these traditional macrobenchmarks, a **microbenchmark** attempts to measure the performance of a very small piece of code, often a single method. The results obtained are used to choose between competing implementations that provide the same functionality deciding the optimization path.

The risk here is to microbenchmark something different than what you think you are measuring. This is something to take into account mainly in the case of JIT compilers as used by Android starting with version 2.2 Froyo. The JIT compiler may compile and optimize your microbenchmark differently than the same code in your application. So, be cautious when taking your decision.

This is different from the profiling tactic introduced in the previous section as this approach does not consider the entire application but a single method or algorithm at a time.

## Caliper microbenchmarks

**Caliper** is Google's Open Source framework for writing, running, and viewing results of microbenchkmarks. There are many examples and tutorials on its website at http://code.google.com/p/caliper/.

It's a work in progress but still useful in many circumstances. We are exploring its essential use here and will introduce more Android related usage in the next chapter.

Its central idea is to benchmark methods, mainly to understand how efficient they are; we may decide that this is the target for our optimization, perhaps after analyzing the results provided by profiling via traveview.

Caliper benchmark extends normally `com.google.caliper.SimpleBenchmark` which implements the `Benchmark` interface. Benchmarks are structured in a similar fashion as JUnit 3 tests and maintain the same structure with the difference that here benchmarks start with the prefix **time** as opposed to **test**. Every benchmark then accepts an `int` parameter usually named `reps`, indicates the number of repetitions to benchmark the code that sits inside the method surrounded by a loop counting the repetitions.

The `setUp()` method is also present.

We need caliper installed in our computer. At the time of this writing, caliper is not distributed as binary but as source code that you can download and build yourself. Follow the instructions provided in its website which basically is getting the source code and building yourself.

Put in a very simple way, you can do it using these command lines. You need Subversion and Ant installed to do it:

```
$ svn checkout http://caliper.googlecode.com/svn/trunk/ caliper-read-only
$ cd caliper-read-only
$ ant
```

The `calliper-0.0.jar` and `allocation.jar` will be found in the `build/caliper-0.0/lib` subdirectory.

## Creating the TemperatureConverterBenchmark project

Let's start by creating a new Java project in Eclipse. Yes, this time is not an Android project, just Java.

For consistency use the package `com.example.aatg.tc.benchmark` as the main package.

Add the `caliper` library and the existing `TemperatureConverter` project to the **Java Build Path** in the project's properties.

Then create the `TemperatureConverterBenchmark` class that is containing our benchmarks:

```
package com.example.aatg.tc.benchmark;

import java.util.Random;
import com.example.aatg.tc.TemperatureConverter;
import com.google.caliper.Param;
import com.google.caliper.SimpleBenchmark;
/**
 * Caliper Benchmark.<br>
 * To run the benchmarks in this class:<br>
 * {@code $ CLASSPATH=... caliper com.example.aatg.tc.
 * benchmark.TemperatureConverterBenchmark.
 * CelsiusToFahrenheitBenchmark} [-Dsize=n]
 *
 * @author diego
 *
 */
public class TemperatureConverterBenchmark {
  public static class CelsiusToFahrenheitBenchmark extends
  SimpleBenchmark {
    private static final double T = 10; // some temp
    @Param
    int size;
    private double[] temps;
```

```java
    @Override
    protected void setUp() throws Exception {
      super.setUp();
      temps = new double[size];
      Random r = new Random(System.currentTimeMillis());
      for (int i=0; i < size; i++) {
        temps[i] = T * r.nextGaussian();
      }
    }
    public final void timeCelsiusToFahrenheit(int reps) {
      for (int i=0; i < reps; i++) {
        for (double t: temps) {
          TemperatureConverter.celsiusToFahrenheit(t);
        }
      }
    }
  }
  public static void main(String[] args) {
    System.out.println("This is a caliper benchmark.");
  }
}
```

We have a `setUp()` method that, similar to JUnit tests, is run before the benchmarks are run. This method initializes an array of random temperatures used in the conversion benchmark. The size of this array is passed as a parameter to caliper and annotated here with the `@Param` annotation. Caliper will provide the value of this parameter automatically.

We use a Gaussian distribution for the pseudo-random temperatures as this could be a good model of the reality.

Then the benchmark itself. As we noted before it should start with the prefix time, as in this instance `timeCelsiusToFahrenheit()`. Inside this method we loop for the repetitions and invoke the conversion `TemperatureConverter.celsiusToFahrenheit()` which is the method we wish to benchmark.

## Running caliper

To run caliper we use a script which is based on the script that comes with the distribution. Be sure to place it in a directory included in the PATH or use the correct path to invoke it:

```
#!/bin/bash
VERSION=0.0
CALIPER_DIR=/opt/caliper-$VERSION
```

```
export PATH=$PATH:$JAVA_HOME/bin
exec java -cp ${CALIPER_DIR}/lib/caliper-${VERSION}.jar:$CLASSPATH
com.google.caliper.Runner "$@"
```

Adapt it to your needs. Before running it, remember that we still need to set our `CLASSPATH` so caliper can find the `TemperatureConverter` and the benchmarks themselves. For example:

`$ export CLASSPATH=$CLASSPATH:~/workspace/TemperatureConverter/bin:~/workspace/TemperatureConverterBenchmark/bin`

Afterwards we can run caliper as:

`$ caliper com.example.aatg.tc.benchmark.TemperatureConverterBenchmark.CelsiusToFahrenheitBenchmark -Dsize=1`

This will run the benchmarks and if everything goes well we will be presented with the results:

 0% Scenario{vm=java, benchmark=CelsiusToFahrenheit, size=1} 8.95ns; σ=0.11ns @ 10 trials

.caliperrc found, reading properties...

ns logarithmic runtime

 9 XXXXXXXXXXXXXXXXXXXXXXXXXXXXXX

vm: java

benchmark: CelsiusToFahrenheit

size: 1

Alternatively we can repeat the benchmark for different number of temperatures to find out if the values itself affect the performance of the conversion. In such cases we run:

`$ caliper com.example.aatg.tc.benchmark.TemperatureConverterBenchmark.CelsiusToFahrenheitBenchmark -Dsize=1,10,100`

Here we added different sizes for the temperatures array and the results obtained are as follows:

  0% Scenario{vm=java, trial=0, benchmark=CelsiusToFahrenheit, size=1} 3.47 ns; σ=0.19 ns @ 10 trials

 33% Scenario{vm=java, trial=0, benchmark=CelsiusToFahrenheit, size=10} 11.67 ns; σ=1.20 ns @ 10 trials

67% Scenario{vm=java, trial=0, benchmark=CelsiusToFahrenheit, size=100} 63.06 ns; σ=3.83 ns @ 10 trials

size    ns linear runtime

   1  3.47 =

  10 11.67 =====

 100 63.06 =============================

vm: java

trial: 0

benchmark: CelsiusToFahrenheit

To help visualize these results there is a service hosted in the Google AppEngine (`http://microbenchmarks.appspot.com`) that accepts your result's data and lets you visualize them in a much better way. To access this service you should obtain an API key providing your Google login. Once obtained this key is placed in the `.caliperrc` file in your home directory and next time you run the benchmarks the results will be uploaded.

The `.caliperrc` would look like this snippet after you pasted the obtained API key:

```
# Caliper API key for myuser@gmail.com
postUrl: http://microbenchmarks.appspot.com:80/run/
apiKey: 012345678901234567890123456789012
```

Now run the benchmarks again using the same command line as before:

```
$ caliper com.example.aatg.tc.benchmark.TemperatureConverterBenchmark.CelsiusToFahrenheitBenchmark -Dsize=1,10,100
```

In addition to the text output, you will receive the instructions to access the results online. You can view current and previous benchmark results online at:

`http://microbenchmarks.appspot.com/run/user@gmail.com/com.example.aatg.tc.benchmark.TemperatureConverterBenchmark.CelsiusToFahrenheitBenchmark.`

> In the previous URL replace `user@gmail.com` with your real Google login username that you used to generate the API key.

## Screenshot

```
com.example.aatg.tc.benchmark.TemperatureConverterBenchmark.
CelsiusToFahrenheitBenchmark
run by ███████

Results
size    ns       linear runtime        %
1       3.48                           103%
10      11.60                          342%
100     64.92                          1,913%
Plain Text - Create Snapshot

Runs
        run      executed                    environment
        A        Sun May 29 13:11:56 -0400 2011   A    Delete

Variables
    run        960014
    vm         java
    trial      0
    benchmark  CelsiusToFahrenheit
    size       ☑1  ☑10  ☑100
```

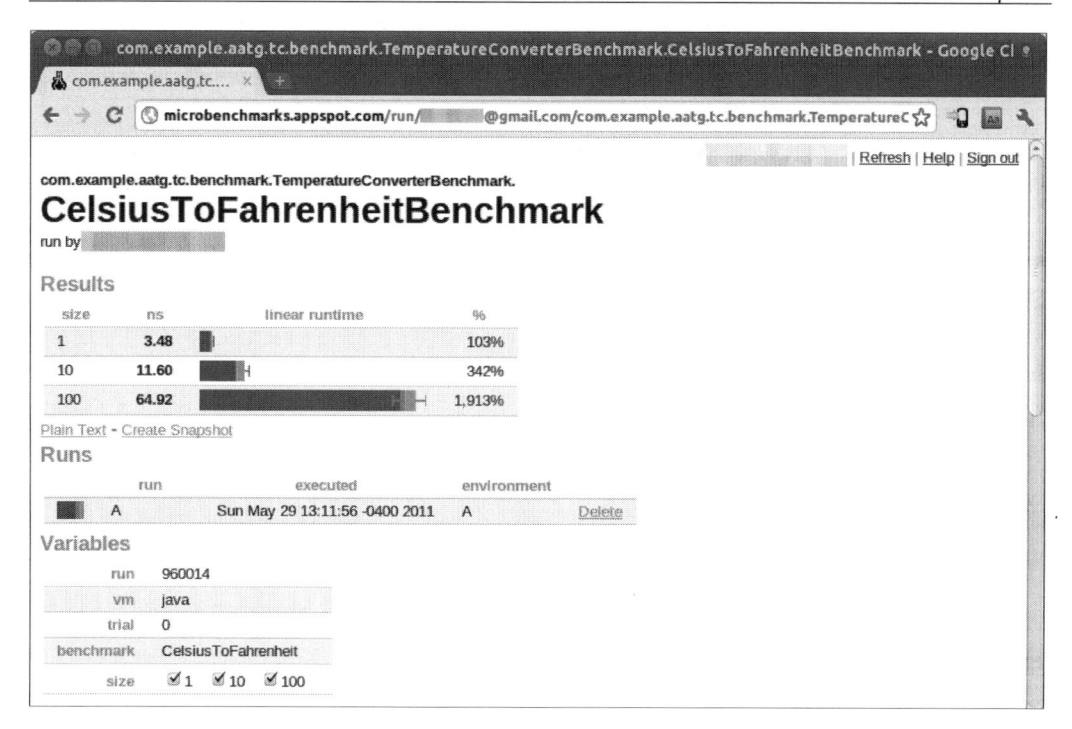

# Summary

In this chapter we dissected the available alternatives to test the performance measures of our application benchmarking and profiling our code.

While some options that should be provided by the Android SDK are not yet completed by the time of this writing, and there is no possibility to implement Android `PerformanceTestCases` because some code is hidden in the SDK, we visited and analyzed some other valid alternatives.

Among these alternatives we found that we can use simple log statements to more sophisticated code extending Instrumentation.

Subsequently we analyzed profiling alternatives and described and exemplified the use of `traceview` and `dmtracedump`.

Finally, we discovered caliper—a microbenchmarking tool that has native support for Android. However, we introduced its most basic usage and postponed more specific Android and Dalvik VM usage for the next chapter.

In the next chapter we will be building Android from source code to obtain an EMMA instrumented build and we will be executing coverage report on our code. We will also introduce alternative tactics and tools by the end of the chapter.

# 10
# Alternative Testing Tactics

Up to this point we have analyzed the most common and accessible tactics to implement testing in our projects. However, there are a few missing pieces in our puzzle and with the current versions of the Android SDK (*Android 2.3 Gingerbread* as of this writing) these features are not yet implemented. Nevertheless, not everything is lost. One of the biggest and strongest benefits of Android is its Open Source nature and the features we are going to exploit here precisely depend on it because we will be using the complete source code to introduce some changes required by what we plan to provide.

Building Android from source code is not for the faint hearted. It is extremely time consuming mainly at the beginning while you are familiarizing yourself with the whole Android environment, and it also requires a lot of disk space and horsepower. To illustrate this assertion, one simple build for one target takes almost 10GB of disk space and almost an hour to build on a 4 core machine. I'm not trying to scare you but warn you and at the same time ask for a little endurance.

They say that great sacrifices come with great rewards and this seems to be another case that follows this rule.

In this chapter we will be covering:

- Building Android from source
- Code coverage using EMMA
- Adding code coverage to our Temperature Converter project
- Introducing Robotium
- Testing on host's JVM
- Introducing Robolectric

# Building Android from source

Perhaps Android's *Achilles' heel* would be the lack of documentation and the number of places you have to visit to get the complete version of what you are trying to find, or what's even worse in many cases the official documentation is incorrect or has not been updated to match the current release. One example of this is the documentation (available at `http://source.android.com/source/download.html` at the time of this writing) of the requirements to build Android from source that still states that Java 6 is not supported and Ubuntu 8.10 (intrepid) 32bit can be used, which is totally wrong. Funnily enough, Java 6 and at least Ubuntu 10.04 (lucid) 64bit are required. Starting with Android 2.3 (Gingerbread), building on 32bit machines is no longer supported. But that's enough for a rant, I will leave them for my personal blog, otherwise if the documentation were complete, books like this one would not be needed and I could be writing one about Windows Phone 7...

Just kidding, I don't think this could happen in the near future.

# Code coverage

One of our objectives in building Android from source is enabling code coverage via EMMA (`http://emma.sourceforge.net/`).

Code coverage is a measure used in software testing that describes the amount of source code that was actually tested by the tests suite and to what degree following some criteria. As code coverage inspects the code directly it is therefore a form of white box testing.

From the several tools available providing code coverage analysis for Java we are using EMMA, an open-source toolkit for measuring and reporting Java code coverage that is supported by the Android project, and the infrastructure to start using it for your own projects is already there, therefore minimizing the effort needed to implement it. EMMA came to fill an existing gap in the vast Open Source ecosystem where no coverage tools existed with compatible licenses. EMMA is based on IBM's Common Public License v1.0 and is thus free for both Open Source and commercial development.

EMMA distinguishes itself from other tools by going after a unique feature combination: support for large-scale enterprise software development while keeping individual developer's work fast and iterative. This is fundamental in a project the size of Android and EMMA shines at its best providing code coverage for it.

# EMMA features

Android 2.3 includes EMMA v2.0, build 5312. The most distinctive set of features, paraphrasing its documentation, which can be found at its website are the following:

- EMMA can instrument classes for coverage either offline (before they are loaded) or on the fly (using an instrumenting application classloader).
- Supported coverage types: Class, method, line, basic block. EMMA can detect when a single source code line is covered only partially.
- Coverage stats are aggregated at method, class, package, and "all classes" levels.
- Output report types: Plain text, HTML, XML. All report types support drill-down, to a user-controlled detail depth. The HTML report supports source code linking.
- Output reports can highlight items with coverage levels below user-provided thresholds.
- Coverage data obtained in different instrumentation or test runs can be merged together.
- EMMA does not require access to the source code and degrades gracefully with decreasing amounts of debug information available in the input classes.
- EMMA can instrument individual .class files or entire .jar files (in place, if desired). Efficient coverage subset filtering is possible, too.
- Makefile and ANT build integration are supported on an equal footing.
- EMMA is quite fast: The runtime overhead of added instrumentation is small (5 to 20%) and the bytecode instrumentor itself is very fast (mostly limited by file I/O speed). Memory overhead is a few hundred bytes per Java class.
- EMMA is 100% pure Java, has no external library dependencies, and works in any Java 2 JVM (even 1.2.x).

Some minor changes were introduced by Android to the EMMA project to fully adapt it and support code coverage:

- Change coverage.out.file location in core/res/emma_default.properties to /data/coverage.ec
- Remove reference to sun.misc.* in core/java14/com/vladium/util/IJREVersion.java
- Remove reference to sun.misc.* and SunJREExitHookManager class from core/java13/com/vladium/util/exit/ExitHookManager.java
- Add java.security.cert.Certificate cast to core/java12/com/vladium/emma/rt/InstrClassLoader.java to fix compiler error

- Move `out/core/res/com/vladium/emma/rt/RTExitHook.closure` (from Emma Ant build) into `pregenerated/` so it does not have to be generated in Android's make-based build, but also doesn't break Emma's build

## System requirements

The Android build for gingerbread requires a 64-bit build environment as well as some other tools:

Required packages:

- Git, JDK, flex, and the other development packages
- Java 6
- Pieces from the 32-bit cross-building environment
- X11 development

The instructions if you are running the recommended Ubuntu 10.04 LTS 64bit are as follows:

```
$ sudo apt-get install git-core gnupg flex bison gperf libsdl-dev \
    libesd0-dev libwxgtk2.6-dev build-essential zip curl libncurses5-dev \
    zlib1g-dev
$ sudo apt-get install gcc-multilib g++-multilib libc6-dev-i386 \
    lib32ncurses5-dev ia32-libs x11proto-core-dev libx11-dev \
    lib32readline5-dev lib32z-dev
```

Set the system to use the right version of java by default:

```
$ sudo update-java-alternatives -s java-6-sun
```

In any case, check the AOSP website (`http://source.android.com/source/download.html`) for updated instructions.

## Downloading the Android source code

The Android project is a large collection of relatively independent projects put under the Android umbrella. All of them use Git as the version control system. You can see what I mean by visiting the **Gitweb** interface for the Android project at `http://android.git.kernel.org/`.

As you can see, dozens of projects are listed and you need all to build the entire platform. To simplify the process of dealing with this great number of Git projects at the same time Google created **repo**, a tool that was built on top of Git to help manage the many Git repositories, uploads to the revision control system, and automate parts of the Android development work-flow.

Repo is a complementary tool that does not replace Git, but just makes it easier to work with Git in the context of Android. The repo command is an Python executable wrapped into a shell script and can be put anywhere in your path.

Detailed information about Git and Repo in the scope of Android project can be obtained from their information page at http://source.android.com/source/git-repo.html.

## Installing repo

As we mentioned before, repo is our key to the Android source code world, therefore the first measure is installing it.

Follow these commands:

```
$ curl http://android.git.kernel.org/repo > ~/bin/repo
$ chmod a+x ~/bin/repo
```

This creates the initial repo script, which will initialize the complete repository and will include the repo.git project as well, so repo is auto-maintained. Every time you synchronize with the repository, changes to repo itself are propagated if necessary. That's a very clever use of the tool.

## Creating the working copy

Our working copy of the repository can be created anywhere in our computer. Just remember that there should be at least 10GB of free space and sometimes much more is needed if you build for different targets.

Let's say that we decide to create the working copy in ~/android/android-2.3, then use the following commands:

```
$ mkdir ~/android/android-2.3
$ cd ~/android/android-2.3
$ repo init -u git://android.git.kernel.org/platform/manifest.git
```

These three simple steps have created our working copy ready to be synchronized. Remember that is a very big download and depending on your network connection speed and the load on the servers it could take some time. So it is very smart to wait some days after a major release is pushed to the servers.

When you are ready to synchronize just invoke this command in your working copy:

```
$ repo sync
```

*Alternative Testing Tactics*

When you run `repo sync`, this is what happens:

- If the project has never been synchronized, then `repo sync` is equivalent to `git clone`. All branches in the remote repository are copied to the local project directory.
- If the project has already been synchronized once, then `repo sync` is equivalent to:
  - `git remote update`
  - `git rebase origin/branch`
  - Where branch is the currently checked-out branch in the local project directory. If the local branch is not tracking a branch in the remote repository, then no synchronization will occur for the project.
- If the `git rebase` operation results in merge conflicts, you will need to use the normal Git commands (for example, `git rebase --continue`) to resolve the conflicts.

Once finished, the complete Android source code has been downloaded to your working copy. We haven't specified any specific branch so we just downloaded the latest Android Open Source Project (AOSP) main branch.

## The Building Steps

We are ready to start our build supporting code coverage analysis.

To achieve this we need to follow the steps to set the environment and chose your combo:

`~/android/android-2.3$ source build/envsetup.sh`

**including device/htc/passion/vendorsetup.sh**

**including device/samsung/crespo/vendorsetup.sh**

`~/android/android-2.3$ lunch`

**You're building on Linux**

**Lunch menu... pick a combo:**

  **1. full-eng**

  **2. full_x86-eng**

3. simulator

4. full_passion-userdebug

5. full_crespo-userdebug

**Which would you like? [full-eng]**

Select **full-eng** in this case.

============================================

PLATFORM_VERSION_CODENAME=AOSP

PLATFORM_VERSION=AOSP

TARGET_PRODUCT=full

TARGET_BUILD_VARIANT=eng

TARGET_SIMULATOR=false

TARGET_BUILD_TYPE=release

TARGET_BUILD_APPS=

TARGET_ARCH=arm

TARGET_ARCH_VARIANT=armv5te

HOST_ARCH=x86

HOST_OS=linux

HOST_BUILD_TYPE=release

BUILD_ID=OPENMASTER

============================================

One more step is needed in this case. As we want to enable EMMA code coverage we need to set this in the environment:

```
~/android/android-2.3$ export EMMA_INSTRUMENT=true
```

Get set, ready, go:

```
~/android/android-2.3$ make -j4
```

> The `-j` or `--jobs` option to make lets you specify the number of jobs (commands) to run simultaneously. This is very useful to speed up lengthy build processes in multiprocessor or multicore machines. If no argument is given to the `-j` option, then make will not limit the number of jobs that can run simultaneously.

After a while and tons of messages, your build will be available. If everything went well you will be seeing a message similar to this one at the end:

**Target system fs image: out/target/product/generic/obj/PACKAGING/systemimage_intermediates/system.img**

**Install system fs image: out/target/product/generic/system.img**

**Installed file list: out/target/product/generic/installed-files.txt**

This is because the last steps are to create the system image and the list of installed files.

If the build fails then try some of the suggestions mentioned below in order to fix it or find out more at the AOSP site (`http://source.android.com/source/building.html`). If there are some problems and things are not so smooth, here is a list of tips you can follow to revert the situation.

> **Tips to revert from a broken build**
> Clean, using `make clean`, and make again.
> Reducing the number of jobs (`make -j` or `make –jobs`) usually helps too.
> Sometimes, just invoking make again after a failed build, can make the build succeed. Yes, I know it sounds like nonsense, but it helps when you have tried everything else.

We now have an instrumented build that will let us obtain code coverage analysis for tests in our projects. So this is our next step.

# TemperatureConverter code coverage

We built Android from source to be able to obtain code coverage analysis reports for our projects mainly for two reasons:

- We need an EMMA instrumented build, which is what we did in previous sections
- To be able to instrument an application, this application should be built as part of the main build tree, and this is what we will be doing now

A possible location for our application and tests inside the main Android tree could be `development/samples`, so we are going to use it. Should you decide on a different location, minor adaption might be needed in the files and commands presented here.

We already have our TemperatureConverter project and its tests `TemperatureConverterTests` somewhere in our filesystem, and if you followed the examples presented before they are probably checked into the version control system of your choice, so the options here are checking out the project again at this location or creating a symbolic link. Let's choose the latter for the sake of simplicity for this example:

`~/android/android-2.3/development/samples$ ln -s ~/workspace/TemperatureConverter .`

`~/android/android-2.3/development/samples$ ln -s ~/workspace/TemperatureConverterTest .`

Following, we need to add the makefiles. We built our projects from Eclipse and later on we added `ant` support. Now we are adding support for a third build system: `make`.

Android built is `make` based and we should follow its conventions and style to be able to build our application and its tests as part of the main build.

Create the following `Android.mk` inside the `TemperatureConverter` project:

```
LOCAL_PATH:= $(call my-dir)
include $(CLEAR_VARS)
LOCAL_MODULE_TAGS := samples
# Only compile source java files in this apk.
LOCAL_SRC_FILES := $(call all-java-files-under, src)
LOCAL_PACKAGE_NAME := TemperatureConverter
LOCAL_SDK_VERSION := current
include $(BUILD_PACKAGE)
```

This makefile will be included as part of the main build if executed.

To build it separately we can use a helper function that was defined in our environment when we set it up at the beginning using `envsetup.sh`. This function is `mm` and is defined as:

```
mm ()
{
    if [ -f build/core/envsetup.mk -a -f Makefile ]; then
        make $@;
```

```
            else
                T=$(gettop);
                local M=$(findmakefile);
                local M=`echo $M|sed 's:'$T'/::'`;
                if [ ! "$T" ]; then
                    echo "Couldn't locate the top of the tree.
                       Try setting TOP.";
                else
                    if [ ! "$M" ]; then
                        echo "Couldn't locate a makefile from the
                            current directory.";
                    else
                        ONE_SHOT_MAKEFILE=$M make -C $T all_modules $@;
                    fi;
                fi;
            fi
        }
```

The boilerplate code to locate and include needed components is provided by this function.

Using it to build the application is simply done by invoking it when our current working directory is the project we want to compile.

`~/android/android-2.3/development/samples/TemperatureConverter$ EMMA_INSTRUMENT=true mm`

Because we enabled EMMA by setting `EMMA_INSTRUMENT=true` in our environment among the messages produced by this command, we should see the following:

**EMMA: processing instrumentation path ...**

**EMMA: instrumentation path processed in 149 ms**

**EMMA: [14 class(es) instrumented, 4 resource(s) copied]**

**EMMA: metadata merged into [/home/diego/android/android-2.3/out/target/common/obj/APPS/TemperatureConverter_intermediates/coverage.em] {in 16 ms}**

This indicates that our build is being instrumented.

We should proceed in a similar manner to build and instrument our tests.

In the `TemperatureConverterTest` project create its corresponding makefile: `Android.mk`, this time containing this information, which is slightly different from the main project:

```
LOCAL_PATH:= $(call my-dir)
include $(CLEAR_VARS)

# We only want this apk build for tests.
LOCAL_MODULE_TAGS := tests

LOCAL_JAVA_LIBRARIES := android.test.runner

LOCAL_STATIC_JAVA_LIBRARIES := easymock hamcrest-core \
  hamcrest-integration hamcrest-library

# Include all test java files.
LOCAL_SRC_FILES := $(call all-java-files-under, src)

LOCAL_PACKAGE_NAME := TemperatureConverterTest

LOCAL_INSTRUMENTATION_FOR := TemperatureConverter

LOCAL_SDK_VERSION := current

include $(BUILD_PACKAGE)

LOCAL_PREBUILT_STATIC_JAVA_LIBRARIES := \
  easymock:libs/easymock-2.5.2.jar \
  hamcrest-core:libs/hamcrest-core-1.2-android.jar \
  hamcrest-integration:libs/hamcrest-integration-1.2-android.jar \
  hamcrest-library:libs/hamcrest-library-1.2-android.jar
include $(BUILD_MULTI_PREBUILT)
```

This is a little more involved because the tests are using external libraries we need to define to be used during the build process.

Again, we should build it using the mm function:

```
~/android/android-2.3/development/samples/TemperatureConverterTest \
  $ EMMA_INSTRUMENT=true mm
```

We have successfully built the TemperatureConverter application and its tests, now as part of the main Android build. At this point we are ready to obtain the code coverage analysis reports, just by following a few more steps.

*Alternative Testing Tactics*

# Generating code coverage analysis report

Having reached this point, we have `TemperatureConverter` and its tests instrumented and compiled residing in our output directory which is `out/target/common/obj/APPS/`.

We need an instance of the emulator that belongs to our instrumented built. This emulator is in the `out` directory too.

In this case we extend the default system partition size up to 256MB and include a sdcard image that should have been created previously. These elements are needed because some data will be collected during the instrumented test run and we need some room to save it.

```
~/android/android-2.3$ ./out/host/linux-x86/bin/emulator -sdcard ~/tmp/sdcard.img -partition-size 256
```

Our intention is now to synchronize the image running on the emulator with our changes.

These steps avoid creating a new image when some changes or updates are available just by copying the modified files.

To be able to do it we first need to enable writing to the system image:

```
~/android/android-2.3$ adb remount
```

This command when finished successfully should give this output:

**remount succeeded**

Followed by the synchronization of changes:

```
~/android/android-2.3/development/samples/TemperatureConverterTest$ adb sync
```

The list of files being copied to the emulator image are displayed. Once everything is updated we can now run the tests using `am instrument` as we previously did. As we mentioned in *Chapter 2, Testing on Android* when we reviewed the available options for this command, `-e` can be used to set various suboptions. In this case we use it to enable code coverage collection:

```
~/android/android-2.3$ adb shell am instrument -e coverage 'true' \
  -w com.example.aatg.tc.test/android.test.InstrumentationTestRunner
```

This following message verifies that our tests are collecting coverage data:

**EMMA: collecting runtime coverage data ...**

The last message indeed informs us where this data was collected:

**Generated code coverage data to /data/data/com.example.aatg.tc/files/coverage.ec**

We can create a directory in the development computer to keep our coverage reports for this project. In this directory we should also copy the off-line coverage metadata and then generate the reports:

`~/android/android-2.3$ mkdir -p out/emma/tc`

`~/android/android-2.3$ cd out/emma/tc`

Then we copy the coverage report from the device:

`~/android/android-2.3/out/emma/tc$ adb pull /data/data/com.example.aatg.tc/files/coverage.ec coverage.ec`

When data is transferred we receive these statistics:

**200 KB/s (22840 bytes in 0.110s)**

And the off-line coverage metadata:

`~/android/android-2.3/out/emma/tc$ cp ~/android/android-2.3/out/target/common/obj/APPS/TemperatureConverter_intermediates/coverage.em .# not the dot (.) at the end`

With all these components present in our working directory, it will be easier to specify the command line options. If you prefer you can use a different organization and leave the files somewhere else and even create symbolic links here.

Having read everything, we can invoke emma to generate the report. The default report shows the overall coverage summary followed by a breakdown by package. In this example we are using HTML output and we are linking to the source.

> If your source folder for the TemperatureConverter main project is other than ~/workspace/TemperatureConverter/src don't forget to adapt the following command, otherwise the command will fail: ~/android/android-2.3/out/emma/tc$ java -cp ~/android/android-2.3/external/emma/lib/emma.jar emma report -r html -in coverage.ec -sp ~/workspace/TemperatureConverter/src -in coverage.em.

And we will be able to see the messages indicating the creation of the report:

**EMMA: processing input files ...**

**EMMA: 2 file(s) read and merged in 20 ms**

*Alternative Testing Tactics*

## EMMA: writing [html] report to [/home/diego/android/android-2.3/out/emma/tc/coverage/index.html] ...

This has created the report files inside the coverage directory, so we can open the index by invoking:

```
~/android/android-2.3/out/emma/tc$ firefox coverage/index.html
```

Then, the coverage analysis report is displayed:

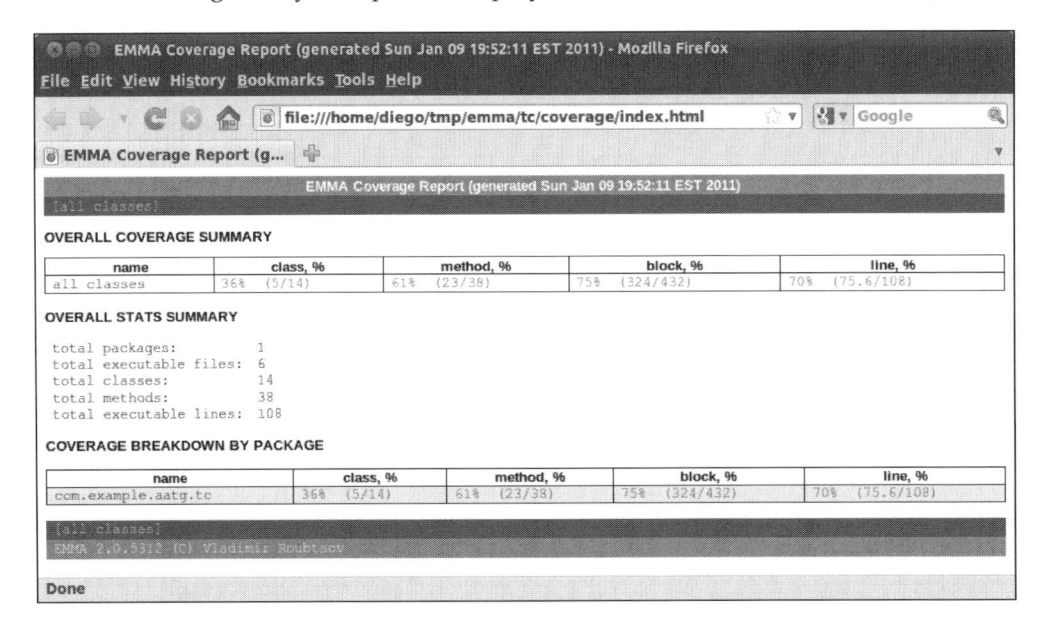

This report has three main sections:

- **Overall coverage summary**: The summary for all classes is presented here.
- **Overall stats summary**: The statistics of the coverage are presented here, for example how many packages, classes, or lines were present.
- **Coverage breakdown by package**: In the case of bigger applications this will display the coverage for particular packages. In this example, it's the same as the total because there is a single package.

The information presented in the report includes coverage metrics in a way that allows for drilling down into data in a top-down fashion, starting with all classes and going all the way to the level of individual methods and source lines (in the HTML report).

The fundamental unit of code coverage in EMMA is the basic blocks; all other types of coverage are derived from the basic block coverage in some way. Line coverage is mostly used to link to the source code.

This table describes the important pieces of information in the EMMA coverage report:

| Label | Description |
|---|---|
| name | The name of the class or package |
| Class, % | The percentage of classes covered over the total and the detailed number. |
| Method, % | The percentage of methods covered over the total and the detailed number. This is a basic java method which is composed by a given number of basic blocks. |
| Block, % | The percentage of blocks covered over the total and the detailed number. A basic block is defined as a sequence of bytecode instructions without any jumps or jump targets. The number of basic blocks in a method is a good measure of its complexity. |
| Line, % | The percentage of lines covered over the total and the detailed number. This is basically used to link to the source code. |

When the values presented are under a threshold coverage metric value, these metrics are presented in red in the report. By default, these values are:

- For methods: 70%
- For blocks: 80%
- For lines: 80%
- For classes: 100%

All of these values can be changed, specifying parameters on the command line or in a configuration file. Please refer to the documentation for details (http://emma.sourceforge.net/docs.html).

We can drill-down from the package to specific methods and the lines covered are presented in green while uncovered ones appear in red and partially covered in yellow.

*Alternative Testing Tactics*

This is an example of this report for the `TemperatureConverter` class:

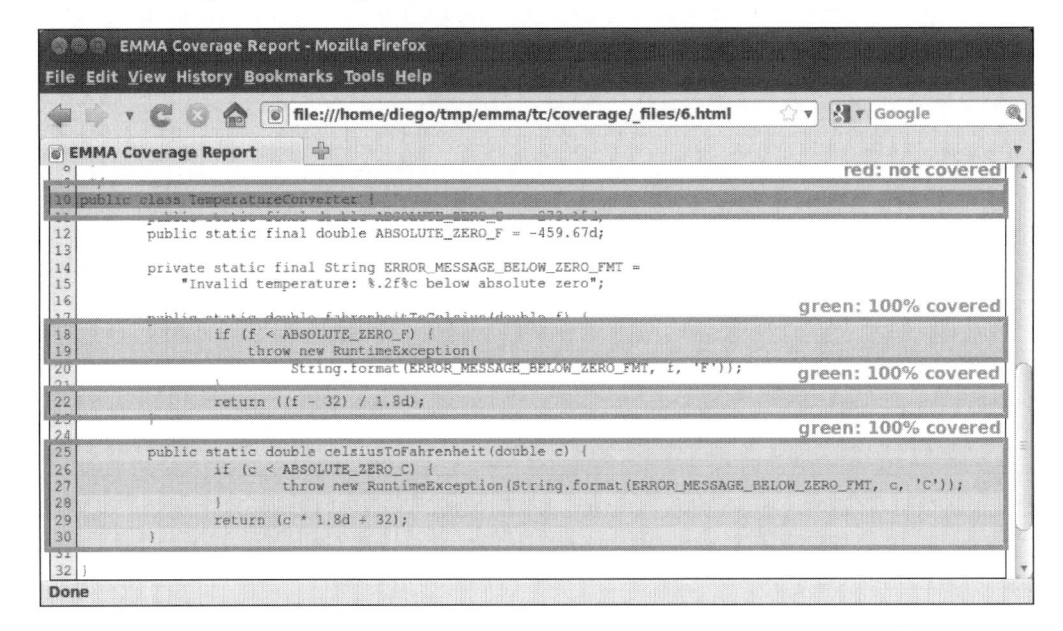

```
10 public class TemperatureConverter {
11     public static final double ABSOLUTE_ZERO_C = -273.15d;
12     public static final double ABSOLUTE_ZERO_F = -459.67d;
13
14     private static final String ERROR_MESSAGE_BELOW_ZERO_FMT =
15         "Invalid temperature: %.2f%c below absolute zero";
16
17     public static double fahrenheitToCelsius(double f) {
18         if (f < ABSOLUTE_ZERO_F) {
19             throw new RuntimeException(
20                 String.format(ERROR_MESSAGE_BELOW_ZERO_FMT, f, 'F'));
21         }
22         return ((f - 32) / 1.8d);
23     }
24
25     public static double celsiusToFahrenheit(double c) {
26         if (c < ABSOLUTE_ZERO_C) {
27             throw new RuntimeException(String.format(ERROR_MESSAGE_BELOW_ZERO_FMT, c, 'C'));
28         }
29         return (c * 1.8d + 32);
30     }
31
32 }
```

In this report we can see that the class `TemperatureConverter` is not 100% covered but all the basic blocks inside it are.

Do you know why ?

Think for a moment...

Yes, because the implicit default constructor has not been tested. But wait a second; this is a utility class which is not supposed to be instantiated at all. We can see here not only how this analysis is helping us to test our code and find potential bugs but also to improve the design.

What we need to do to prevent `TemperatureConverter` from being instantiated is to create a private default constructor:

```
public TemperatureConverter {
    ...
    private TemperatureConverter() {
    }
    ...
}
```

Once we add this private constructor and run the tests and coverage again we can see now that even though the class is not yet 100% covered and thus not green we can assure that this constructor won't be invoked from any other class.

## Covering the restoring the instance state

There is another case that we will analyze. In the report for `TemperatureConverterActivity` we can see that some blocks are still not covered and they are red. One of such blocks is the partial support for restoring a saved instance we added before, though this block is not yet functional and its only logging a message we should cover it with a test.

The code mentioned in `TemperatureConverterActivity.java` is:

```
/** Called when the activity is first created. */
@Override
public void onCreate(Bundle savedInstanceState) {
    super.onCreate(savedInstanceState);
    setContentView(R.layout.main);

    if ( savedInstanceState != null ) {
      Log.d(TAG, "Should restore state from " +
        savedInstanceState);
    }
...
```

To test this block we must control the invocation of the `onCreate()` method and inject a mock `Bundle` to simulate the actual Android lifecycle.

We may think of using one of our previously created test classes to add the needed test, but if you remember from our previous chapters we stated that when we need a higher degree of control over the creation of the `Activity` under test, instead of `ActivityInstrumentationTestCase2<T>` we should use `ActivityUnitTestCase<T>`, which is also derived from `InstrumentationTestCase` (see the UML class diagram for `ActivityInstrumentationTestCase2<T>` in Chapter 3, Building Blocks on the Android SDK).

The test case based on `ActivityUnitTestCase<T>` allows us to inject the desired values to `onCreate()` while starting the Activity by using `startActivity(Intent intent, Bundle savedInstanceState, Object lastNonConfigurationInstance)`.

## Alternative Testing Tactics

The following code snippet shows the test case we are adding to our already existing `TemperatureConverterActivityUnitTests` class:

```
package com.example.aatg.tc.test;

import com.example.aatg.tc.TemperatureConverterActivity;
import com.example.aatg.tc.TemperatureConverterApplication;

import android.app.Instrumentation;
import android.content.Intent;
import android.os.Bundle;
import android.test.ActivityUnitTestCase;

public class TemperatureConverterActivityUnitTests extends
    ActivityUnitTestCase<TemperatureConverterActivity> {

  public TemperatureConverterActivityUnitTests(String name) {
    super(TemperatureConverterActivity.class);
    setName(name);
  }

  protected void setUp() throws Exception {
    super.setUp();

    mStartIntent = new Intent(Intent.ACTION_MAIN);
    mInstrumentation = getInstrumentation();
    setApplication(new TemperatureConverterApplication());
  }

  protected void tearDown() throws Exception {
    super.tearDown();
  }

  // other tests not displayed here …

  public final void testOnCreateBundle() {
    Bundle savedInstanceState = new Bundle();
    savedInstanceState.putString("dummy", "dummy");
    setApplication(new TemperatureConverterApplication());
    Intent intent = new Intent(mInstrumentation.getTargetContext(),
      TemperatureConverterActivity.class);
    startActivity(intent, savedInstanceState, null);
    TemperatureConverterActivity activity = getActivity();
    assertNotNull(activity);
  }
}
```

We are creating a `Bundle` containing only dummy values as nothing special is expected in the Activity. Additionally we are injecting a real `TemperatureConverterApplication` object instead of an Application mock because it is used, and casted, inside the Activity's `onCreate()` method and it would fail.

No additional tests were added to this class as nothing special is done when the saved state is restored. For your particular application probably you would like to check that some values were restored correctly.

Should we run the test coverage report again we would see that now the mentioned block is now covered.

## Covering the exceptions

Continuing with our examination of the coverage report will lead us to discover another block that is not exercised by our current tests. The block in question is the last catch in the following try-catch block in `TemeratureConverterActivity`:

```
try {
  final double temp = Double.parseDouble(str);
  final double result = (mOp == OP.C2F) ?
    TemperatureConverter.celsiusToFahrenheit(temp) :
    TemperatureConverter.fahrenheitToCelsius(temp);
  final String resultString = String.format("%.2f", result);
  mDest.setNumber(result);
  mDest.setSelection(resultString.length());
} catch (NumberFormatException e) {
  // WARNING
  // this is generated while a number is entered,
  // for example just a '-'
  // so we don't want to show the error
} catch (InvalidTemperatureException e) {
  mSource.setError("ERROR: " + e.getLocalizedMessage());
}
```

We should provide a test, or better a pair of tests, one for each temperature unit, that furnishing an invalid temperature verifies that the error is displayed. This is the test in `TemperatureConverterActivityTests` for the Celsius case and you can easily convert it to provide the other case:

```
public void testInvalidTemperatureInCelsius() throws Throwable {
  runTestOnUiThread(new Runnable() {
    @Override
    public void run() {
      mCelsius.clear();
      mCelsius.requestFocus();
    }
  });
  // temp less than ABSOLUTE_ZERO_C
```

```
            assertNull(mCelsius.getError());
            sendKeys("MINUS 3 8 0");
            assertNotNull(mCelsius.getError());
    }
```

We clear and request the focus for the field under test. As we did before, we should achieve this by using a Runnable on the UI thread otherwise we will receive an exception.

Then we check there's no previous error, set the invalid temperature, and retrieve the error message to verify that is not null. Running the end-to-end process again we can attest that the block is now covered giving us total coverage as intended.

This is the iterative process you should follow to change as much as possible of the code to green. Ideally this should be 100% but sometimes this is not achievable mainly for some blocks that are not reachable during the tests.

# Bypassing access restrictions

One of the blocks we added to satisfy our needs, the private constructor for TemperatureConverter, is now unreachable by our tests and is marked red. In cases like this we can leave it as it is or we can use a more convoluted solution using reflection to bypass the access restrictions and create a test. Though this is not really advisable because strictly speaking you should limit to test the public interface, we are including this as an illustration of this technique.

This is the test we are adding to the TemperatureConverterTests class:

```
    public final void testPrivateConstructor() throws
        SecurityException, NoSuchMethodException,
        IllegalArgumentException, InstantiationException,
        IllegalAccessException, InvocationTargetException {
        Constructor<TemperatureConverter> ctor =
            TemperatureConverter.class.getDeclaredConstructor();
        ctor.setAccessible(true);
        TemperatureConverter tc = ctor.newInstance((Object[])null);
        assertNotNull(tc);
    }
```

This example uses reflection to bypass the access restriction and create a new TemperatureConstructor instance and then verify that it was successfully created.

If you are not familiar with this technique or Java reflection in general you can read the excellent tutorial at The Java Tutorials by Oracle (http://download.oracle.com/javase/tutorial/reflect/).

# Covering the options menu

Taking another look at the coverage report, we can yet identify a method that's not covered by our tests. It is the `TemperatureConverterActivity.onCreateOptionsMenu()` which creates the menu holding the Preferences option in our particular situation. What it does is very simple and straightforward. It creates a `MenuItem` that when clicked invokes the `TemperatureConverterPreferences` Activity through the corresponding intent. This is right what we are going to test. From our experience we know that if we are interested in knowing if an Activity was launched from our Activity under tests, then what we need is an `ActivityMonitor`, so we are establishing the test based on this component.

This is the new test we will add to the `TemperatureConverterActivityTests` class:

```
public final void testOnCreateOptionsMenu() {
  final Instrumentation instrumentation = getInstrumentation();
  final ActivityMonitor preferencesMon =
    instrumentation.addMonitor(
    "com.example.aatg.tc.TemperatureConverterPreferences",
    null, false);
  assertTrue(instrumentation.invokeMenuActionSync(
    mActivity, TemperatureConverterActivity.
    MENU_ID_PREFERENCES, 0));
  final Activity preferences =
    preferencesMon.waitForActivityWithTimeout(3000);
  assertNotNull(preferences);
  preferences.finish();
}
```

Firstly we get the Instrumentation as in other cases. We then add a monitor using `addMonitor()`, a convenience wrapper that also creates the `ActivityMonitor` for us and returns it, defining the name of the Activity class to monitor, null as a result as we are not interested in it, and false not to block the start of the Activity. This monitor will be hit if an Activity that matches the class is launched.

Next, we invoke the menu option with ID 0, as it was defined in `onCreateOptionsMenu()`, and passing no flags (0 again). We assert that the invocation was successful as `invokeMenuActionSync()` returns true in such cases.

We wait for the Activity to start, verify that it was actually started as `waitForActivityWithTimeout()` returns null if the timeout expires before the Activity was started, and finally `finishing()` the Activity.

*Alternative Testing Tactics*

This is a good example of `ActivityMonitor` utilization. However, the way we used to invoke the particular menu item and the limitations we would face if we intended to continue testing the new Activity for a real functional test led us to believe that there should be another way, and actually there is!

We will explore such ways in the following section.

## The undocumented Ant coverage target

If building with make doesn't appeal to you very much there is still another alternative. Latest versions of Android tools include an undocumented option that adds to the documented targets we mentioned before: help, clean, compile, debug, release, install, and uninstall.

This target is `coverage` and can be used like in the following example in the `TemperatureConverterTest` project.

> To be able to successfully complete all its subtasks a suitable emulator or device should be running.

```
$ ant coverage
```

This will generate the following output (parts of the output were trimmed in order to include it here):

```
Buildfile: <path/to>/TemperatureConverterTest/build.xml
    [setup] Android SDK Tools Revision 11
    [setup] Project Target: Android 2.3.1
...
-set-coverage-classpath:

-install-instrumented:
...
-package-with-emma:
...
-install-with-emma:
...
coverage:
    [echo] Running tests ...
    [exec]
    [exec] com.example.aatg.tc.test.EditNumberTests:.......
    [exec] com.example.aatg.tc.test.
              TemperatureConverterActivityTests:...............
    [exec] com.example.aatg.tc.test.
              TemperatureConverterActivityUnitTest:...
```

```
    [exec] com.example.aatg.tc.test.
               TemperatureConverterApplicationTests:....
    [exec] com.example.aatg.tc.test.TemperatureConverterTests:.......
    [exec] com.example.aatg.tc.test.robotium.
               TemperatureConverterActivityTests:..
    [exec] Test results for
               InstrumentationTestRunner=.........................
    [exec] Time: 61.931
    [exec]
    [exec] OK (38 tests)
    [exec]
    [exec]
    [exec] Generated code coverage data to
               /data/data/com.example.aatg.tc/files/coverage.ec
    [echo] Downloading coverage file into project directory...
    [exec] 14 KB/s (751 bytes in 0.050s)
    [echo] Extracting coverage report...
...
    [echo] Saving the report file in <path/to>/
               TemperatureConverterTest/coverage/coverage.html
BUILD SUCCESSFUL
Total time: 1 minute 31 seconds
```

This automates several of the steps we described before. However it is not documented yet so it can be removed or changed in the future. On the other hand, when the projects are complex or there are a lot of dependencies this build target may fail when the makefile succeeds, so use it with caution.

# Introducing Robotium

One component of the vast emerging robotic fauna is Robotium (`http://code.google.com/p/robotium/`), a test framework created to simplify the writing of tests requiring minimal knowledge of the application under test. Robotium is mainly oriented to write powerful and robust automatic black-box test cases for Android applications. It can cover function, system, and acceptance test scenarios, even spanning multiple Android activities of the same application automatically.

Robotium can also be used to test applications that we don't have the source code for, or even pre-installed applications.

Robotium has full support for Activities, Dialogs, Toasts, Menus, and Context Menus.

Let's put Robotium to work creating some new tests for `TemperatureConverter`. To keep our tests organized we create a new package named `com.example.`

*Alternative Testing Tactics*

`aatg.tc.tests.robotium` in the `TemperatureConverterTest` project. In this package we are creating the class for our test cases, because we will be initially testing `TemperatureConverterActivity`. It is reasonable to call it `TemperatureConverterActivityTests` even though we have a class with the same name in another package also extending `ActivityInstrumentationTestCase2`. After all, this class will be containing tests for this same `Activity` too.

## Downloading Robotium

We need to download the `robotium-solo` JAR file and its Javadoc so we can add them to our project. Go to the Robotium download site (`http://code.google.com/p/robotium/downloads/list`) and pick the latest version available, which at the time of this writing is `robotium-solo-2.1.jar`.

## Configuring the project

In the properties of our `TemperatureConverterTest` project we need to add this JAR to **Java Build Path | Libraries**. Once added, you can expand this node and add the Javadoc location to point to the companion JAR file using the **Javadoc in archive** option.

## Creating the test cases

From previous chapter we know that if we are creating test cases for an Activity that should run connected to the system infrastructure, we should base it on `ActivityInstrumentationTestCase2`, and that is what we are going to do.

### The testFahrenheitToCelsiusConversion() test

More or less the test cases have the same structure as other Instrumentation based tests. The main difference is that we need to instantiate Robotium's Solo in the test `setUp()` and `finalize()` it in the `tearDown()`:

```
package com.example.aatg.tc.test.robotium;

import android.test.ActivityInstrumentationTestCase2;

import com.example.aatg.tc.TemperatureConverterActivity;
import com.jayway.android.robotium.solo.Solo;

/**
 * @author diego
 *
 */
public class TemperatureConverterActivityTests extends
```

```
ActivityInstrumentationTestCase2<TemperatureConverterActivity> {
  private Solo mSolo;
  private TemperatureConverterActivity mActivity;
  /**
   * @param name
   */
  public TemperatureConverterActivityTests(String name) {
    super(TemperatureConverterActivity.class);
    setName(name);
  }
  /* (non-Javadoc)
   * @see android.test.ActivityInstrumentationTestCase2#setUp()
   */
  protected void setUp() throws Exception {
    super.setUp();
    mActivity = getActivity();
    mSolo = new Solo(getInstrumentation(), mActivity);
  }
  /* (non-Javadoc)
   * @see android.test.ActivityInstrumentationTestCase2#tearDown()
   */
  protected void tearDown() throws Exception {
    try {
      mSolo.finalize();
    }
    catch (Throwable ex) {
      ex.printStackTrace();
    }
    mActivity.finish();
    super.tearDown();
  }
}
```

To instantiate `Solo` we have to pass a reference to the `Instrumentation` and to the `Activity` under test.

On the other hand, to finalize `Solo` we should precisely call the `finalize()` method, then finish the `Activity`, and invoke `super.tearDown()`.

Solo provides a variety of methods to drive UI tests and some assertions. Let's start by re-implementing the `testFahrenheitToCelsiusConversion()` that we previously implemented using the conventional approach, but in this case using `Solo` facilities:

```
public final void testFahrenheitToCelsiusConversion() {
    mSolo.clearEditText(CELSIUS);
    mSolo.clearEditText(FAHRENHEIT);

    final double f = 32.5d;
    mSolo.clickOnEditText(FAHRENHEIT);
    mSolo.enterText(FAHRENHEIT, Double.toString(f));
    mSolo.clickOnEditText(CELSIUS);
    final double expectedC =
        TemperatureConverter.fahrenheitToCelsius(f);
    final double actualC =
        Double.parseDouble(mSolo.getEditText(CELSIUS).
        getText().toString());
    final double delta = Math.abs(expectedC - actualC);
    final String msg = "" + f + "F -> " + expectedC +
        "C but was " + actualC + "C (delta " + delta + ")";
    assertTrue(msg, delta < 0.005);
}
```

This is pretty similar, however the first difference you may have noticed is that in this case we are not getting references to the UI elements as we previously did in the `setUp()` method using `findViewById()` to locate the View. However, we are using one of the biggest advantages of Solo that is locating the Views for us using some criteria. In this case the criteria are used in the order in which they appear on the screen and since they are counted an index is assigned. The method `mSolo.clearEditText(int index)` expects an integer index of the position on the screen starting from `0`. Consequently we should add these constants to the test case, as in our UI the Celsius field is on top and Fahrenheit beneath:

```
private static final int CELSIUS = 0;
private static final int FAHRENHEIT = 1;
```

The other methods follow the same convention and we are supplying these constants when necessary. This test is very similar to the one in `com.example.aatg.tc.test.TemperatureConverterActivityTest` but you may have noticed that there is a subtle difference. Here we are located at a much higher level and we don't have to worry about internals or implementation details; for example when in our previous test we invoked `mCelsius.requestFocus()` to trigger the conversion mechanism, but here we just simulate what the user does and issue a `mSolo.clickOnEditText(CELSIUS)`.

Because of this, we don't want to cast and use `EditNumber.getNumber()` either. We just obtain the textual data that is on the screen, convert it to a `Double`, and then compare it against the expected value.

We simplified the test sensibly but the biggest advantage of using `Solo` is yet to come.

# The testOnCreateOptionsMenu() revisited

You may have been waiting for this since the announcement in our preceding `testOnCreateOptionsMenu()` implementation. This time we are situated at a much higher level and we don't deal with implementation details. It is not our problem if a new Activity is launched when we click on the menu item; we only treat this case from the UI perspective.

This is a screenshot showing the preferences dialog for **Decimal places**:

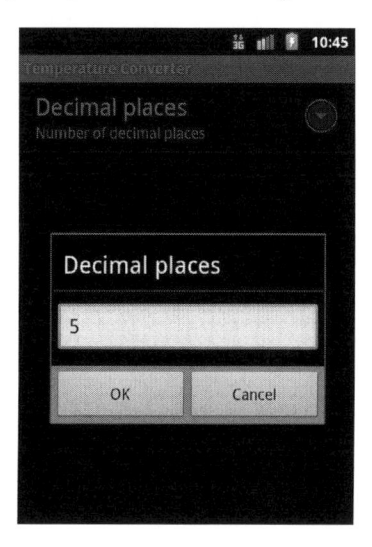

Our purpose is also to change the value of **Decimal places** preferences to 5, and verify that the change actually took place.

The following code snippet illustrates the details of the test:

```
public final void testOnCreateOptionsMenu() {
    final int decimalPlaces = 5;
    final String numberRE = "^[0-9]+$";

    mSolo.sendKey(Solo.MENU);
    mSolo.clickOnText("Preferences");
    mSolo.clickOnText("Decimal places");
    assertTrue(mSolo.searchText(numberRE));
    mSolo.clearEditText(DECIMAL_PLACES);
    assertFalse(mSolo.searchText(numberRE));
    mSolo.enterText(DECIMAL_PLACES,
        Integer.toString(decimalPlaces));
    mSolo.clickOnButton("OK");
    mSolo.goBack();
```

```
        mSolo.sendKey(Solo.MENU);
        mSolo.clickOnText("Preferences");
        mSolo.clickOnText("Decimal places");
        assertTrue(mSolo.searchText(numberRE));
        assertEquals(decimalPlaces, Integer.parseInt(
           mSolo.getEditText(DECIMAL_PLACES).
             getText().toString()));
   }
```

Can you already appreciate the difference? There are no gory details about how all this is implemented. We only test its functionality.

We start by pressing the MENU key, clicking on **Preferences**.

Wow, we just specify the menu item title and that's it!

The new Activity is started but we don't have to worry about it. We continue and click on **Decimal places**.

We verify that some field containing a number, the prior value of this preference, appeared. Do you remember what I said about regular expressions: they always come in handy in one way or another; here to match any decimal integer number (any digit followed by zero or more digits). Then we clear the field and verify that it was in fact cleared.

We enter the string representing the number we want to use as a preference, 5 in this case. Click on the **OK** button, and the preference is saved.

It remains to verify that it actually happened. The same procedure is used to get the menu and the field and finally we verify that the actual number is already there.

You may wonder where DECIMAL_PLACES comes from. We previously defined CELSIUS and FAHRENHEIT index constants for the fields on the screen and this is the same case, because this will be the third EditText we should define in our class:

```
        private static final int DECIMAL_PLACES = 2;
```

Tests can be run from Eclipse or the command line according to your preferences.

I hope you have enjoyed this simplicity as much as I did and that your brain is now bubbling with ideas to implement your own tests.

# Testing on host's JVM

We left this subject for the end of this chapter as it seems this is the *Holy Grail* of the Android platform.

You know that Android is based on a virtual machine named Dalvik, after a village in Iceland, optimized for mobile resources with limited capabilities such as constrained amount of memory and processor speed. Certainly a very different environment than our development host computer, which may have plenty of memory and processor speed to enjoy.

Ordinarily, we run our applications and tests on an emulator or device. These targets have a much slower real or emulated CPU and thus running our tests is a time consuming activity mainly when our project starts to grow, and applying Test Driven Development techniques compels us to run hundreds of tests to verify every change we introduced.

> It's worth noticing that this technique can be used only as a workaround during the development process to speed things up and it should never replace final testing on the real platform as incompatibilities between the Dalvik and JavaSE runtime may affect the accuracy of the tests.

Later, we should find out a method that allows us to intercept the standard *compilation-dexing-running* on an emulator or a device sequence and be able to run on our host computer directly.

# Creating the TemperatureConverterJVMTest project

Let's put the ideas presented here into practice. This time we are creating a Java project in Eclipse, as opposed to our previously created Android projects.

*Alternative Testing Tactics*

These are the steps needed to do it:

1. First we create the project and select **JavaSE-1.6** as the execution environment:

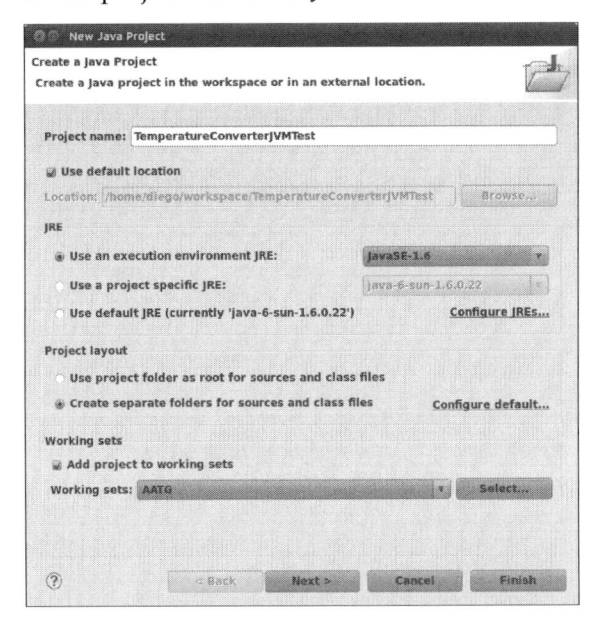

2. Pressing **Next >** we can select the **Java Settings** for the project and as our intention is to create the tests for the `TemperatureConverter` project we should add it as a **Required project on the build path**:

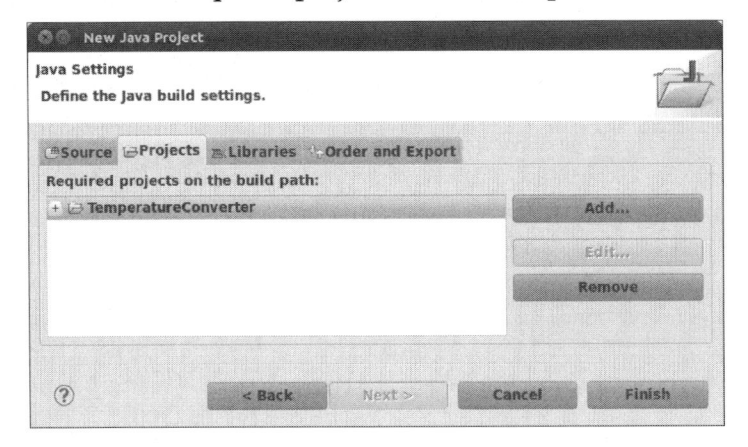

3. Then we create a new package in this project to keep our tests, named `com.example.aatg.tc.test`. In this package we create a new **JUnit Test Case**, named `TemperatureConverterTests`, using JUnit version 4, as opposed to the supported JUnit version 3 used in standard Android test cases. Select **TemperatureConverter** as the **Class under test**:

*Chapter 10*

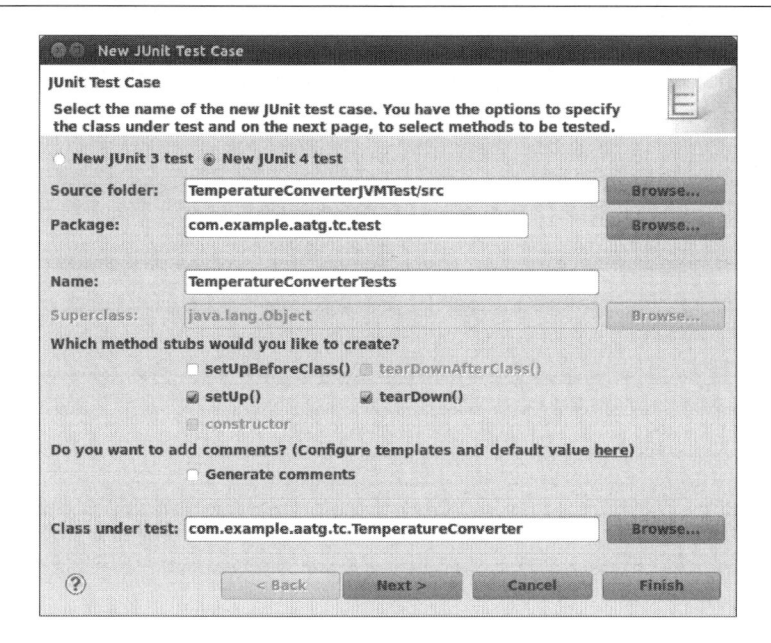

4. Pressing **Next >** this time we can select the methods to test and the method stubs will be generated automatically:

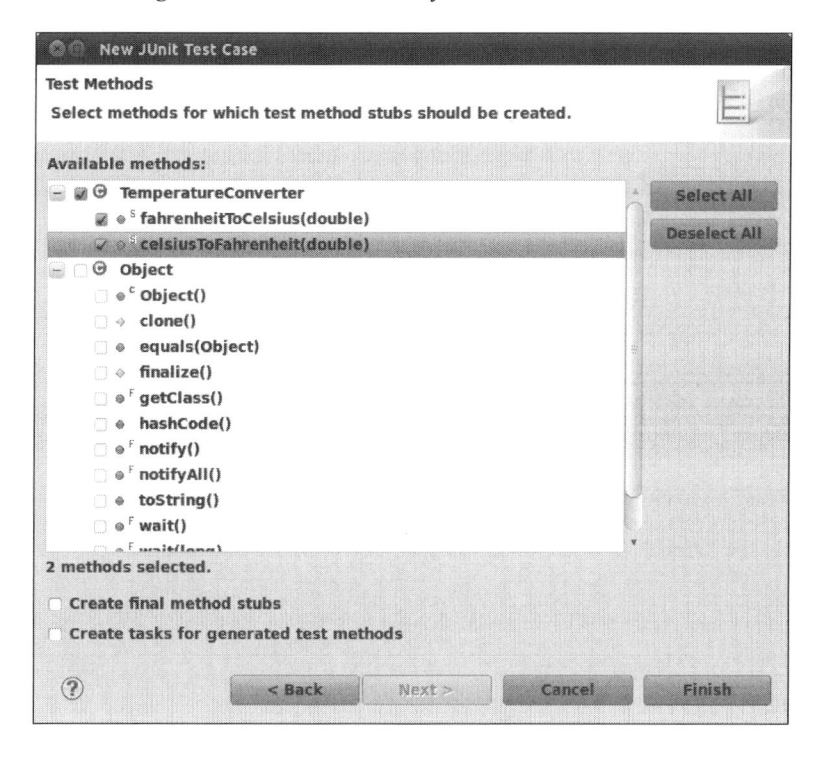

*Alternative Testing Tactics*

Now we have the test case template and the method stubs completed. We now need to enter the test code we created in previous chapters for `TemperatureConverter` in these stubs:

```
package com.example.aatg.tc.test;

import static org.junit.Assert.*;

import java.util.HashMap;

import org.junit.After;
import org.junit.Before;
import org.junit.Test;

import com.example.aatg.tc.TemperatureConverter;

public class TemperatureConverterTests {
  private static final HashMap<Double, Double> conversionTableDouble =
     new HashMap<Double, Double>();
  static {
    // initialize (c, f) pairs
    conversionTableDouble.put(0.0, 32.0);
    conversionTableDouble.put(100.0, 212.0);
    conversionTableDouble.put(-1.0, 30.20);
    conversionTableDouble.put(-100.0, -148.0);
    conversionTableDouble.put(32.0, 89.60);
    conversionTableDouble.put(-40.0, -40.0);
    conversionTableDouble.put(-273.0, -459.40);
  }
```

The previous code snippet shows the imports and the definition of the `TemperatureConverterTests`. This is almost exactly the same as before but with the sole addition of JUnit 4 annotations:

```
@Before
public void setUp() throws Exception {
}

@After
public void tearDown() throws Exception {
}

/**
 * Test method for {@link com.example.aatg.tc.
    TemperatureConverter#fahrenheitToCelsius(double)}.
 */
@Test
public void testFahrenheitToCelsius() {
  for (double c: conversionTableDouble.keySet()) {
```

```java
      final double f = conversionTableDouble.get(c);
      final double ca = TemperatureConverter.fahrenheitToCelsius(f);
      final double delta = Math.abs(ca - c);
      final String msg = "" + f + "F -> " + c + "C but is " + ca +
        " (delta " + delta + ")";
      assertTrue(msg, delta < 0.0001);
   }
}
/**
 * Test method for {@link com.example.aatg.tc.
    TemperatureConverter#celsiusToFahrenheit(double)}.
 */
@Test
public void testCelsiusToFahrenheit() {
   for (double c: conversionTableDouble.keySet()) {
      final double f = conversionTableDouble.get(c);
      final double fa = TemperatureConverter.celsiusToFahrenheit(c);
      final double delta = Math.abs(fa - f);
      final String msg = "" + c + "C -> " + f + "F but is " + fa +
        " (delta " + delta + ")";
      assertTrue(msg, delta < 0.0001);
   }
}
```

Again, this code snippet shows no changes against our previous version of the test case but with the sole addition of JUnit 4 annotations:

```java
@Test
public final void testExceptionForLessThanAbsoluteZeroF() {
   try {
      final double c = TemperatureConverter.fahrenheitToCelsius(
        TemperatureConverter.ABSOLUTE_ZERO_F-1);
      fail("Less than absolute zero F not detected");
   }
   catch (InvalidTemperatureException ex) {
      // do nothing
   }
}

@Test
public final void testExceptionForLessThanAbsoluteZeroC() {
   try {
      final double f = TemperatureConverter.celsiusToFahrenheit(
        TemperatureConverter.ABSOLUTE_ZERO_C-1);
      fail("Less than absolute zero C not detected");
   }
```

# Alternative Testing Tactics

```
      catch (RuntimeException ex) {
        // do nothing
      }
    }
  }
}
```

The code is exactly the same with just a few minor differences. One such difference is that we are now annotating the tests with `@Test`, as JUnit 4 finds the test methods by this annotation and not by their name. So in this example we are using the same names for tests methods as we used before, but strictly speaking we could have used something different, for example `shouldRaiseExceptionForLessThanAbsoluteZeroC` instead of `testExceptionForLessThanAbsoluteZeroC`.

# Comparing the performance gain

Once the tests are finished we can run them from Eclipse by selecting the appropriate test launcher, **Eclipse JUnit Launcher**:

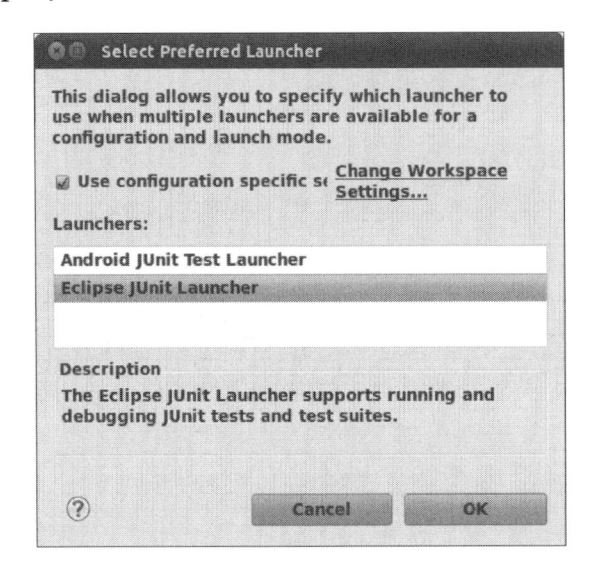

The distinction is evident. There is no emulator start up, any device communication and therefore the speed gain is important. Analyzing the evidence we can find out these differences.

Running all tests in my development computer takes 0.005 seconds, with some tests taking so little time that they are not even accounted for, and are displayed as 0.000 seconds:

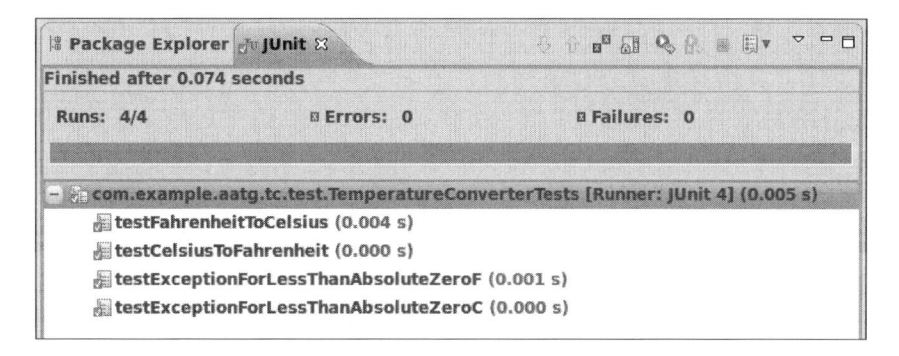

```
┌─────────────────────────────────────────────────────────────────┐
│ ▤ Package Explorer │ JUnit ⊠      ↓ ↑ ▪ ▩ ◉ ⁑ ▪ ▦ ▼    ▽ ▭ □ │
├─────────────────────────────────────────────────────────────────┤
│ Finished after 0.074 seconds                                    │
│                                                                 │
│  Runs: 4/4           ⊡ Errors: 0         ⊡ Failures: 0          │
│ ▬▬▬▬▬▬▬▬▬▬▬▬▬▬▬▬▬▬▬▬▬▬▬▬▬▬▬▬▬▬▬▬▬▬▬▬▬▬▬▬▬▬▬▬▬▬▬▬▬▬▬▬▬▬▬▬▬▬▬▬▬  │
│                                                                 │
│  ⊟ ▦ com.example.aatg.tc.test.TemperatureConverterTests [Runner: JUnit 4] (0.005 s) │
│       ▦ testFahrenheitToCelsius (0.004 s)                       │
│       ▦ testCelsiusToFahrenheit (0.000 s)                       │
│       ▦ testExceptionForLessThanAbsoluteZeroF (0.001 s)         │
│       ▦ testExceptionForLessThanAbsoluteZeroC (0.000 s)         │
└─────────────────────────────────────────────────────────────────┘
```

Comparing this with the time it took to run the same tests on the emulator makes this huge difference evident:

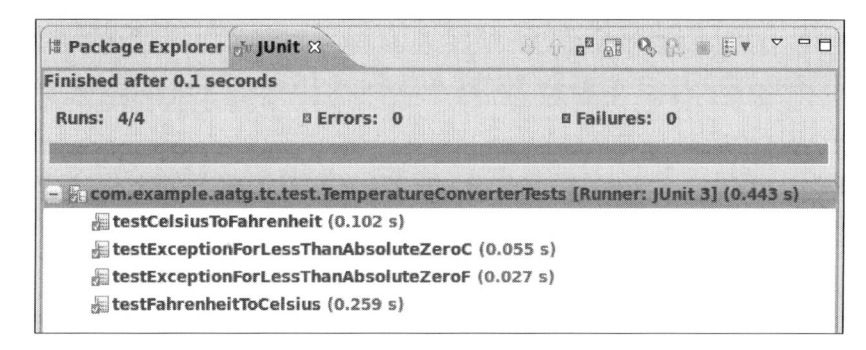

```
┌─────────────────────────────────────────────────────────────────┐
│ ▤ Package Explorer │ JUnit ⊠      ↓ ↑ ▪ ▩ ◉ ⁑ ▪ ▦ ▼    ▽ ▭ □ │
├─────────────────────────────────────────────────────────────────┤
│ Finished after 0.1 seconds                                      │
│                                                                 │
│  Runs: 4/4           ⊡ Errors: 0         ⊡ Failures: 0          │
│ ▬▬▬▬▬▬▬▬▬▬▬▬▬▬▬▬▬▬▬▬▬▬▬▬▬▬▬▬▬▬▬▬▬▬▬▬▬▬▬▬▬▬▬▬▬▬▬▬▬▬▬▬▬▬▬▬▬▬▬▬▬  │
│                                                                 │
│  ⊟ ▦ com.example.aatg.tc.test.TemperatureConverterTests [Runner: JUnit 3] (0.443 s) │
│       ▦ testCelsiusToFahrenheit (0.102 s)                       │
│       ▦ testExceptionForLessThanAbsoluteZeroC (0.055 s)         │
│       ▦ testExceptionForLessThanAbsoluteZeroF (0.027 s)         │
│       ▦ testFahrenheitToCelsius (0.259 s)                       │
└─────────────────────────────────────────────────────────────────┘
```

These same tests took 0.443 seconds to run, almost 100 times more and that's a huge difference if you consider hundreds of tests running tens of times a day.

It is also good to notice that other advantages exists beside the speed gain and they are the availability of several mock frameworks and code coverage tools.

# Adding Android to the picture

We intentionally left Android outside our picture. Let's analyze what happens if we include a simple Android test. Remember that for these tests to compile `android.jar` from the SDK should also be added to the project libraries.

Add this test to a new JUnit test case named `TemperatureConverterActivityUnitTests`:

```
package com.example.aatg.tc.test;
import static org.junit.Assert.assertNotNull;

import org.junit.After;
import org.junit.Before;
```

```java
import org.junit.Test;
import android.app.Application;
import android.content.Intent;
import com.example.aatg.tc.TemperatureConverterActivity;
import com.example.aatg.tc.TemperatureConverterApplication;
public class TemperatureConverterActivityUnitTests {
  @Before
  public void setUp() throws Exception {
  }

  @After
  public void tearDown() throws Exception {
  }

  @Test
  public final void testApplication() {
    Application application = new TemperatureConverterApplication();
    assertNotNull(application);
  }
}
```

And here is what we obtain:

**java.lang.RuntimeException: Stub!**

  at android.content.Context.<init>(Context.java:4)

  at android.content.ContextWrapper.<init>(ContextWrapper.java:5)

  at android.app.Application.<init>(Application.java:6)

  at com.example.aatg.tc.TemperatureConverterApplication.<init>(TemperatureConverterApplication.java:27)

  ...

The reason is that `android.jar` provides only the API, not the implementation. All methods throw `java.lang.RuntimeException: Stub!` when used.

If we want to circumvent this limitation to test some classes outside of the Android operating system, we should create an `android.jar` that mocks every class. However, we will also find problems for subclasses of Android classes like `TemperatureConverterApplication`. This would be a daunting task and a significant amount of work, so we should look for another solution.

# Introducing Robolectric

**Robolectric** (http://pivotal.github.com/robolectric/) is a unit test framework that intercepts the loading of Android classes and rewrites the method bodies. Robolectric re-defines Android methods so they return default values, like `null`, `0`, or `false`, and if provided it forwards method calls to shadow objects giving Android behavior.

A large number of shadow objects are provided, but this is far from complete coverage, however it is improving constantly. This should also lead you to treat it as an evolving Open Source project, for which you should be ready to contribute to make it better, but also to depend on it with caution because you may discover that what you need for your tests has not been implemented yet. This is not in any way to diminish its promising future.

# Installing Robolectric

Robolectric can be installed by downloading the `robolectric-<version>-jar-with-dependencies.jar` from the Maven central repository (http://repo1.maven.org/maven2/com/pivotallabs/robolectric/). By the time of this writing the latest JAR available is `robolectric-0.9.8-jar-with-dependencies.jar` and this is what we are going to use in our samples.

Conveniently you can also download the corresponding Javadoc and attach it to the library in you project properties so you can access the documentation from Eclipse.

# Creating a new Java project

To keep our tests organized we are creating a new Java project as we did in our previous section. This time we are adding the following libraries:

- `robolectric-<version>-jar-with-dependencies.jar`.
- `android.jar` from your Android SDK.
- `maps.jar` also from your Android SDK. Note that this is an optional package when you install the SDK.
- JUnit 4.

# Writing some tests

We will get acquainted with Robolectric by reproducing some of the tests we wrote before.

*Alternative Testing Tactics*

One good example can be re-writing the `EditNumber` tests. Let's create a new `EditNumberTests` class, this time in the newly created project, and copy the tests from the `EditNumberTests` in `TemperatureConverterTest` project:

```
package com.example.aatg.tc.test;

import static org.junit.Assert.assertEquals;
import static org.junit.Assert.assertNotNull;

import org.junit.After;
import org.junit.Before;
import org.junit.Test;
import org.junit.runner.RunWith;

import com.example.aatg.tc.EditNumber;
import com.xtremelabs.robolectric.RobolectricTestRunner;

@RunWith(RobolectricTestRunner.class)
public class EditNumberTests {
  private static final double DELTA = 0.00001d;
  private EditNumber mEditNumber;
```

In the previous snippet we defined the package. In this case using `com.example.aatg.tc.test` as usual. Also we declare the test runner with the `@RunWith` annotation. Later we defined the `mEditNumber` field to hold the reference to the `EditNumber`:

```
  @Before
  public void setUp() throws Exception {
    mEditNumber = new EditNumber(null);
    mEditNumber.setFocusable(true);
  }

  @After
  public void tearDown() throws Exception {
  }

  @Test
  public final void testPreconditions() {
    assertNotNull(mEditNumber);
  }

  /**
   * Test method for {@link com.example.aatg.tc.EditNumber#
       EditNumber(android.content.Context, AttributeSet attrs,
       int defStyle)}.
   */
  @Test
  public final void testEditNumberContextAttributeSetInt() {
    final EditNumber e = new EditNumber(null, null, -1);
    assertNotNull(e);
```

}

This snippet comprises the usual `setup()` and `tearDown()` methods followed by the `testPreconditions()` test. In the `setUp()` method we created an `EditNumber` with a null context and then we set it as focusable:

```
/**
 * Test method for {@link com.example.aatg.tc.EditNumber#clear()}.
 */
@Test
public final void testClear() {
    final String value = "123.45";
    mEditNumber.setText(value);
    mEditNumber.clear();
    String expectedString = "";
    String actualString = mEditNumber.getText().toString();
    assertEquals(expectedString, actualString);
}
/**
 * Test method for {@link com.example.aatg.tc.EditNumber#
     setNumber(double)}.
 */
@Test
public final void testSetNumber() {
    mEditNumber.setNumber(123.45);
    final String expected = "123.45";
    final String actual = mEditNumber.getText().toString();
    assertEquals(expected, actual);
}
/**
 * Test method for {@link com.example.aatg.tc.EditNumber#
     getNumber()}.
 */
@Test
public final void testGetNumber() {
    mEditNumber.setNumber(123.45);
    final double expected = 123.45;
    final double actual = mEditNumber.getNumber();
    assertEquals(expected, actual, DELTA);
}
}
```

In this last snippet we have the basic tests which are the same as the `EditNumber` tests of our previous examples.

## Alternative Testing Tactics

We are highlighting the most important changes. The first one is to specify the test runner JUnit will delegate the processing of the tests to, by using the annotation `@RunWith`. In this case we need to use `RobolectricTestRunner.class` as the runner. Then we create an `EditText` using a null `Context` as this is a class that cannot be instantiated. Finally, a `DELTA` value is specified in `testGetNumber` as `assertEquals` since the floating point number requires it in JUnit 4. Additionally we added the `@Test` annotation to mark the method as tests.

The other test methods that existed in the original `EditNumberTests` cannot be implemented or simply fail for a variety of reasons. For example, as we mentioned before, Robolectric classes return default values, like `null`, `0`, `false`, and so on, and this is the case for `Editable.Factory.getInstance()` which returns null and causes the test to fail; because there is no other way of creating an `Editable` object we are at a dead end.

Similarly, the `InputFilter` that `EditNumber` sets is non functional. It is futile to create a test that expects some behavior.

The alternative to these shortcomings would be to create `Shadow` classes but this requires alteration of the Robolectric source and the creation of `Robolectric.shadowOf()` methods. This procedure is described in the documentation that you may follow if you are interested in applying this approach to your tests.

Before being able to run your tests you need to create symbolic links for `TemperatureConverter` project's `AndroidManifest.xml` and resources which are used by Robolectric.

```
$ cd ~/workspace/TemperatureConverterJVMTests
$ ln -s ../TemperatureConverter/AndroidManifest.xml
$ ln -s ../TemperatureConverter/res . # note the dot at the end
```

Having identified these issues we can proceed to run the tests from inside Eclipse and they will run in the host's JVM with no need to start or communicate with an emulator or device.

## Summary

This chapter has been a little more involved than previous ones, with the sole intention of facing realistic situations and state-of-the-art Android testing.

We started analyzing the requirements and steps to build Android from source. This measure is needed to be able to activate code coverage through EMMA, which we did and later on we ran our tests obtaining a detailed code coverage analysis report.

We then used this report to improve our tests and we created some to cover areas we were not aware that have not been tested. This led us to better tests and in some cases improved the design of the project under test.

We introduced Robotium, a very useful tool to ease the creation of test cases for our Android applications and we improved some tests with it.

Then we analyzed one of the hottest topics on Android testing as it is testing on the development host JVM optimizing and reducing considerably the time needed to run the tests, something that is highly desirable when we are applying Test Driven Development to our process. Within this scope, we analyzed JUnit 4 and Robolectric and created some tests as demonstrations and to get you started on these techniques.

We have reached the end of this journey through the available methods and tools to Android testing. You should now be much better prepared to start applying this to your own projects. The results will be visible as soon as you begin to use them.

Finally, I hope that you have enjoyed reading this book as much as I did writing it.

Happy testing!

# Index

## Symbols

@DomainStep annotation  160
@DomainSteps annotation  160
@FlakyTest annotation  36
@LargeTest annotation  36
@MediumTest annotation  36
@Param annotation  258
-prop command line  136
@SmallTest annotation  36
@Smoke annotation  36
@Supress annotation  37
@UIThreadTest annotation  37, 56, 105
@UIThredTest  18
@VeryImportantTest  44

## A

activities
  testing  175-181
ActivityInstrumentationTestCase2 class
  about  74
  constructor  75
  setUp method  75, 76
  tearDown method  76
  testPreconditions method  76
  UML class diagram  74
ActivityInstrumentationTestCase2.
    getActivity() method  97
Activity Manager, test application
  running  25
ActivityMonitor inner class
  about  66
  example  66
ActivityTestCase class
  about  72, 73
  scrubClass method  73

adb shell command  42
addBookmark()  190
addMonitor()  283
am instrument command  41
Android
  about  7
  adding, to JUnit test case  297, 298
  applications, testing  170
  assertions  50
  building, from source  264
  command-line options  47
  Dalvik JIT compiler  23
  demonstration application  50
  EasyMock  196
  EMMA features  265
  history  7, 8
  JUnit  28
  JUnit 3, using  13
  Mock Objects  58
  mock objects, in android.test.mock
      package  12
  Package explorer  31
  test case, creating  32-35
  Test Driven Development  85
  testing on  27
  tests, debugging  45
  tests, running  37
Android ADT plugin  18
Android applications
  building manually, Ant used  218-223
Android assets  209
Android, building from source
  Android source code, downloading  266
  building steps  268-270
  code coverage  264
  repo, installing  267

system requisites 266
working copy, creating 267
**Android CTS test suite 167**
**Android Development Challenge (ADC1) 8**
**Android emulator**
  supporting options, for latency 138
  supporting options, for network speed 137
**Android Emulator Plugin 226**
**android.jar 299**
**AndroidManifest.xml 40**
**Android project**
  creating 28
  external libraries, using 80-83
**Android sample project**
  creating 88
**Android SDK**
  dmtracedump, using 251
  performance tests 246
  Traceview, using 251
**Android SDK and AVD Manager 130**
**Android source code**
  downloading 266
**AndroidTestCase base class**
  about 62, 63
  assertActivityRequiresPermission() method 63
  assertReadingContentUriRequiresPermission method 64
  assertWritingContentUriRequiresPermission() method 65
**Android testing framework**
  about 23
  features 23
  instrumentation framework 23, 25
  targets, testing 25
**android.test.mock package 17**
**android.test.mock package, classes**
  MockApplication 58
  MockContentProvider 58
  MockContentResolver 58
  MockContext 58
  MockCursor 58
  MockDialogInterface 59
  MockPackageManager 59
  MockResources 59
**Android Test Project**
  creating 29

**Android test results**
  obtaining 231-240
**android:text property 100**
**Android Unit tests**
  about 167-169
  BrowserProvider tests 185-190
**Android Virtual Devices.** *See* **AVD**
**ApiDemos sample application 192**
**applications**
  RenamingMockContext class, testing 170, 171
  TemperatureConverterApplicationTests class, testing 171-175
  testing 170
**assertActivityRequiresPermission() method**
  about 63
  className parameter 64
  description 64
  example 64
  packageName parameter 64
  permission parameter 64
**assertAssignableFrom 55**
**assertBaselineAligned 54**
**assertBottomAligned 54**
**assertContainsInAnyOrder 55**
**assertContainsInOrder 55**
**assertContainsRegex 55**
**assertEmpty 55**
**assertEquals 55**
**assertGroupContains 54**
**assertGroupIntegrity 54**
**assertGroupNotContains 54**
**assertHasScreenCoordinates 54**
**assertHorizontalCenterAligned 54**
**assertInsertQuery() 187, 190**
**assertions**
  about 50, 51
  assertAssignableFrom 55
  assertBaselineAligned 54
  assertBottomAligned 54
  assertContainsInAnyOrder 55
  assertContainsInOrder 55
  assertContainsRegex 55
  assertEmpty 55
  assertEquals() 53, 55
  assertGroupIntegrity 54
  assertGroupNotContains 54

assertHasScreenCoordinates 54
assertHorizontalCenterAligned 54
assertLeftAligned 54
assertMatchesRegex 55
assertNotContainsRegex 55
assertNotEmpty 55
assertNotMatchesRegex 55
assertOffScreenAbove 54
assertOffScreenBelow 54
assertOnScreen 54
assertRightAligned 54
assertTopAligned 54
checkEqualsAndHashCodeMethods 56
custom messages 52
static imports 52, 53
**assertLeftAligned 54**
**assertMatchesRegex 55**
**assert* methods 16**
  assertEquals() 16
  assertFalse() 16
  assertNotNull() 16
  assertNotSame() 16
  assertNull() 16
  assertSame() 16
  assertTrue() 16
  fail() 16
**assertNotContainsRegex 55**
**assertNotEmpty 55**
**assertNotMatchesRegex 55**
**assertOffScreenAbove 54**
**assertOffScreenBelow 54**
**assertOnScreen 54**
**assertOnScreen method 55, 101**
**assertQueryReturns() 190**
**assertReadingContentUriRequiresPermission method**
  about 64
  description 64
  example 65
  permission parameter 65
  uri parameter 65
**assertRightAligned 54**
**assertVerticalCenterAligned 54**
**assertWritingContentUriRequiresPermission() method**
  about 65
  description 65

example 66
permission parameter 65
uri parameter 65
**AVD**
  cleaning up 135
  creating 129-132
  emulator configurations 136
  emulator, terminating 136
  hardware properties 130
  headless emulator 133
  keyguard, disabling 134, 135
  monkey application 142
  running, from command line 132
  scripting, testing with monkeyrunner 144

# B

**Behavior Driven Development**
  about 21, 149
  Given/When/Then words 150
  history 149, 150
**benchmarking 255**
**benchmarks**
  about 255
  macrobenchmarks 255
  microbenchmark 256
**BrowserProvider tests 185-190**
**bugs 8, 9**
**buildfile**
  targets 220

# C

**Caliper**
  about 256
  running 258, 260
**Caliper microbenchmarks**
  about 256
  TemperatureConverterBenchmark project, creating 257, 258
**celsiusToFahrenheit 123**
**checkEqualsAndHashCodeMethods 56**
**clear() functionality 116**
**clear() method 107**
**code coverage**
  about 264
  enabling, via EMMA 264

code coverage analysis report,
    TemperatureConverter
  generating 274-277
**command line options**
  -e annotation <annotation-name> 43
  -e func true 43
  -e log true 44
  -e <NAME> <VALUE> 41
  -e perf true 43
  -e size {small | medium | large} 43
  -e unit true 43
  -p <FILE> 41
  -r 41
  -w 41
**ContentProviders**
  about 12
  testing 181-184
**ContentProvider test 78**
**Continuous Integration**
  about 11, 217
  features 217
  with Hudson 225
**coverage reports 10**
**createApplication() 172**
**createMock() 200**
**createNiceMock() 200**
**createStrictMock() 200**
**custom annotation**
  creating 43

# D

**Dalvik JIT compiler 23**
**Dalvik virtual machine 25**
**databases**
  testing 181-184
**debugging**
  Android tests 45, 46
**Debug.stopMethodTracing() 253**
**Debug.waitForDebugger() 45**
**default constructor, TestCase base class 61**
**demonstration application, Android 50**
**disableKeyguard() 135**
**dmtracedump**
  about 252
  using 252

# E

**EasyMock**
  about 196
  benefits 196
  demonstrating 196
  easymock JAR file, adding to Test
    project 197
  amcrest, introducing 202
  libraries, importing 198
  testTextChanged test 198-200
**EasyMock2Adapter 204**
**EditNumber class 105**
**EditNumber tests 114**
**Electron 8**
**EMMA**
  about 10
  code coverage report, displaying 10
  URL 264
**EMMA features 265**
**emulator configurations, AVD**
  about 136
  network conditions, simulating 137-139
  Qemu options 140, 141
**exceptions**
  testing 191, 192
**external libraries, using**
  using, in Android project 80-83

# F

**fahrenheitToCelsius 123**
**fail method 35**
**files**
  testing 181-184
**findViewById() 179, 180**
**finish() method 248**
**FitNesse**
  about 151
  features 151
  running, from command line 151
  TemperatureConverterTests subwiki,
    creating 152
  test systems 156
  URL 151
**functionality, TemperatureConverterActivi-
    tyTests project**
  adding 104

EditNumber class  105-110
EditNumber tests  114-119
InputFilter tests  125, 126
TemperatureChangeWatcher class  119-122
temperature conversion  104
TemperatureConverter tests  123-125
TemperatureConverter unit tests  110-113
**functional or acceptance tests**
  about  20, 21
  test case scenario  22

# G

getActivity()  74, 97, 179
getBookmarksSuggest()  190
getContext() method  63
getDecorView()  101
getNumber() method  107
getPackageName()  174
getprop command  136
getSharedPreferences()  175
getStartedActivityIntent()  180
**Git**
  about  224
  downloads  224
  local git repository, creating  224, 225
  URL  224
**Gitweb interface  266**
**given name constructor, TestCase base class  62**
**GivWenZen**
  about  158
  downloading  159
  features  158, 159
  test scenario, creating  159-164
**Gravity class  103**

# H

**hamcrest**
  about  202
  matchers  203
  using  202
**hamcrest library**
  URL  202
**hamcrest matchers**
  allOf  203
  anyOf  203
  anything  203
  array  204
  Beans  204
  closeTo  204
  Collections  204
  containsString  204
  core  203
  describedAs  203
  endsWith  204
  equalTo  203
  equalToIgnoringCase  204
  equalToIgnoringWhiteSpace  204
  greaterThan  204
  greaterThanOrEqualTo  204
  hasEntry  204
  hasItem  204
  hasItemInArray  204
  hasItems  204
  hasKey  204
  hasProperty  204
  hasToString  203
  hasValue  204
  instanceOf  203
  is  203
  isCompatibleType  203
  lessThan  204
  lessThanOrEqualTo  204
  logical  203
  not  203
  notNullValue  203
  nullValue  203
  number  204
  object  203
  sameInstance  203
  startsWith  204
  Text  204
**hardware properties, AVD**
  accelerometer  131
  audio playback support  131
  audio recording support  131
  battery support  131
  cache partition size  131
  cache partition support  131
  camera support  131
  device RAM size  131
  DPAD support  131
  GPS support  131

GSM modem support  131
keyboard support  131
maximum horizontal camera pixels  131
maximum vertical camera pixels  131
SD Card support  131
touch-screen support  131
track-ball support  131
**hasToString matcher  204**
**headless emulator  133**
**Hudson**
  about  225
  Android test results, obtaining  231-240
  configuring  226
  downloading  226
  installing  226
  jobs, creating  227-230
  new job screen options  228, 229
**Hudson GIT plugin  226**

# I

**InputFilter tests  125**
**instrumentation  66**
**instrumentation framework, Android testing framework  23, 25**
**instrumentation tag  40**
**InstrumentationTestCase class**
  about  68
  launchActivity method  69
  launchActivityWithIntent method  69
  runTestOnUiThread helper method  71, 72
  sendKeys method  69-71
  sendRepeatedKeys method  69-71
**InstrumentationTestCase class, subclasses  68**
  ActivityInstrumentationTestCase2<T extends Activity>  68
  ActivityTestCase  68
  ActivityUnitTestCase<T extends Activity>  68
  ProviderTestCase2<T extends ContentProvider>  68
  SyncBaseInstrumentation  68
**InstrumentationTestCase.launchActivity()  74**
**integration tests  20**
**invokeMenuActionSync()  283**

**isFinishCalled()  180**
**IsolatedContext class  59**
**ItelliJ  19**

# J

**jbehave**
  about  22
  URL  22
**JUnit**
  about  13, 28
  Eclipse and other IDEs support  18
**junit.framework.Assert class  35**
**JUnit TestCase  32**
**JVM virtual machine  25**
**Jython**
  URL  145

# K

**keyguard**
  disabling  134, 135
**KeyguardManager  135**

# L

**launchActivity method  69**
**launchActivityWithIntent method  69**
**LaunchApp() method  248**
**LaunchPerformanceBase instrumentation**
  creating  246, 247
**LinearLayout  101**
**local and remote services**
  testing  192-195
**local git repository**
  creating  224
**LocalService class  193**
**logcat command  135**
**Log.i() method  245**

# M

**macrobenchmarks  255**
**mActivity field  96**
**maps.jar  299**
**memory leaks**
  testing  212, 213
**mFahrenheit.setNumber(f) method  109**

microbenchmark 256
mMessage.getRootView() 55
MockApplication class 58
MockContentProvider class 58
MockContentResolver class 58, 60
MockContext class 58, 59
MockCursor class 58
MockDialogInterface class 59
Mock Objects
  about 17, 58
  IsolatedContext class 59
  MockContentResolver class 60
  MockContext class 59
mock objects, in android.test.mock package
  MockApplication 17
  MockContentProvider 17
  MockContentResolver 17
  MockContext 17
  MockCursor 17
  MockDialogInterface 17
  MockPackageManager 17
  MockResources 17
MockPackageManager class 59
MockResources class 59
monkey application
  client-server monkey 143
  running 142
MonkeyRecorder 147
monkeyrunner
  about 144
  features 145
  test screenshots, acquiring 145, 146
MyFirstProjectTest project 31

# N

Netbeans 19
Neuro Linguistic Programming (NLP)
        techniques 149

# O

onCreate(Bundle) 96
onCreate() method 180, 279
onDestroy() 180
onDestroy() event 12
onPause() event 12
Open Handset Alliance 7

# P

Package explorer 31
parser Activity 210, 211
parsers
  testing 209
parser test 211
performance gain
  comparing 296, 297
performance tests
  about 22-246
  launching 246
  LaunchPerformanceBase instrumentation,
        creating 246, 247
  running 249, 251
  temperatureConverterActivityLaunch
        Performance class, creating 248, 249
performClick() 180
Positron 7
ProviderTestCase2<T> class
  about 76
  constructor 77
  example 78
  UML class diagram 76
public void methods 16
Python
  URL 145

# Q

Qemu
  about 140
  URL 140
qemu-specific options 140, 142

# R

reenableKeyguard() 135
RenamingDelegatingContext class 60
RenamingMockContext class 170, 171
repo
  about 266
  installing 267
  URL 267
Robolectric
  about 299
  installing 299
  new Java project, creating 299

tests, writing 299-302
URL 299
**robolectric-<version>
-jar-with-dependencies.jar 299**
**Robotium**
  about 285, 286
  downloading 286
  project, configuring 286
  test cases, creating 286
  testFahrenheitToCelsiusConversion()
    test 286-288
  testOnCreateOptionsMenu() 289
**runTestOnUiThread helper method 71, 72**

# S

**scripting**
  testing, monkeyrunner used 144-146
**scrubClass method 73**
**sendKeys method 69-71**
**sendRepeatedKeys method 69-71**
**ServiceTestCase<T>**
  about 78
  constructor 79
  UML class diagram 78, 79
**setActivityIntent(Intent intent) 74**
**setAutomaticPerformanceSnapshots()
    method 247**
**setContext() method 171**
**setName() method, TestCase base class 62**
**setNumber() method 107**
**setUp() method 15, 75, 96, 97, 172, 256, 301**
**special methods, Android test case**
  setUp method 36
  tearDown method 36
  testSomething method 36
**startActivity() 179**
**startService(startIntent) method 195**
**stringCmp() 200**
**stringCmp() Comparator 204**
**system tests 23**

# T

**targetPackage attribute 66**
**TDD**
  about 85, 86
  advantages 88

code, refactoring 87
  requisites 88
  sample project, creating 88
  TemperatureConverterActivityTests
    project, creating 92
  test case, writing 86
  tests, running 87
  UML activity diagram 86
**tearDown() method 15, 73, 76, 180, 301**
**TemperatureConverterActivityLaunch
    Performance class**
  creating 248, 249
**TemperatureConverterActivityTests project**
  creating 92-96
  empty fields 100
  final application, viewing 126, 127
  fixture, creating 96, 97
  functionality, adding 104
  IDs, defining 98, 99
  preconditions, testing 97
  requirements, translating to tests 99
  screen layout 104
  user Interface components, testing 98
  user interface, creating 97, 98
  views properties 100-103
**Temperature Converter, Android sample
    project**
  creating 88-91
  requisites 89
  user Interface concept design 89
**TemperatureConverterApplicationTests
    class 171-175**
**TemperatureConverter.celsiusTo
    Fahrenheit() 258**
**TemperatureConverterCelsiusTo
    FahrenheitFixture 154**
**TemperatureConverter code coverage**
  about 270-273
  access restrictions, bypassing 282
  code coverage analysis report,
    generating 274-279
  exceptions, covering 281, 282
  options menu, covering 283
  restoring instance state, covering 279, 280
**TemperatureConverter.
    fahrenheitToCelsius(f) 109**

TemperatureConverterJVMTest project
  creating 291-296
TemperatureConverter methods 156
TemperatureConverterTests subwiki
  acceptance test fixture, adding 155
  child pages, adding 153, 154
  creating 152, 153
  supporting test classes, adding 156-158
TemperatureConverter utility class 107
testAccessPrivateData() method 170
test annotations, Android
  @FlakyTest 36
  @LargeTest 36
  @MediumTest 36
  @SmallTest 36
  @Smoke 36
  @Supress 37
  @UIThreadTest 37
testBindable() test 195
test case, Android
  creating 32, 34, 35
  special methods 36
  test annotations 36
TestCase base class
  about 61
  default constructor 61
  given name constructor 62
  setName() method 62
  UML class diagram 61
testClear() method 116
testConversionError() 16
testConversionToString() 16
Test Driven Development. *See* TDD 9
testFahrenheitToCelsiusConversion()
    test 286-288
test fixture 15
testFullFirstTitleWord() 187
testFullFirstTitleWordPartialSecond() 187
testFullTitle() 187
testFullTitleJapanese() 188
testHasDefaultBookmarks() 187
testing
  activity lifecycle events 12
  characteristics, of devices 12
  code 11
  database and filesystem operations 12
testOnCreateBundle method 96

testOnCreateOptionsMenu() 289, 290
testParseXml() 212
testPartialFirstTitleWord() 187
testPartialTitleJapanese() 188
testPreconditions method 76
testPreconditions() method 16, 194
tests, Android
  all tests, running 42
  debugging 45, 46
  dry run 44
  performance tests, running 44
  running 37
  running, from command line 41, 42
  running, from Eclipse 37
  running, from emulator 39-41
  running, from specific test case 42
  single test case. running from Eclipse 38
  specific test, running by name 42
  specific tests, running by category 43
test scenario, GivWenZen
  creating 159-163
testSomething() method 34, 43
testSoundmarkTitleJapanese() 188
testStartable() test 195
tests, types
  functional or acceptance tests 20
  integration tests 20
  performance tests 22, 23
  system tests 23
  unit tests 13
testSubLaunch() test 180
TestSuiteBuilder.FailedToCreateTests
    class 80
testTextChanged() method 205
testTextChanged test 198
testValues() 16
TextWatcher 119
TextWatcher mock 198
timeCelsiusToFahrenheit() 258
TouchUtils class
  about 57
  usage 57
TouchUtils helper class 18
Traceview
  about 251
  using 252

# U

**UI tests** 18
**UML class diagram**
  ActivityInstrumentationTestCase2 class 74
  ActivityTestCase class 72, 73
  AndroidTestCase base class 62, 63
  InstrumentationTestCase class 68
  ProviderTestCase2<T> class 76
  ServiceTestCase<T> 79
  TestCase base class 61
**undocumented Ant coverage target** 284
**unit tests**
  about 13
  actual tests 16
  setUp() method 15
  tearDown() method 15
  test fixture 15
  testPreconditions() method 16

# V

**VCS** 224
**verifyConversion() method** 162
**View.getRootView()** 55
**views**
  testing, in isolation 205-208

# W

**waitForActivityWithTimeout()** 283

# Y

**Ye Olde Logge method** 244, 245

# [PACKT PUBLISHING] Thank you for buying Android Application Testing Guide

## About Packt Publishing

Packt, pronounced 'packed', published its first book "*Mastering phpMyAdmin for Effective MySQL Management*" in April 2004 and subsequently continued to specialize in publishing highly focused books on specific technologies and solutions.

Our books and publications share the experiences of your fellow IT professionals in adapting and customizing today's systems, applications, and frameworks. Our solution based books give you the knowledge and power to customize the software and technologies you're using to get the job done. Packt books are more specific and less general than the IT books you have seen in the past. Our unique business model allows us to bring you more focused information, giving you more of what you need to know, and less of what you don't.

Packt is a modern, yet unique publishing company, which focuses on producing quality, cutting-edge books for communities of developers, administrators, and newbies alike. For more information, please visit our website: www.packtpub.com.

## Writing for Packt

We welcome all inquiries from people who are interested in authoring. Book proposals should be sent to author@packtpub.com. If your book idea is still at an early stage and you would like to discuss it first before writing a formal book proposal, contact us; one of our commissioning editors will get in touch with you.

We're not just looking for published authors; if you have strong technical skills but no writing experience, our experienced editors can help you develop a writing career, or simply get some additional reward for your expertise.

## Selenium 1.0 Testing Tools: Beginner's Guide

ISBN: 978-1-849510-26-4  Paperback: 232 pages

Test your web applications with multiple browsers using the Selenium Framework to ensure the quality of web applications

1. Save your valuable time by using Selenium to record, tweak and replay your test scripts
2. Get rid of any bugs deteriorating the quality of your web applications
3. Take your web applications one step closer to perfection using Selenium tests

## Python Testing: Beginner's Guide

ISBN: 978-1-847198-84-6  Paperback: 256 pages

An easy and convenient approach to testing your powerful Python projects

1. Covers everything you need to test your code in Python
2. Easiest and enjoyable approach to learn Python testing
3. Write, execute, and understand the result of tests in the unit test framework
4. Packed with step-by-step examples and clear explanations

Please check **www.PacktPub.com** for information on our titles

# [PACKT] PUBLISHING

### Moodle 1.9 Testing and Assessment

ISBN: 978-1-849512-34-3  Paperback: 392 pages

Develop and evaluate quizzes and tests using Moodle modules

1. Create and evaluate interesting and interactive tests using a variety of Moodle modules
2. Create simple vocabulary or flash card tests and complex tests by setting up a Lesson module
3. Motivate your students to excel through feedback and by keeping their grades online

### Django 1.1 Testing and Debugging

ISBN: 978-1-847197-56-6  Paperback: 436 pages

Building rigorously tested and bug-free Django applications

1. Develop Django applications quickly with fewer bugs through effective use of automated testing and debugging tools.
2. Ensure your code is accurate and stable throughout development and production by using Django's test framework.
3. Understand the working of code and its generated output with the help of debugging tools.

Please check www.PacktPub.com for information on our titles

Printed in Great Britain
by Amazon.co.uk, Ltd.,
Marston Gate.